Catch a Wave

Catch a Wave

A Case Study of Hawaii's New Politics

TOM COFFMAN

With a Foreword by Stuart Gerry Brown

The University Press of Hawaii

Honolulu

First edition published 1972 by Star-Bulletin Printing Company

Second edition published 1973 by The University Press of Hawaii

Library of Congress Catalog Card Number 72-98011

ISBN 0-8248-0270-5

Manufactured in the United States of America

To my son
Harry

Contents

Foreword

In 1970 John A. Burns, a onetime police captain turned politician
—one of the more remarkable of his generation in American politics—was elected to his third term as governor of Hawaii. In 1954
he had led the Democratic party, largely molded by himself, to its
first great victory over the Republicans, who had dominated Hawaii since annexation in 1898. Two years later he had gone to
Congress as elected delegate and played a leading role in organizing
the congressional coalition which admitted Alaska and Hawaii to
statehood in 1959. After an upset defeat for governor that year he
had quietly consolidated his hold on his party and rebuilt his
following in the state electorate. In 1962 he won the first full term
as governor in the new 50th state. In 1970, after two terms and
eight boom years, Burns was challenged by formidable opponents,
first in his party primary and then by the Republicans in the
general election. Tom Coffman's book is a study of these two
elections, an analytical account of the reasons Burns was threatened and how he won.

But *Catch a Wave* (the title is drawn from the Burns television
campaign) is much more than a narrative of recent history. It is a
case study in politics, both the older and the newer versions. Political scientists in recent years have taken an increasingly critical view
of the traditional "structure and function" type of text to introduce
the subject of government to students. Even in secondary schools
old-fashioned civics is on the way out. The new approach is
through political behavior. Attention is focused on questions like
why do people in this or that district vote as they do? what draws
some voters to a candidate while others are repelled? why do many
people not vote? who are the nonvoters? what relation do national
origin, income, church, age, occupation, and other factors bear to
citizen participation in the political process? what role do the

parties actually play? what are the sources of tension within as well as between parties? how effective are advertising, television, radio, and newspapers? what role is played by major contributors? etc., etc. Some political scientists are mainly engaged in gathering data bearing on such matters, formulating hypotheses, and feeding computers to test them. Mathematics, often at a very high level, is a requisite for this kind of study of political behavior. But behavior is also studied, perhaps more effectively from the point of view of general readers and students, by means of case studies. Tom Coffman's book is a remarkably useful case study.

To be more than a tract a case study must take account, so far as possible, of all the factors that enter into a political event. This is what Tom Coffman has done. He sketches the history of partisan politics in modern Hawaii in terms of the changing social structure —from plantation to industry, from exclusive boardroom to union bureaucracy, from sparse rural population to dense urban concentration. He gives a brief but sufficiently accurate account of the transition from a sugar economy to contemporary diversification —tourism, the military, development construction, expanding higher education. But above all he pays close attention to the variety of people who give Hawaii its unique quality: the early domination of public—and private—decision-making by haoles (Caucasians recently or remotely from the mainland); the prominent political role of Hawaiians and part-Hawaiians; the emergence of people of Asian background, first in economic life and then in politics; the surge to power of the Japanese-descended minority—much the largest; and finally the tensions, political and otherwise, which hold the communities of Hawaii today in precarious balance.

Into this context Coffman places the political personalities and groupings which came into decisive combat in 1970. But despite the intrinsic interest of this story, its value as a case study in modern politics for anyone, student, teacher, plain citizen, interested in "what really happens" would be limited were it not for the methods used by all parties in the Hawaiian campaign of 1970. It is no accident that both the American Society of Political Consultants and its international counterpart heard special reports on the Hawaiian campaign in their convention the following year, or that a collage of campaign films for television won an award for political advertising at an international film festival. For old-fashioned canvassing, for political polling, for advertising consultation, and for television programming probably more money was spent per vote than in any previous election in the country. Coffman deals expertly not only with how the money was spent but with the decisions on how to spend it—and who contributed.

A book of this kind must stand or fall on the craft of its author. Political journalism is itself a part of the political process. National attention is commanded by the dispatches and columns of the Washington press corps. One of the prime elements in the success or failure of a president is his ability to deal with the press effectively, to project his personality and views on television. So it is with governors or mayors as they interact with the reporters around state capitols and city halls and seek to reach their constituencies through radio and television. Tom Coffman is young enough to take a fresh and absorbing interest in the politics of his state—and mature enough neither to be fooled by political pretense nor by the cover of smart-alec cynicism that protects some older reporters from their own failure to see the political process as a whole, with its failures, corruption, hope, talent, and remarkable achievement of keeping some degree of access to public decision-making open to all kinds and conditions of people.

STUART GERRY BROWN

Acknowledgements

For the time to research and write this book, I am indebted to my employers at the *Honolulu Star-Bulletin*. Hobart Duncan, executive editor, made the assignment; Edwin Edwards, city editor, initially edited the manuscript; and John Scott, publisher, carried the project through to completion. For background I drew on the work of many good reporters, particularly that of Byron Baker. The *Star-Bulletin*'s librarians helped tremendously. Most of the book's photo section is the work of *Star-Bulletin* photographers. Ron Youngblood edited the photos. Dr. Dan W. Tuttle's papers on Hawaii politics provided a valuable starting point, as did Lawrence Fuchs' excellent book *Hawaii Pono*. Many people gave valuable time for interviews. I particularly appreciated the candor of those who risked a measure of ill will from their respective political camps in the interest of written history. Jean Sadako King edited the manuscript. Such errors as the story may contain are, of course, mine alone. Here I add a word of peace and love for those who have cared selflessly through good times and bad: Herman and Helen Doi, Wayne and Mary Protheroe, Ulu, Bob Browne, Scoops Kreger, David Butwin, Jocelyn Fujii, Vicki Arbas, and others. As Donne wrote, *"Angels affect us oft."*

Reading Note
for Newcomers

For both Polynesian and Oriental words and names, it is usually correct if each vowel and syllable is pronounced phonetically. For the original Polynesian migrants, the word *Hawaiian* is reserved. All others, despite the awkward construction, are not Hawaiians but rather are residents of Hawaii, the people of Hawaii, and so forth. Throughout this book an American of Japanese ancestry is referred to as an AJA, which is standard in Hawaii. A *nisei* is an AJA born of immigrant Japanese parents. A *haole*, literally an outsider, is a Caucasian. Where other Polynesian and Asian words have been used, the author has attempted to provide the meaning in context.

People

John A. Burns—For sixteen years he had dominated the politics of Hawaii. Now, in 1970, he sought a third term as the new state's governor.

Thomas P. Gill—Within the Burns-dominated Democratic party, Gill had played the role of young upstart. By 1970 it appeared that his time had come.

Joseph Napolitan—Known nationally as a manager of Democratic presidential candidates, Napolitan in 1970 served Burns as strategist for the new politics of total media campaigning.

Jack Seigle—He coordinated the media campaign.

George Ariyoshi—Campaigning for lieutenant governor, Ariyoshi played the role of Burns' dream for Hawaii come true.

Robert C. Oshiro—He managed the Burns campaign.

Samuel P. King—King ran for governor on the Republican ticket.

Dates

1941—Pearl Harbor.

1946—The young American war veterans of Japanese ancestry returned to Hawaii as heroes, determined to become first-class citizens.

1954—Led by John A. Burns, with Thomas P. Gill playing a supporting role, the young war veterans captured the Hawaii legislature as Democrats.

1959—Hawaii became the 50th state, and for the first time elected its own governor.

Catch a Wave

1

To Govern Hawaii

The year 1970 was only the eleventh year of statehood, so that as a state Hawaii was still young, still enthralled by the right to self-government, still feeling out its role as America's newest state. Yet as a society Hawaii had a grand tradition, a long tradition, of which it was perhaps not altogether aware. Perhaps not in the sense of a collectively shared awareness of a rich past, because the struggle *to become* was still intense, the pace of movement always headlong. The modern history of the Islands had been one of precipitous, sometimes chaotic change, change that had come fast and faster still, so that events tumbled upon events rather than flowing. And in the rush of things there was little time to reflect.

In 1970, because thinking turned so heavily on who next would govern, there was little time to reflect on the fact that the eight islands—embracing more than a thousand years of Polynesian culture—first had been governed by a king, a monarch.

Historically the Asian and European peoples who had poured into the Polynesian kingdom likewise had been governed by kings and emperors, by men who in their time had been accepted as a fusion of God and state.

And even after the Polynesian kingdom had been annexed as a United States territory, it was governed not by popular consent but by a higher authority, by a governor imposed on the Islands by the president of the United States. For six decades following annexation, Hawaii had had to struggle for full membership in the United States, for voting representatives in Congress, and for the right to elect a governor.

All that lay in the past.

Statehood. In the staid *Honolulu Star-Bulletin* the big red headline in 1959 was itself a revolution. It was six inches high, and this was twice as high as an earlier headline—"War"—which had appeared on December 7, 1941. With statehood Hawaii's people became first-class citizens. And no doubt this meant something more in Hawaii than it had in other new states, because in Hawaii a majority of the people had known in more ways than one what it was like to be second-class citizens.

There immediately had been a gubernatorial election in 1959. The second was in 1962, and after that the election was held at intervals of four years, which meant that the third gubernatorial election was in 1966, and the fourth would be in 1970.

Nineteen seventy would yield the most remarkable campaign in the state's eleven years, but it would be more than that. It would be one of the most extraordinary campaigns ever waged for control of a state capitol.

It would be waged as Hawaii was reaching a vital turning point, at a time when the new post-World War II forces were only just being reconciled to the old. And it would be waged at a time when this new consensus—in the person of John Burns—would in turn be assaulted by forces of even more contemporary origin.

As lightning in the night may briefly illumine the contour of breaking waves, so the campaign would capture in stark outline a time of transition.

Once underway, the campaign season would run on far longer than had any before it in Hawaii, dominating conversation much as it dominated the news.

Yet the length of it alone was enough to numb the mind, and much of what was most telling was, at the time, either politely overlooked or a well-guarded secret.

Only afterward was it apparent that race and ethnicity had played such a large role, and that historic attachments proved to be so persistent, each racial group reacting in its own way to style, image, and issues. If not contrary to the Pacific Golden Man mystique which is Hawaii's special halo, the ethnic undercurrents of the campaign reaffirmed the historic view of Hawaii as a series of immigrant waves, each contending for its place in the sun.

An amazing degree of sophistication went into the campaign, a near-revolutionary refinement of technique that departed radically from traditional Island politicking.

To be sure, everyone was aware that the old-time neighborhood rally—the hula dancers and the flamboyant, fiery speechmakers—had slipped into the past. But just how far into the past was a matter that escaped most people.

Although there is no national clearinghouse for evaluating campaigns, it well may be that in 1970 Hawaii experienced the most sophisticated application of polling, technology, and electronics in the history of American politics.

The winning campaign was to receive national, then international recognition. As a small and isolated laboratory, Hawaii proved ideal for the scientific engineering of images and issues.

The struggle over governing a state of fewer than 800,000 people attracted the talents of professionals who had handled campaigns for the United States presidency, foreign heads of states, and dozens of governors, U.S. senators, and congressmen across the country.

Yet during the campaign only a handful of people in Hawaii recognized the names of technicians who had participated in revamping the nature of Mainland campaigning in the 1960s.

The marriage of highly professionalized strategy to Island politics meant unprecedented campaign costs, too. But, again, few appreciated the quantity expended in the pursuit of power.

The total reported bill ran to nearly $2 million, almost four times the cost of the 1968 battle for control of Honolulu's City Hall.

The winner alone spent nearly a million dollars on Hawaii's tiny electorate, amounting to almost a tenth of the money which Democrat Hubert Humphrey had spent two years earlier campaigning for the nation's presidency.

Fittingly, the prelude was not a mere year or two, but many years, dating to the early 1950s, when John Burns was struggling to organize the Democratic party. And Tom Gill was a bright and brash young man just graduated from law school.

By 1966, the two were on a collision course in public, visibly so when, as governor, John Burns attempted to frustrate Gill's short-range ambition of capturing the state's second-highest office, that of lieutenant governor. Burns was no doubt being wary of Gill's larger ambitions.

At the outset of the 1966 political season, John Burns was at the height of his powers. He had been the prime maker of the triumphant Democratic party, a two-term delegate of the territory to Congress, and had managed the Hawaii Statehood Bill through Congress. In 1966 he was well into the fourth year of his first term as the state's governor, having won his office by a landslide vote. He commanded a working majority in the state legislature. His closest allies ran the Honolulu City Council, and his influence extended into the office of mayor, even though the occupant was a nominal Republican.

There was no real threat to his own reelection in sight.

For a running mate in 1966, Burns had placed his considerable prestige on soft-spoken, part-Hawaiian Kenneth F. Brown, an architect and corporate businessman who was untested in the field of political combat.

Burns' candidate had not just lost. He had been swamped.

While the defeat in a narrow sense had not mattered that much —by law, the lieutenant governor's only real job is administering the elections—in a general way it mattered enormously, because Burns had lost far more than working control of this spare-part office.

He had lost a potential successor of his choosing, someone who —properly groomed—could be elected to govern Hawaii when his own day was done, presumably in 1970. And in the process, Burns and his powerful allies had lost face. The governor had campaigned ineptly, alienated people who previously had been either content or indifferent, and then had nearly lost the general election to the Republicans.

The impression that the Burns power bloc could direct the course of events just so, just as it saw fit—an impression which then was very widespread—had evaporated as the votes were tallied.

The worst of it from Burns' viewpoint was the new spare part, who for years had been anathema to the power structure of the Island chain, Thomas Gill.

In the initial low-stakes bout of 1966, Tom Gill had beaten not only Burns' man, Kenny Brown. He had beaten the Burns organization. He had won office against the will of the party's prime maker.

Gill had, with a large assist from Burns by virtue of Burns' opposition, enhanced his reputation as the gutsy and unyielding underdog. And in this there was a special irony, because the underdog role was the role which John Burns had played in an earlier day, and on this role his political legend had been built.

From the 1966 election day on, the question of future power over direction of the Islands intensified, sometimes subtly behind the scenes, sometimes publicly. And as each year passed, the 1970 race for the governorship loomed larger. The prospect of impending conflict ranged through the chambers of the state legislature, through both political parties, through political lobbies big and little, and down to the most obscure community organizations, in which one faction might attach itself to John Burns and another to Tom Gill.

It fed story after story to the press, created a mood of uncertainty among businessmen, aggravated the chronic factional warfare within organized labor, and gradually propelled droves of spectators into the combined drudgery and fever of campaign politics.

This was a confrontation of strong personalities, a pairing of heavyweights, a contest that would open the new decade.

In part, the tension reflected the more tangible stakes of the campaign, a political office of incomparable influence in Hawaii, for reasons unique to Hawaii.

The governor of Hawaii mixes with admirals and generals, business giants, celebrities, and the continuous stream of foreign and domestic dignitaries who traverse the Pacific. He is chauffeured in a black limousine.

He resides near the new $30 million capitol building in a mansion constructed for the last of the monarchs, called Washington Place, where he is served by a staff of cooks, maids, and uniformed guards who beep messages among themselves on walkie-talkies, and also carry revolvers on their belts.

The governor is also Hawaii's first host, and for that role he has a generous slush fund, administered by a protocol office which dispatches the engraved invitations to that endless string of early-evening state receptions.

To the uninitiated there is something a trifle awesome about that first walk up the steps of the mansion—the official greeting, and the tinkling ice in cocktail glasses on the mansion's east lanai. Here and there you spot people of particular influence, the governor drifting among them, and you are left to wonder if something of importance transpired in conversation.

From the mist of past days, there remain the overtones of supreme authority, of an office that is more than a political office, and this is accentuated by the state's isolation in the Pacific, some 5,500 miles from Congress and the president.

The governor sets the tone for Island life. He is not only the first creator of policy, but also the foremost creator of values. John Burns when first elected was asked to join the all-haole Pacific Club. He declined. By the decade's end, this spa of the haole elite had members from all the races, first on a token basis, then in substantial numbers.

As a public forum, the office of governor can command more attention than any other in Hawaii. With a word to his press secretary, the governor can assemble reporters from every major media in his chambers at a moment's notice.

In exercising his power, a governor is damned and praised, courted and pressured. In any case, it is testimony to his importance.

In a policy sense, he is a far more powerful figure in his domain than are his Mainland counterparts.

The tradition of the kingdom had found its way into the state's constitution and into the law, and the strategy for securing statehood also had played its part.

This is because Hawaii's constitution was drafted in a convention in 1950, and this was a time when the concept of a strong chief executive had come into its own nationally. And above all, the drafters of the constitution wanted to be in tune with national sentiment, because the convention's real agenda was to demonstrate the territory's readiness for self-government and statehood. For the nine years between 1950 and statehood in 1959, the constitution was really nothing but a page of testimony before Congress.

But after experience with statehood, Hawaii's 1968 Constitutional Convention merely reaffirmed the concept of centralizing authority in the chief executive.

The result is an assignment of power to the governor far surpassing most Mainland states, whose antiquated constitutions were drafted during periods of general mistrust of government.

For an executive of such power, the annual salary is modest but adequate, $42,000.

It was this office which John Burns, an enigmatic and solitary figure, would defend. During the campaign he still would be introduced occasionally as the Great White Father, and this introduction would be made without self-consciousness. To a Tom Gill, such a thing was preposterous.

2

Greening of Hawaii

In the climate of the 1970 election, one central fact stood out from the 1960s: rapid growth—a fast-growing economy and a fast-growing population.

For every eighty people in Hawaii in 1960, there were over a hundred by 1970. In ten years, the population jumped from 633,000 to 770,000, making Hawaii the eighth fastest-growing of the fifty states.

Although the Neighbor Islands had experienced a slight growth for the first time since World War II, 137,000 of Hawaii's new people had packed themselves into Honolulu and its sprawling suburbs. In a decade, the city's skyline shot up from the dominant quaintness of two-story and three-story buildings to twenty- and thirty-story skyscrapers.

The greatest mass of high-rise buildings was concentrated in Waikiki, the locus of Hawaii's tourism, which in the 1960s displaced sugar and pineapple as the Islands' leading local industry.

The number of hotel rooms more than tripled. From the 1960 total of 300,000 people, the number of tourists arriving in Hawaii increased fivefold.

Retail sales doubled. Contracting nearly tripled.

Defense spending almost doubled, stimulated by the war in Vietnam.

Wages and salaries increased by about 50 per cent, and the number of cars on the road by 70 per cent. Virtually every household in Hawaii had a TV set. Unemployment dropped below the theoretical possible low of 3 per cent to 2.7 per cent.

Tax revenues far more than doubled, much of the new money going into the education system which, everyone agreed, was improved dramatically.

In the American tradition, growth was progress, and progress was good.

It provided work and membership for the labor unions, spiraling profits to the businessman, and revenue to finance government.

In truth, Hawaii was undergoing an economic and social revolution. Statehood had put Hawaii on the map, had made it psychologically accessible, had shrunk the vast Pacific expanse. Hawaii became a state just as the big jets hit the runways, and to the expanded air routes was added yet another factor. Only a year after statehood, John F. Kennedy became president, and the Kennedy-Johnson regimes precipitated an unprecedented national affluence.

By the late 1960s, Hawaii was undergoing yet another revolution, this one in values and attitudes. Or, more rightly, it was a reaction. The firmest of American tenets, that growth is progress and progress is good, was suddenly thrown open to question.

Hawaii was fairly aching with growth and progress.

Horace Sutton, America's leading travel writer, would describe Waikiki to the nation as a "concrete jungle, a raucous sideshow . . . a billion-dollar cement mistake. It got that way because of need, greed, and neglect."

Except for its far Diamond Head end, Waikiki Beach had been all but taken over by tourists, and Waikiki's resident population had actually declined while the state's population mushroomed.

While hotel construction boomed, the Islands were feeling a housing squeeze of crisis proportions. Study and restudy varied on the magnitude of the problem, but all suggested that it was staggering. During the decade, rents doubled, placing Hawaii's rent rates second only to Alaska's. Less than half of the houses were owned by their occupants. And home ownership was priced out of the hands of anyone who made less than thirteen or fourteen thousand dollars a year.

The cost of an average house was twice the national average. About a fifth of the existing housing was classified as overcrowded. And at least an eighth was classified as dilapidated. The latest of many studies concluded that Hawaii was short 50,000 reasonably priced housing units and suggested that the situation would grow worse.

University students put up a tent city on campus in early 1970, and a family who had lost its house made front-page news by pitching a lean-to on the grounds of Iolani Palace.

House- and apartment-sharing became so common that Hawaii led the nation in average number of people per housing unit.

The first air pollution stories appeared in 1965, to be read by a public which was largely convinced that an island swept by gentle trade winds could never be polluted. By 1970, air pollution—most of it coming from the ever-increasing number of cars—was a fact of life. One could smell it and see it.

Rush-hour bumper-to-bumper traffic became a reality, too, particularly in downtown Honolulu and in the sprawling new suburban districts of Leeward and Windward Oahu.

Water pollution and the dying plant and animal life of streams, bays, and off-shore reefs were a new fact of Hawaii's life. And the noise of airplanes, street traffic, jackhammers, and piledrivers became ever more of an irritant. One out-of-town writer seized on the plight of a Japanese crane in Honolulu zoo, which purportedly was "near a nervous breakdown . . . [because] the crane is so busy tilting its crested head to follow each warplane or tourist plane zooming in to land on Hawaii's golden beaches."

At the far end of the gloom spectrum, a Youth Congress—after four days of agonizing in the summer of 1970—voted by a two-to-one margin that the ultimate solution was secession from America, something which eleven southern states had tried in 1861 without success.

The mental health of the crane in the zoo was not to be a campaign issue, nor was secession from the Union. But, however bizarre, these things reflected an expanding feeling that the old reverence for growth and progress was being discarded for good.

So far as issues played a role in the campaign (issues were increasingly obscured as election day neared), this change in values was a major turning point in Hawaii politics. Yet beneath such tangible growth issues as housing, traffic, and pollution there was something more subtle at work, a something of compelling political importance. There was a nagging anxiety that the wave of newly arrived Mainland haoles, the Caucasians attracted by tourism and big jets and statehood, was eroding Island tradition. There was a feeling seldom openly voiced that the new wave was jeopardizing the comfortable ways of Island life, and likewise was threatening the prominent role of non-Caucasians in Island politics.

Those of Asian descent no sooner had begun enjoying their liberation from rule by an elite haole oligarchy than they were faced with a tide of new settlers from mainland America.

The 1960 federal census found that Caucasians had risen to 32 per cent of the population, compared to 32.2 per cent of Japanese ancestry, with the balance distributed among smaller ethnic groups

—mainly part-Hawaiians, 14.4 per cent; Filipinos, 10.9 per cent; and Chinese, 6 per cent.

Annual tallies of "intended residents"—widely circulated in the press—started at 14,000 in 1961 and consistently ran over 30,000 in the last four years of the decade. (The impression created by these reports was highly misleading, because well over half of the intended residents came and left.)

At a Governor's Conference on Immigration, the state's planning director estimated the net Mainland migration at 90,000.

A state manpower official claimed that the immigrant wave suggested a haole majority within a decade.

A bank official erroneously fixed the haole population at 41 per cent, predicting that a haole majority was not far off.

At the same conference, State Statistician Robert Schmitt took issue with the fear "voiced by local residents that Hawaii will soon have a haole majority," estimating that AJAs still slightly outnumbered haoles, and that a whopping remainder of 42 per cent was distributed among other groups—many of mixed blood. He conceded, however, that Caucasians might go over the 50 per cent mark in twenty years or so.

The incumbent governor, while upholding his "Open Society" theme, meaning that all must be welcomed, added, "We want to keep in balance the unique character of our society, that character which makes us the envy of the world."

In private, Governor Burns would put it more succinctly. At his desk on the fifth floor of the State Capitol, Burns would write down the number 51. "If any group goes over that," Burns would tell a reporter, "then Hawaii is in trouble—everyone is in trouble." Fifty-one per cent.

In the private offices of non-Caucasian state legislators, particularly it seemed AJA legislators, there would be occasional talk of the new immigrant wave, of how best to survive it, and of how to integrate the new immigrants politically by bringing them into the given order.

The new immigrants, for their part, were a mixed lot, but tended to be young, aggressive, and well educated—they fell disproportionately into professional, technical, and managerial positions, but some simply hit the beach, as had many an adventurer before them.

While many eagerly sought to fit in, to adapt, to learn Island ways, others tended to be traditionally WASPish and ethnocentric, not *haole* but white, reacting to all slights, real or otherwise, being used as they were to having things their way. And the apprehension generated by this strain of the new immigrants no doubt was magnified by the national experience of the 1960s, in which the blacks had struggled endlessly against white society to secure the most basic rights of Western democracy.

Although the data was hopelessly confusing, the idea had become widespread that Mainland haoles were upsetting Hawaii's ethnic balance.

But while it is certain that haole influence was—and is—on the upsurge, the impression of a heavy impact on the 1970 campaign may have been almost totally in error.

A researcher for the Burns camp, after a study of voters expected to participate in the all-important Democratic primary, concluded that AJAs still outnumbered haoles two-and-a-half to one. The ethnic breakdown—the only statewide analysis known to exist—was as follows:

—AJA, 45.8%	—Filipino, 9.7%
—Caucasian, 20%	—Chinese, 5.3%
—Part-Hawaiian and Hawaiian, 16.9%	—Unclassified, 2.3%

The 1970 census breakdown would come as a footnote, published after the election. It registered a climb of Caucasians to 38.8 per cent and a drop of AJAs to 28.3 per cent. (Robert Schmitt, Hawaii's most distinguished demographer, would sharply disagree with the method of the census—contending that it skewed the Caucasian percentage upward, mainly at the expense of part-Hawaiians.)

It could be debated endlessly how much, and in what way, the crash of the Mainland wave on Island ethnic history affected the campaign. It could not be ignored.

3
John Burns: Consensus

As the 1970 election year loomed, John Burns was in peculiar straits. Even though he was a two-term incumbent, his base of popular support was remarkably narrow. A poll by the *Star-Bulletin* found that Burns was the first choice of only 25 per cent of the electorate. Even though most of the major power centers in Hawaii politics supported him, he was trailing badly behind the upstart lieutenant governor, Tom Gill, in trial-heat polls, by as much as 20 per cent on populous Oahu, according to one of his own polls.

Burns had held the state's highest office for seven years, but most voters didn't know what he had been doing as governor, as a $27,000 research project would later reveal.

And even though he had been in the public eye for more than twenty years, Jack Burns' personal and political history was not widely known.

A further riddle was the governor's attitude toward the coming campaign. Throughout 1969, he was publicly dropping hints that he planned to run again, but privately he was indicating a strong desire to retire from public life.

In truth, he later would say, he was undecided throughout 1969.

Candidate or not, the old political warhorse presented a striking figure. His thinning hair was snow-white, his long face deeply wrinkled around the eyes and mouth, ruddy and sunburned from his twice-a-week rounds on the golf course. He remained lean and fantastically erect, as if he were still in police blue.

He was sixty-one, and he had lived to see his early hopes for Hawaii largely come to pass.

Sixty-one, he would say, is a nice age to retire. The year before, Burns' wife of thirty-nine years, Beatrice, had been seriously ill.

Burns had just finished building a new house, in Kailua on the windward side of Oahu, which sat empty most of the time awaiting occupants.

He had devoted more than half of his adult life to politics and, although not wealthy, he was assured of a comfortable government retirement.

His place in the history of the young state was secure, yet the early polls were so consistently bad that he faced a strong possibility of ending his career in defeat.

Further, he once had proposed that no one hold the office of governor for more than two terms, an indication that he shared the conventional American distrust of anyone holding power too long.

And, in a curious sort of way, he seemed perpetually amazed that he had ever risen to such heights.

Burns once described himself as "the most accidental goshdamned office-holder you ever saw."

He would ask, in his typically rambling way, "You tell a kid from Kalihi—a high school graduate whose mother took in laundry at one time, and whose highest job was a post office clerk—that he would be a member of Congress and then governor of a state?"

It was true—his life story was mostly a hard-times story, and perhaps because of it he possessed an uncanny instinct for people who had known hard times.

His father was an Army sergeant, Harry Burns, and had been stationed at a fort in Montana when John Anthony was born, the first of four children, two boys and two girls. Four years after the birth of his first son, Harry Burns was reassigned to Oahu's Fort Shafter. Five years later, when Jack Burns was nine, Harry Burns vanished, never to be seen by his son again. Mrs. Burns was left to raise the future governor and her three other children in Honolulu's rough Kalihi district.

John Burns, many years later, seldom talked of his childhood, but when asked he would hint broadly—mischievously, even—that he had been a tough little rebel.

He endured nine years of priestly discipline at Saint Louis School, then was packed off to Catholic schools in Kansas for another dose, first at Leavenworth's Immaculata High School in his sophomore year, then at Atchison's St. Benedict's High School in his junior year. He spent more time on basketball and football than in study. And after his junior year he dropped out, did a year's hitch in the Army, then worked for his ship passage back to the Territory of Hawaii. At 19 he reenrolled in Saint Louis, finished his senior year and picked up a diploma. More bouncing around: Burns landed a job as a night-desk cub on the *Star-Bulletin,* then enrolled at the University of Hawaii. For him college was an aimless venture. He didn't know what he wanted out of it, and he abandoned it quickly—before the semester was up.

More odd jobs followed and then, at twenty-two, Burns married Beatrice Van Fleet, an Army nurse, who perhaps could not have guessed that one day she would be a First Lady. The young couple took off for California, where Burns ran a fruit farm (pears and grapes) owned by his wife's uncle. Those were the worst of the depression years, 1931, 1932, and 1933. And Burns' fling at farming came to an end when his wife's family, strapped for money, took over operation of the farm.

So Burns returned to Hawaii, worked briefly in a pineapple cannery, then as a driver-salesman for a dairy.

At twenty-five he made it onto the Honolulu police force, where he would spend eleven crucial years of his life. Like every cop he started at the bottom, as a beat patrolman, then a detective. But he made rank fast. In seven years, at the age of thirty-two, he was promoted to captain. The year was 1941.

War was raging in Europe and Asia, and for isolationist America it was only a matter of time. History dropped a bizarre assignment in Jack Burns' lap, to head a five-man intelligence group. Its job was to probe Honolulu's Japanese community for possible espionage and subversion in the event of war with Japan.

Looking back, it would be hard to dream up a more unlikely twist: Jack Burns was tapped to play the agent of suspicion, a bit part in what would be a national travesty. By the very nature of the assignment, Burns seemed bound to make enemies throughout the Japanese community, but just the opposite occurred. It was the beginning of a mutual allegiance which, after years of struggle, would change the course of Hawaii's history.

It would endure the next twenty-nine years, down through the election of 1970.

But in early 1941, no one could see beyond the specter of international war. And the immediate problem was the so-called loyalty question.

As Burns himself told the story, the first significant event was a meeting of young Americans of Japanese ancestry at McKinley High School. Anticipating the coming war, they organized "with the idea they were going to be placed on the spot." As a way of demonstrating allegiance to America, a group from the McKinley meeting went to the police department offering to serve on the reserve police force. The department's top brass took a dim view of the offer, but Burns proposed that they be deployed as an extension of his espionage operation. Burns organized a network of young AJAs who were to serve as contacts in every Japanese neighborhood throughout Oahu.

Like the police department, the FBI, Army, and Navy also were at work on the same question, the possibility of espionage.

Burns submitted the names of his contact group to the FBI, which eventually came through with security clearances for its members.

Burns felt the U.S. agencies liked the idea: "The FBI and G-2 (Army intelligence) couldn't get anything out of them. They couldn't speak pidgin or anything else. They were running into stone walls."

Finally a date was set for the first meeting of the contact group, a Monday evening, December 8, 1941.*

It was canceled by the Sunday morning waves of Japanese bombers which devastated Pearl Harbor and threw the Islands into a fit of hysteria. Rumors, all later proven false, bombarded police and military authorities. Local Japanese had poisoned the water. Arrows had been cut in the cane fields pointing the way to Pearl Harbor. Clandestine radio operators were transmitting information to the Japanese military. Caches of guns, ammunition, and dynamite were buried in various Japanese communities. Japanese pilots shot down in the air raid were wearing McKinley High School rings.

On the West Coast, the Japanese communities were being interned en masse in concentration camps which eventually swelled to over 100,000 people.

In Honolulu, on December 7, Burns met with the FBI and Army intelligence.

The Army had a contingency plan for arrests, but in the confusion of the attack it seemed unworkable.

It fell to Burns to direct the arrests, and, in his words, "I went along at the time with the idea, which was to take the leadership."

Shinto priests, the principals of Japanese language schools, and affiliates of the Japanese consulate made up the bulk of the roundup —370 on December 7 and 8, around 1600 within a week.

---

*According to one Contact Group member, who years later still referred to Burns as "Captain Burns": "Some of our own people called us *inu*, dogs, and held us in suspicion. They misunderstood our purpose."

In an office set up in the old Dillingham Building near the waterfront, three people pored over the arrest list. They were Burns, Robert Shivers of the FBI, and George Bicknell of Army intelligence.

Of the three, as Burns saw it, he and Shivers had the more intimate knowledge of the Japanese community. The three men voted their way down the list: "I'd come to a name of a person I knew and I would say, 'I think he's a damned fine American through and through.' Shivers would generally be in agreement with me."

Several hundred people were released.

The remainder were impounded on Sand Island (most accounts estimate the number at a thousand, including Neighbor Islanders), then shipped to the Mainland.*

With the assignment imposed by the national government behind him, Burns set out to help stabilize the Japanese community and minimize the continued suspicions of disloyalty.

By order of martial law, all Japanese-language radio stations and newspapers had been closed down.

In January, Captain Burns revived his idea of a police contact group as a vehicle for internal communication—a system for checking out scare rumors, quieting the sense of fear, outlining the harsh realities of martial law, and translating information to those of the immigrant generation who spoke no English. Flanked by two nisei, dentist Ernest Murai and Masa Katagiri, an insurance salesman, Burns enlisted AJAs in groups of threes and fours until an Islandwide network was reestablished.

*Many writers have stressed that the AJAs of Hawaii suffered little, at least numerically, in comparison to their Mainland counterparts, thanks to the forces of Hawaii economics and interracial aloha. Writers also have created an impression that AJAs unanimously accepted their fate passively and stoically, and that the whole affair was rather quickly forgotten. This is not altogether true. For example, in 1941 a teen-age AJA—years later a legislator—awoke to find his father's temple surrounded by GI's. The soldiers sacked the temple and took his father away. "I was a kid, but still I was the oldest, so I took care of the other kids. Through the whole war we ate only rice balls and *miso* soup, or nothing. That's why I'm in politics— I said 'Never again.' " A high state official during the 1960s was eighteen in 1941, and was making plans to become a doctor. His father also was taken away to the Mainland, leaving him with heavy family responsibilities which precluded his gaining a formal education. He once told me, "I carry this around in my guts even now. It made me forever sympathetic to the underdog." A year after the gubernatorial election, Hawaii's AJA representatives in the U.S. Congress would lead the successful drive to repeal the "emergency detention" provision of the Internal Security Act—this, at a time when many blacks and dissenters actively feared being thrown into concentration camps. Particular credit goes to U.S. Rep. Spark M. Matsunaga. Generally, in contemporary Hawaii, I venture to speculate that cultural identity is still a crippling thing for some people, flowing in large part from the suppression of the AJA ethnic culture in the now long-ago years of World War II.

Burns' Police Contact Group was one of several overlapping organizations which were to shepherd Honolulu through the war years. It was linked closely to the military-sanctioned Morale Committee and its AJA subcommittee, the Emergency Service Committee.

Burns was involved with each, which in turn were instrumental in promoting the historic military volunteer movement of the nisei, the Varsity Victory Volunteers and the 442nd Regimental Combat Team.

Bit by bit, the young police captain was backing into politics. His personal contacts were multiplying to the hundreds and thousands, ranging from his organizing campaigns to managing a Japanese baseball team, the Asahis (Morning Sun), who for wartimes' sake changed their name to the Athletics.

Some of his contacts were fleeting, others intimate. The effect was cumulative.

As a direct consequence of December 7, 1941, in the dark night of war, modern Hawaii was born. In the global sense, the Pacific would become an American lake. But within Hawaii, the emergence of a modern and egalitarian society would result—more than for any other reason—from the trauma and injustice brought down on Hawaii's Japanese-Americans, and from their determination to endure and to secure an equal status as Americans. This, their hour of trial, was to be regarded one day as their hour of greatness, and Jack Burns was on hand to give them moral support.

In the early days of panic following December 7, two who came to know of Burns as a helping friend were Ted Tsukiyama and Edwin Honda.

Both were in the Reserve Officers Training Corps (ROTC) at the university when the bombs fell.

They reported to the old armory on Beretania Street—now the site of the State Capitol—and were issued khakis and Springfield bolt-action rifles, the type that is loaded and fired one bullet at a time.

Renamed the Hawaii Territorial Guard, the ROTC unit was posted around the island on beaches, roads, bridges, water pumping stations, and communication centers in anticipation of a ground invasion.

Honda guarded the bridge over the Ala Wai canal between the city and Waikiki, which then was covered more by kiawe than hotels. The Territorial Guard was to last only six weeks. Then, abruptly, the armed AJAs were disbanded by the military government on January 21, 1942, stripped of their rifles and uniforms.

Honda was in tears, as were other guardsmen. He would remember "a feeling of complete frustration—a mixture of being totally angry, sad, and helpless."

Stunned, the would-be soldiers turned to older leaders on the Morale Committee, who encouraged them to try again. Tsukiyama, with the help of Honda and several others, drafted a letter to the territory's military governor, Lt. Gen. Delos Emmons.

Given the hysterical climate of the moment, the letter was one of the important first steps in settling the loyalty business. In part the letter to Emmons said: ". . . we were deeply disappointed when we were told that our services in the Guard were no longer needed." But, it continued, "Hawaii is our home; the United States our country. We know but one loyalty, and that is to the Stars and Stripes. We wish to do our part as loyal Americans in every way possible. . . ."

The Morale Committee was working behind the scenes to bring Emmons around to the idea of giving the young AJAs a chance, and finally Emmons sanctioned an assembly at the University of Hawaii on February 25. About 150 ex-Guardsmen were dubbed the Varsity Victory Volunteers and attached to the Army, albeit for dirty work.

There was little glamor in the VVV. Stationed at Schofield Barracks, the VVV was commanded by a Caucasian whose second-ranking officer was a Chinese-American. The top sergeant was the famous part-Hawaiian athlete, Tommy Kaulukukui. The VVV built roads and bridges, dug ditches, strung barbed wire, and fought boredom by playing Ping-Pong, courting the girls, watching movies, listening to lectures.

They donated blood to the blood bank, bought war bonds avidly ($27,000 in a ten-month period), and waited it out for a more dignified chance to prove themselves loyal citizens.

The records of a slogan contest give a glimpse into the collective feel of the VVV. The winning slogan was: "Work up a sweat and the sun will set." Another winner was: "Let not our efforts be in vain." Patience, endurance.

Burns went to Schofield and enlisted Ted Tsukiyama to talk in AJA plantation towns—"just to calm them, to smooth them over."

"It was morale work, wiping out the tendency toward hysteria," as Tsukiyama would remember the talks.

While the VVV sweated it out at Schofield Barracks, AJAs from established National Guard units were assembled in June 1942, shipped to the Mainland for training, and renamed the 100th Battalion. However, Selective Service remained closed to AJAs until January of 1943, when General Emmons, impressed by the VVV and the 100th, announced a call for 1,500 volunteers.

The Emergency Service Committee campaigned for a big turnout, perhaps needlessly. The pace-setting Victory Volunteers dissolved and signed up almost to a man to fight. Of an estimated 17,000 AJAs who would have been draft eligible under normal circumstances, 10,000 volunteered to fight. Eventually the resulting outfit, the 442nd, swelled to 7,500 men, almost half of whom were to be wounded, a thousand of them seriously. Seven hundred would die on the battlefields of Europe.

On the home front, Burns continued working with the AJAs, primarily through the Emergency Service Committee, whose members overlapped heavily with his own Police Contact Group.

The AJA Emergency Service Committee led the avid demonstration of loyalty to America. It encouraged donations to blood banks, ran a Speak-American campaign, helped close down the Japanese language schools, collected flowers from Japanese flower farmers for the graves of those killed on December 7, removed Japanese signs and "other visible sources of irritation."

One of the committee's most eye-catching projects was a $10,-000 Bombs on Tokyo fund-raising campaign. When the check was presented to the military, it was accompanied by a statement that said: "We are real Americans and we are going to act and fight like Americans. We hope that this money will be used for bombs which will give Tojo and his cutthroats bloody hell."

The Emergency Service Committee's executive secretary was Mitsuyuki "Mits" Kido, who in 1959 would run with Burns as a candidate for lieutenant governor. Kido first met Burns in the early days of the war, and in Kido's eyes, "During this period he absorbed our aspirations."

By 1944, Burns, Kido, and three others were meeting almost weekly to lay plans for postwar times, their efforts stimulated by messages from the warfront which Kido summarized as saying:

"Here we have sacrificed ourselves. Now what is our place in Hawaii when we come back?*

"We asked each other, 'What the hell are we going to do when these kids come home?' That made a politician out of me." They settled on the Democratic party as the vehicle for reordering the feudal system. "We said we would stand for equality of opportunity, regardless of race. We wanted acceptance as first-class citizens. Our second goal was to raise the standard of living and the standard of education."

The other three participants in the weekly meetings were Ernest Murai, who had helped Burns organize the Police Contact Group; Jack Kawano, an ILWU (International Longshoremen's and Warehousemen's Union) organizer; and politician Chuck Mau.

After four long years, the war came to an end.

Almost immediately Burns turned in his resignation to the police department, intent on reorganizing a party that had never controlled an elected legislative body in the history of Hawaii.

He was thirty-six, the father of three children, and his wife was permanently crippled by polio. He would support himself the next three years on a real estate license and a liquor store, then for six years as Oahu's Civil Defense director.

A latter-day Burns would particularly like to recall a 1946 encounter with Roy Vitousek, a former house speaker and chairman of the entrenched majority Republican party.

Over lunch at the Pacific Club, Vitousek offered to back him for a race in the next election if Burns would sign up as a Republican. Burns said no thanks, he wasn't interested, that he intended instead to build the Democrats into the majority party.

Vitousek said it could never be done.

*The depth of feeling behind these messages is not to be underestimated. One soldier wrote that he and his comrades had "risked life and limb time and time again that persons of Japanese descent may walk the streets in dignity." Another letter, likewise recorded by author Thomas Murphy: "If we return home to find that we are still Japs in the eyes of the guys who have grown fat with dough during the war, we are going to find beautiful platitudes like equality of opportunity and such blown, as we are being blown here; and then we are going to suffer as we have never before suffered. . . ." The 100th and 442nd received enormous press coverage, numerous Presidental Unit Citations, and were honored by President Truman as follows: "You fought not only the enemy but you fought prejudice—and you have won. Keep up that fight and we will continue to win—to make this great Republic stand for just what the Constitution says it stands for—the welfare of all the people all of the time. Bring forward the colors." The political struggle in Hawaii, excepting Burns and a few others, had yet to begin.

Burns recalled telling the Republican powerhouse, "It won't be for lack of trying."

By 1948, Burns had gathered enough support to become the Oahu chairman of the Democratic party.

In the fall of 1948 he made his first run for elective office, a last-minute move to fill the ticket.

It was a patently impossible race for delegate to Congress against the popular Republican incumbent, Joseph Farrington.

Burns lost dismally, receiving only a quarter of the total vote. But in his eyes it was an important turning point. His fondest memory of the 1948 campaign was a telephone call from a young war veteran studying at the university, Dan Inouye.

" 'Are you serious about running?' Inouye asked.

" 'Yes, but I'm not going to get elected.'

" 'But if you're serious I still want to work for you.'

"I said, 'Fine, that makes two of us.' And after that the young guys really started coming in."

One of the new young men was Inouye's war-front first sergeant, Dan Aoki, who would become Burns' top political sergeant.

By 1950 Aoki was president of the 442nd Veterans Club, and Sakae Takahashi was head of the Club 100.

Burns' group was growing—Inouye, Aoki, Mike Tokunaga, Takahashi, Herman Lum, Bill Richardson, Shigeto Kanemoto, Matsuo Takabuki.

In 1950, Takahashi won a seat on the old Honolulu Board of Supervisors. Then, partly as a result of behind-the-scenes dealing by Burns and Kido, Takahashi was appointed by Democratic Gov. Oren E. Long to be the first AJA treasurer of the territory.

In 1952 Burns rose from Oahu chairman to territorial chairman of the Democratic party, which was slowly chipping out a base of elected power. The same year, Matsuo Takabuki won a seat on the Honolulu Board of Supervisors.

To people like Aoki, Burns' organizing drive was a constructive outlet for frustration accumulated during decades of economic and racial discrimination—suppression unbearable in light of the bitter sacrifices of war.

Aoki remembered the days when Democrats weren't allowed on the plantations, "and how the plantation laborers were being treated, and I saw what the unions had to go through to organize."

"It was boiling inside of us," Aoki would say. "It took a guy like Jack Burns to bring it out and bring us together."

The Democratic takeover was on its way, accelerating a bit each time a war veteran returned from school on the Mainland, often a law school, with a degree financed by the GI Bill of Rights.

Sociologist Lawrence Fuchs, a student of Burns' early years, wrote in his sociological history, *Hawaii Pono,* that Burns and his faction "indefatigably exploited the accumulated resentments of Japanese, Chinese, Hawaiians, and Filipinos against the injustices, real and imagined, of the past."

Fuchs recorded Burns as charging in one of his early campaigns that the Republicans wanted to keep power out of the hands of "an unruly mass of natives and Orientals."

In 1954, thirteen years after the bombing of Pearl Harbor, the now-vital Democratic party stormed to victory, capturing solid majorities in both houses of the legislature.

That same year, a half-hour before the deadline for filing nomination papers, Dan Aoki was out negotiating on behalf of Burns for a top-name candidate for delegate to Congress. The deal fell through and Burns himself jumped into the race, for a second time.

This time Burns lost by less than a thousand votes, running against Joseph Farrington's widow, Mrs. Elizabeth Farrington.

Two years later, in 1956, Burns beat Mrs. Farrington in a landslide to win the most prestigious elective office then available in Hawaii. A Democratic delegate in a Democrat-controlled Congress, Burns cultivated Southern congressmen, the long-time stumbling block to statehood. He worked under the wing of two powerful Texans, House Speaker Sam Rayburn and Senate Majority Leader Lyndon B. Johnson. At the risk of his own political future, Burns opted in 1958 for the so-called Alaska strategy, separating the questions of statehood for Alaska and Hawaii, and allowing Alaska to go up first. It worked.

The Alaska bill passed, and Burns won reelection in 1958 on the promise that statehood for Hawaii was just around the corner.

The Hawaii bill came out of committee early in 1959, passing the House on a 323–89 vote and then the Senate by 76 to 15. At last, eighteen years after Pearl Harbor, Hawaii's people were first-class citizens. Delegate Burns came home to Hawaii to run for governor.

In the referendum, Hawaii voters ratified statehood by the overwhelming margin of 17 to 1. But Burns fared badly. He lost the governorship to the appointed incumbent Republican, Bill Quinn, by 4,000 votes.

Burns was fifty and, some thought, a political has-been. He whiled away his time playing golf and talking politics. In his last act as delegate, he introduced the newly elected congressman Dan Inouye to the House. Early in 1960 he worked out of Washington trying to round up state delegations to support Lyndon Johnson's bid for the Democratic presidential nomination.

Two years later, and this time far better organized, Burns took on Quinn in a rematch. No doubt he was helped by James Kealoha, Quinn's lieutenant governor, who had turned on Quinn and challenged him in the Republican primary, dividing the already skimpy resources of the Republican party. But probably it was more a case of the great strength of the Democratic party, and the large role Burns had played in it, asserting itself. And this time Burns won in a landslide. The vote was 114,000 for Burns, a mere 82,000 for Quinn.

Burns had been the supreme figure in the rise of the Democratic party, had managed the statehood bill, and now he was governor. For four years he was the unquestioned authority in Hawaii, and then there had come in 1966 that strange turn of events, the overheated dispute over the inconsequential office of lieutenant governor, and Thomas P. Gill. In the 1966 elections Burns scraped past Republican Randolph Crossley to win his second four-year term by a mere 5,000 votes.

Fuchs, who focused on Burns' pregubernatorial role as party organizer, described Burns as "aligned with the 'outs,' the downtrodden and the oppressed. He passionately hated the 'ins,' the high and mighty. . . ."

The description suggests something of the fire-breather, but once in power, Burns prided himself on working with the most diverse power blocs of the Islands, so that his administration was dubbed "consensus," like that of his Washington mentor, Lyndon Baines Johnson. For the most part he managed to remain above the fray but not above the crowd. (His ill-fated venture on Brown's behalf was an exception.) He was generally grey, uncontroversial, and publicly dispassionate, consistently obscuring his own role in public affairs. As the years passed, Burns progressively shunned the executive role of program advocate and public opinion-maker.

His public appearances were few, and his major addresses fewer still.

Rather, he ruled quietly in his sphere of influence, operating simultaneously as foremost state caretaker, as conciliator, as The Old Man, The Boss, The Great Stone Face, The Great White Father, and as enunciator of broad principles.

"Jack Burns," one political analyst would say, "is the closest thing to a metaphysical politician in America," Burns being at once earthy and imperial. A mystic, in his way.

His sphere of influence, however quietly ruled, was of course considerable.

As governor, he directly controlled fifteen departments of the government through appointed directors and deputy directors. Of these fifteen departments, only three were subject to policy boards, and the governor appointed all the board members.

The remaining two departments, the University of Hawaii and the Department of Education, fell more or less in his domain as governor. He appointed the statewide University system's Board of Regents. The elected state school board was also heavily dependent on him, owing to his gubernatorial power of fiscal control, and also owing to the fact that the school board chairman, Dr. Richard Ando, was one of the faithful.

This was no ordinary state aparatus, because its constitutional powers covered many functions, such as public health, welfare, and housing, which traditionally fall to city governments on the Mainland.

There also was the state government's highly centralized court system. The governor appointed all five justices of the supreme court, and also appointed all judges of the lower circuit court. In turn, state-administered justice reached down to the pettiest of cases, even to the traffic courts, whose magistrates were appointed by the Burns-appointed chief justice of the supreme court.

As this was no ordinary system of state government, neither was it an ordinary economic situation. Here too the governor held great sway.

Through the Department of Land and Natural Resources, the Hawaii government owns 38 per cent of the Island land mass. The State Tax Office sets tax valuations on both land and capital improvements on the land, and it also advises the legislature on budgetary and tax matters, always first clearing both informational and policy statements with the governor, of course.

Burns also organized and appointed the nation's first statewide zoning board, the land use commission, which exerts great influence over land values, over location of land development, and over the distribution of Hawaii's population. As governor, he exercised a related power to shape development through his Department of Transportation, which controls all of Hawaii's harbor and airport work and also the construction of all major highways.

Further, because the legislature had consistently overloaded the pork-barrel capital improvements program budget, Burns by the late 1960s could pick and choose from a backlog of hundreds of millions of dollars in public works—among them schools, libraries, hospitals, parks, civic centers, the development of houselots, water lines, sewers, and so forth. (In effect, the legislature had abdicated to the governor one of its most crucial fiscal powers.)

Burns' Department of Planning and Economic Development, previously two departments which Burns had fused into a single agency, housed a variety of industrial, agricultural, and commercial promotion programs, which were coupled to research and development projects and to capital loan funds—that is, to low-interest money.

All these things and more fell in Burns' immediate *kuleana,* his bailiwick, and in turn these institutions of state gave him entree—and often influence over—most of the other major institutions in Hawaii, public and private.

Burns exercised his influence in a low-key fashion, and was in fact greatly impressed not by the breadth and depth of a governor's reach, but by the limitations on a governor's power. On occasion he would say, when confronted by a stubborn element of the legislature, or when frustrated that his own underlings were working in conflicting directions, "People think I have so damned much power. But look at this."

It was the influence of public educator, of advocate, that Burns seemed to understand least, seemed to like the least, and certainly exercised the least.

Rather, Burns was at home in behind-the-scenes meetings and was fond of remarking, "It's the game, not the name," which was his way of saying that he wanted only to get the job done as he saw the need, and that he cared little for recognition.

When questioned by reporters, he was prone to go off-the-record or ask that he not be quoted directly. He often left himself with so much elbow room that at best a reporter might muster something like, "The governor today indicated he might. . . ." Burns complained in private that most reporters were an ill-informed lot who frequently distorted his views. Headline writers, he said, were worse.

The fact was he often expressed himself badly. If at times he was self-conscious on this score when faced by the new tyranny of the TV cameras, he also seemed to enjoy being obscure. He might ramble for hours if he warmed to a conversation, but more often he was terse, clipped. His expression and gestures transmitted more of the message than his words. To a given question, he might purse his mouth, arch his right eyebrow, arch his left eyebrow, arch both eyebrows, frown solemnly, grin lopsidedly, wink, pull an ear, raise both hands in mock surrender, lean back casually, lean forward intently—in the space of a minute, he might do all these things in succession.

As this was a matter of style, it also was a matter of strategy and political posture. Just prior to the legislative session of 1969, he was asked which bills he considered to be of the most importance. He gave this a moment of thought, then he replied that there was no point in answering the question.

He explained, "To say this thing is more important or that thing is more important only invites argument."

In the 1970 campaign that was to come, his most remarkable statement would be that any damned fool could take a stand.

But despite such confounding utterances, there was a long-range thrust by Burns' administration that amounted to priorities, and these priorities were deeply rooted in his political and personal history.

One was improving the quality of education at all levels, financed by expanding tax revenues. A second essential ingredient was rapid expansion and diversification of the economy.

Both served the common interests of organized labor, served the rising aspirations of underdog classes and races who had originally voted the Democrats into office in 1954, and also served all but the most backward-looking elements of business.

To one who spent nearly three years covering the State Capitol, the impression was that Burns maintained a lively interest in education trends while devoting most of his personal attention to the state government's fiscal position and to the vitality and stability of the economy.

He aimed consistently at decentralizing private investment and public institutions to the Neighbor Islands, and at encouraging a broader Pacific role for Hawaii through such institutions as the university, the foreign trade zone, and the Hawaii International Services Agency.

He seemed particularly preoccupied with developing tourism, scientific research, and oceanography—above all, with tourism and particularly with his grand plan to create a vast hotel-resort complex on the Big Island's Kona Coast, with construction of an airport and the franchising of airline routes throughout Hawaii and the Pacific.

He was constantly in touch with the progress of labor-management contract negotiations, pressuring for economic stability and also timing state economic development efforts and public construction so as to maintain full employment.

He also kept careful track of the flow of tax revenues, preserving a cash cushion from the state budget (Burns personally approved the hiring of every new civil servant, from janitor to engineer), and closely followed Wall Street interest rates for advantageous bond sales to finance public construction projects.

To be sure, Burns' interests were not limited to government finance and economics; but those seemed to be his central interests.

As criticism of the pace of business development began to set in, Burns countered by equating the reaction to the old feudal order which he and his allies had assaulted. So far as he was a creature of his past, the past blinded him. To put it charitably, Burns was slow to see that the old value attached to economic growth, and to the hallowed idea that growth-is-progress, was rapidly giving way.

In his annual state of the state message to the legislature in 1968, which is a governor's most important forum, Burns dismissed criticism of mass tourism as "myopic thinking which must be discouraged.

"Hawaii must not become a closed society—as it was in past years when the vast ocean and certain political, business, and social interests effectively guarded the gates.

"Let us welcome all."

In his 1969 state of the state message, he took issue with "cries of alarm from those of lesser spirit and faint heart who say 'Enough, enough! Slow down!' as the pace of Hawaii's growth and progress leaves them breathless.

"They would close down again the doors we have opened, and are determined to keep open."

In this same 1969 address, he interjected one of the most interesting if, to some, enigmatic statements of his career: "To be perfectly candid, I sense among some elements of our community—particularly those who are descended from our immigrant plantation workers—a subtle 'inferiority of spirit'. . . ."

This subtle sense of inferiority, Burns said, was totally unwarranted. But it "becomes for them a social and psychological handicap in life."

Burns, his silver hair glistening in the light of the new House chamber's podium, peered sternly through his black, horn-rimmed glasses. He added: "You who have grown up with me here in the Islands, and who remember the pre-World War II climate, know full well what I mean."*

Burns in 1969, as he would be in 1970, was first and foremost the politician of first-class citizenship, as he had been in 1954 and 1959. This was the real point of the consensus, a point of importance which was mistakenly thought to have been largely diminished by the passage of time.

To those who believed that postplantation sentiment had faded into the past, Burns' "sense of inferiority" speech was but further evidence that the Great White Father was out of touch.

Because despite the general adherence of major elements of business, labor, and the legislature to Burns' low-profile consensus, signs abounded that change was in the air.

Burns himself would remark wryly, "I may have outworn my welcome."

His candidate Kenneth Brown had lost so badly in 1966. In the same primary, stemming from the heated battle for the lieutenant governorship, Burns had been chastised by 22,000 protest votes for a George Fontes, an eccentric whom voters had never heard of until they stepped into the balloting booth. The same year Burns' old friend, Mitsuyuki Kido of the Emergency Service Committee, had lost his seat in the state senate.

In the 1968 city and county elections, the maverick hairshirt Frank F. Fasi beat a Burns protege, Herman Lemke, in the Democratic mayoral primary on an anti-Establishment campaign, then

---

*Legislative reaction divided generally along two lines among non-Caucasian Democrats. Those more ethnically oriented praised it as a large gem of wisdom. Others sniffed, suggesting that given the tangible problems of the day Burns should have outlined an Executive program. Among the latter group were men who in 1970 would resent implied suggestions of an ethnic debt to Burns, men who ascribed their own success to education and hard work.

won Honolulu's top office in the general election. In the same 1968 election Matsuo Takabuki, widely regarded as the governor's closest political advisor, lost the city council seat he had held since 1952.

Clearly an urge to clean house had dominated Oahu in 1968.

And, in a vague but unmistakable way, the mood of national unrest over the Vietnam war was infecting Hawaii.

Specifically, Burns lost his direct line to the White House when President Johnson, dragged down in the Vietnam quagmire, withdrew himself from the 1968 presidential elections, prompting murmurings in Hawaii that Burns "might pull an LBJ."

And one day in the early fall of 1969, Burns was showing his new Capitol office to two priests. As he emerged from his inner chambers a reporter had heard him say, "I'd just as soon retire and play golf."

Downstairs, in the senate Republican caucus room, an influential minority senator related the story of a conversation with Burns in which Burns indicated that he yearned to call it quits. But, so the story went, there were two people he decidedly did not want to take over his office. One was the Republican Randolph Crossley, whom he had narrowly beaten in 1966.

The other was the lieutenant governor of Hawaii, Thomas Gill.

Burns said he regarded both as too headstrong to bring diverse elements of the community together, each therefore being unsuited to perpetuate what Burns well may have seen as the overriding accomplishment of his years in office: a sense of harmony among the major forces of Hawaii.

As the story had it, Burns also implied a sense of pessimism about his own chances if he were to stand for reelection.

Nevertheless, the public signal was still go—that the governor would run again.

As early as January of 1969 Burns dropped by ILWU headquarters, whose news sheet, *The Voice* reported that "he hopes he will be supported again in 1970." Later that month the pro-Burns party chairman, David C. McClung, proposed a "harmony ticket" which would have Gill run against the seemingly unbeatable Republican, Hiram Fong, for the U.S. Senate and have Burns run for reelection. Burns portrayed himself as "very interested" in the proposal, but added, "I'm not announcing my candidacy."

In March of 1969 on the governor's birthday, at a huge party in Waikiki's Royal Hawaiian Hotel, U.S. Sen. Daniel Inouye hoped aloud that "as his gift to us tonight he would give his personal assurance" that he would run for a third term.

Burns did not reply directly, but acknowledged Inouye's statement and went on to talk of unfinished business and "a dream, and the energy to reach that dream."

Reporter Byron Baker, after studying the Burns-Gill question at length, wrote that Burns' inner circle was confident that Burns would run "if Gill runs, if for no other reason than to keep Gill from becoming governor of Hawaii."

While Burns pondered the question, his wardrobe underwent a gradual metamorphosis. Underneath the dark-suit uniform, Burns took to wearing colored shirts and modish wide ties, the style of the day.

John A. Burns

Delegate

Party chairman

Burns and mentor, Lyndon Johnson

Burns and Tom Gill campaigning, 1966

Burns and the Ariyoshis, Ryozo and George

George Ariyoshi   Daniel Inouye

Jack Seigle

Robert Oshiro

Daniel Aoki

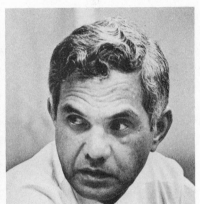

Myron Thompson

Jack Hall

Nadao Yoshinaga

Art Rutledge and Gill, 1970

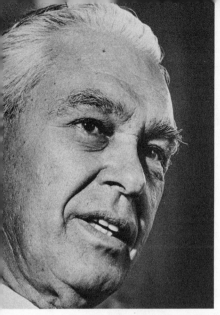

Hebden Porteus

D. G. Anderson

Samuel P. King

Inouye and Burns

4
Tom Gill: Dissent

Tom Gill had played a role, as Burns had played a role, in the hallowed old days of the Democratic party. Always he had been the up-and-coming young man, the bright one destined for large things—perhaps brighter than a politician can be, and certainly discomforting in his abrasiveness. As Tom Gill could not tolerate stupidity and dishonesty, neither could he bring off an air of modesty about his own gifts.

Although Gill had fought the political wars of 1954, by the mid-1960s he saw the Democratic party as having grown fat through years of accumulated power and affluence. So, at once, Tom Gill was an apostle of new priorities and a throwback to the old-fashioned Democratic militance—to the politics of the dispossessed and the disenchanted.

As the 1970 election year approached he was forty-seven, neither young nor old. His hair was starting to turn a gubernatorial grey, but his face still had a boyish look that didn't quite make it as a stereotyped image of a governor.

Unlike John Burns, who qualified as a Democrat by virtue of humble family origins, Gill's Democratic credentials were based on liberal ideology. His father had been an architect and had accumulated enough wealth for a family compound on Tantalus and a tract of land in Waikiki. His mother had been a society editor of the *Honolulu Star-Bulletin.*

Thirteen years younger than Burns, Gill had been fighting in the South Pacific during World War II while Burns was at home laying the groundwork for a new Democratic party.

(Gill, incidentally, had been decorated for bravery in combat, a fact which he refused to exploit politically, and was even reluctant to discuss in private.)

After the war, when Burns was piecing together such people as Mits Kido, Ernest Murai, Dan Aoki, and Bill Richardson, Gill had been on the Mainland earning his law degree.

Although outwardly they had traveled many of the same political roads, Burns and Gill were a study in contrasts.

On the national political spectrum, Gill could easily be classed as a liberal reformer. Burns defied labeling.

Burns was a regular, a Lyndon Johnson man, then a Hubert Humphrey man. Gill was for Bobby Kennedy. Burns was a Vietnam warhawk. ("Freedom! This is what the war in Vietnam is about today. This is why Hawaii's sons—as their fathers before them in World War II and the Korean War—have died in that embattled land.") Gill was an outspoken dove.

Burns worried over an American retreat from Asia. Gill couldn't wait for the day when America would abandon its role as world policeman.

As delegate to Congress, Burns had cultivated Southerers like Johnson and Sam Rayburn in the pursuit of statehood. Gill, in Congress later, aligned himself with the Northern liberal bloc.

Burns marveled at man's first walk on the moon; Gill dismissed it as another technological exercise which a nation plagued by domestic decay could ill afford.

While Burns systematically shunned explicit priorities, Gill made his own crystal clear—regardless of whom he alienated.

While Burns inclined to behind-the-scenes workings, Gill was at home on the podium or, better yet, in public hearings, where he could bring to bear his power for give and take. Gill was widely recognized as an intellect and an idea man. Burns made a virtue of not having all the answers. Foremost, Gill dealt in ideas and issues, Burns in balancing conflicting power drives; Gill in advocacy, Burns in conciliation.

Burns projected a sense that, at the core of things, all was well, or could be made so; Gill that the world had gone awry. Burns would look at a problem and insist on calling it a challenge. To Gill, it was a crisis.

Burns was comforting, Gill the antithesis thereof. Gill was out. Burns was in.

Burns had tasted a great deal of power, Gill only a little.

Yet over the years Gill had become more and more of a force to be reckoned with—the towering figure in a political network which, for lack of a better word, had earned the label "independent."

However loosely organized, the independent Democrats were bound together by style, by a preoccupation with issues, and often by a shared distaste for the Burns faction, for corporate business, for the powerful and Burns-allied International Longshoremen's and Warehousemen's Union, or for all three.

Almost from the day when Gill returned from law school in 1951, he had been at odds with the Burns faction.

Story piled on story, slight on slight, resentment on resentment, so that what may have begun as a conflict in personalities broadened into a conflict of policy and philosophy—and into a conflict of ambition and power drives.

The first meeting between Burns and Gill was in 1951, preserved by Dan Aoki, Burns' political organizer. Although in later years neither Burns nor Gill remembered it clearly, the incident lived vividly in Aoki's mind, which was a sort of repository of the anti-Gill tales told by the Burns camp.

According to Aoki, it went like this: Matsuo Takabuki had known of Gill at the University of Hawaii, and told Burns that Gill was bright and aggressive and could be a major asset to the undermanned Democratic movement. Gill was well educated, and was determined to be a labor lawyer, which in those years was no way to get ahead in life.

A lunch was set at the old South Seas restaurant in Waikiki, to be attended by Burns, Gill, Takabuki, and Aoki.

Takabuki introduced Gill to Burns, then outlined to Gill what had been done to build the Democratic party. By this time, Burns for three years had been the Oahu county chairman, was soon to be territorial chairman, and Takabuki was planning his successful race for Honolulu's Board of Supervisors.

Aoki, the storyteller, recalled, "The lunch was short." Gill was asked if he would get behind the movement, join up. He was told he was needed. "Gill just looked at us. Then he said, 'Join you guys? How about you guys joining me?'

"That was the end of the lunch."

A second Aoki story had it that Gill subsequently dropped by Aoki's office in the Labor Department, where Aoki was running a rehabilitation program for war veterans.

"Tom said, 'Hey, we've got to get rid of this stupid s.o.b.'

"I said, 'Who do you mean?'

" 'I mean Burns,' " Gill was said to have answered.

Aoki was furious, the kind of anger which still showed when he would tell the story years later.

"I told him if that's your attitude, get the hell out of here. That's really the last time I talked to him about anything."

Others close to Burns embellish the story by contending that Aoki also would remark on occasion, quizzically, "If the Old Man (Burns) is stupid, what does that make me?"

Etched in Gill's own memory was a series of meetings in early 1952 with members of the Heen family political clan and with a functionary of Art Rutledge's Teamsters' union. Burns and the Heens had been at odds, and in Gill's view the meetings "immediately stamped me as anti-Burns."

Notwithstanding the friction with Burns, Gill came out of the 1952 Oahu county convention as county campaign chairman. And typically revealing his faith in the power of words, Gill organized the Democrats' first radio talkathon as a campaign tactic.

It was the same year Burns won the chairmanship of the territorial Democratic party.

In the spring of 1954, with Democratic victory just around the corner, Burns and Gill clashed at the county convention. This time Gill won, beating a 442nd veteran who ran as a stand-in for the Burns forces, Tadao Beppu, later speaker of the state house.

It was Gill's only convention victory over the many years of struggle, and he used the county chairmanship to run the Democratic party campaign on Oahu while Burns made his near-miss race for delegate against Joseph Farrington's widow, Betty Farrington.

Again, Aoki had a story to tell about Gill's county convention victory: "After the vote, Tom made a sort of acceptance speech. He turned and looked at our group and said something like, 'Even you guys will work with me.'" Complaints in the Burns camp of Gill's cockiness were not unlike those which circulated among independents who resented Burns. To the independent faction, as the sociologist Fuchs read them, Burns seemed "cold, aloof, inflexible and dictatorial. He appeared to mistrust any Democrat who had not been reared in the slums or on hard plantation labor."

Factionalism from the party conventions inevitably spilled over into the legislature.

In 1959 Gill, as a freshman legislator, engaged in a fight for control of the Hawaii House of Representatives while Burns was working as delegate in Washington.

Allied with former House Speaker Vincent Esposito, Gill originally counted a slim majority of the votes. Esposito was to again be house speaker and Gill was to chair not one but two house committees, two of the most important: the Judiciary Committee and the Land Reform Committee. Fuchs, who made an extensive study of the legislative power fight, wrote: "Certain they had the votes, and determined to accomplish major land-reform legislation, Gill and Esposito refused to make significant concessions until it was too late."

Republicans and ILWU Democrats laid the groundwork for a coalition. And when enough Democrats from the Burns faction joined them, Gill and Esposito were defeated.

Conflicting attitudes toward race and toward the ILWU particularly impressed Fuchs.

The Gill forces impressed him as "more cosmopolitan in spirit," that is, less inclined to deal in racial politics.

The Burns and ILWU Democrats, on the other hand, "thought that the independents tried too hard for respectability to interpret correctly the militant aspirations of Hawaii's underprivileged."*

Fuchs quoted one of Gill's opponents as claiming the independents were "more concerned about being smeared as friends of the ILWU or afraid of giving the impression that the Democratic Party is a branch of the 442nd Club than with building a militantly liberal program."

Delegate Burns had opposed the coalition, but once it was organized, he wired his congratulations from Washington to the new house speaker, Elmer F. Cravalho of Maui.

---

*True and not true. Only truly complex. Fuchs may have somewhat mistaken the rhetoric of an essentially ethnic movement for deeply held political ideology. He covered the 1950s. Increasingly the 1960s suggested that as AJA aspirations were fulfilled, the movement splintered across the political map—some forever restless, some snug, some strangely torn between old ideals and new comforts. Gill, for his part, was forever the ideologue, for him a real strength and also a real limitation. Gill as liberal, constitutionalist, and Democrat clung fiercely to the ideal that all men are equal. As sardonic humorist, Gill also would say of some powerful Establishment and non-Caucasian politicians in the late 1960s: "They call it Murphy's law—anybody can screw something up."

The same Tom Gill, while occasionally preaching ethnic pride, would have mixed emotions about Brown Power once the Hawaiian people started moving—this, even though Gill as antipoverty director had by happenstance helped start the movement. After hearing the Maoist Kalani Ohelo talk of Brown Power, Gill would dismiss him by saying, "Brown power, black power, green power, purple power—they're all the same, all just people." Ohelo was put off —struggling, as he was, to save his life-style from extinction, and also having seen what Jeffersonian democracy had done to Polynesia. Burns' ethnic dimension was even more complex. Born poor, white, and Catholic, Burns was from a group which had been exploited (but unlike the blacks never glamorized), and Burns understood better in his guts how other ethnics felt. Accordingly Burns' critics would look on him as simply a racial politician, and therefore as retarding Hawaii's emergent cosmopolitan spirit. Not so simple as that.

The telegram, Gill was to recall, "burned a lot of people up," himself included.

When Burns came home later in the year for the new state's first governor's race, he was, in the view of the Gill camp, late in arriving and slow to seek their support.

Then Burns lost to the incumbent Republican, Quinn, by a scant 4,000 votes.

Regardless of which side of the factional fence one sat on, Burns' defeat could be ascribed largely to factionalism.

It is significant, too, that this election, 1959, was the only time in the sixteen-year span between 1954 and 1970 that the Democratic grip on Hawaii was seriously threatened. The Democrats lost not only the governorship but a majority in the state senate.

The next time around, in 1962, under the party chairmanship of Robert C. Oshiro, the party worked at piecing together a unity ticket which would bring together both factions and both of the big labor unions, the AFL-CIO and the ILWU.

But even when the Democratic party's future was in doubt, there was friction in the making of a slate.

As negotiators for the Gill faction recalled it, at one meeting someone tossed out the idea of Gill running for lieutenant governor along with Burns. Burns resisted, saying that "the boys" wanted Bill Richardson. Pressed, Burns made the point that Richardson as a part-Hawaiian would give the slate a desirable and politically attractive racial balance.

State Sen. Nelson K. Doi, volatile and eloquent, blew his stack. One report was that he said: "To hell with the boys, Jack, what do you want." Another had it that Doi said: "Dammit, I joined the Democratic party to get away from this race business. This is a democratic country. We shouldn't go on race, but on merit."

Despite the back-room friction, a slate was worked out. Burns defeated Quinn in a landslide to become governor of Hawaii. Gill and Spark M. Matsunaga won U.S. House seats.

While, for once, there were no complaints about disunity during the campaign, the motives of Burns and his faction remained suspect in Gill's eyes. "I think there was some method in their madness. The thought was to get me out of town."

In 1964, two years later, Gill challenged incumbent Republican Hiram L. Fong for the U.S. Senate after handily defeating the ILWU-aligned Nadao Yoshinaga in the primary. Always distrustful of the Burns faction, Gill would remember his general election campaign with a sense of bitter irony: "I wasn't exactly overwhelmed by their support." Opposed by the ILWU, Gill lost the general election by 15,000 votes.

In 1966, for the first time, the two factions clashed directly in a statewide election campaign in the fight for the lieutenant governorship.

The details were as follows: Burns, following Gill's loss to Fong, had appointed Gill to organize Hawaii's new Office of Economic Opportunity, the glamor agency of President Johnson's short-lived war to end poverty in America. Gill was in fact well qualified for the job, and it was to Burns' credit that he gave Gill the appointment. As a U.S. House member, Gill had worked on the antipoverty bill, was thoroughly familiar with its provisions, and was likewise familiar with the Washington bureaucracy which administered the law. Gill also knew a network of people in the poverty target areas, such as Kalihi and Nanakuli, and he organized them quickly to meet the antipoverty law's demand for neighborhood participation. Soon he had millions of dollars pouring into Hawaii, and by early 1966 he was receiving superb reviews on the new agency, which was reputed to be the best in the nation. It also was a political gold mine, although it no doubt alienated many who thought the antipoverty program was somehow dangerously radical.

Burns, in the meantime, had appointed his lieutenant governor, Bill Richardson, to be the chief justice of the supreme court.

Burns sounded out several people who might eventually rise to the governorship to take Richardson's old job. Prominent among them were Attorney General Bert Kobayashi and House Speaker Cravalho. Neither wanted the job, so it fell to the state treasurer, Andrew Ing, on a strictly temporary basis.

Gill had had his fill of bureaucratic life. He was eager to return to elective politics, and in the shuffle he saw an opening. He traveled to Burns' chamber in Iolani Palace, technically as an employee of the governor's but actually as a political power in his own right. As ever he was suspicious of Burns, and perhaps he saw in the antipoverty post an attempt by Burns to co-opt him politically. Burns for his part was at least willing to have Gill on the payroll, but was most unwilling to have Gill on the ticket. They had collaborated together on the Great Society program, but the breach had not healed. At most this visit, in Gill's mind, was probably a ritual call, as most political figures call on the governor before declaring for political office.

Accounts of the courtesy call, as they eventually leaked out, had it that Gill asked, "Jack, would you get the hives if I ran for lieutenant governor?"

Burns countered, "What the hell do you mean by hives? Hives? I don't know what you mean by hives, but if you give me my druthers I can think of several other people I'd rather have than you."

Then Gill asked if Burns could work with him if he were lieutenant governor.

Burns parried by saying he wouldn't have given Gill the antipoverty agency if there had been no mutual ground for cooperation, but could Gill work with him? Meaning, of course, would Gill play his role loyally?

(A Burns aide would claim that Burns came on even stronger, saying, "I can work with the devil if I have to.")

Gill said he thought he could function smoothly with Burns if he had his say in administration affairs.

But, Burns asked, once a final decision on a given question was made, would Gill abide by it?

The gist of Gill's answer was that it depended on the decision.

Burns, recalling the talk, would fume, "There are a lot of things I run into in life that I can't agree with, but I have to accept."

To those deeply loyal to Burns, Gill's move was proof positive that Gill could not be trusted, that Gill knew no such thing as indebtedness. Burns had magnanimously scraped Gill off the floor after the Fong race, and now? The antipoverty agency had broadened Gill's personal following, and he was using it to run against the wishes of the governor.

And the phrasing—"Jack, would you get the hives. . . ."

At this point the politically unknown Kenneth F. Brown emerged stage-center as Burns' annointed candidate for the office of lieutenant governor, an act that provoked an equally strong sense of outrage among Gill supporters.

Gill had labored long years for the party. He had been a legislator for three years, a U.S. Congressman for two years, and he had brought credit to Burns for the antipoverty program. Did not Gill, as the state's top out-of-office Democrat, deserve the only prestige post that was open in 1966?

And who was Kenneth Brown—an officer of numerous corporations, a Pacific Club member, from a Republican family—but a symbol of the worst of consensus politics: Burns' newly found coziness with big business.

Undeterred, Gill announced his candidacy. He campaigned cheerfully, secure in the knowledge that Burns had undertaken a politically infeasible task.

Brown for his part seemed a little awed by it all, like an army recruit in his first days of boot camp.

And Burns did Gill the favor of taping a series of TV spots for Brown, urging on the electorate the candidate of his choosing—this was Jack Burns at his stiffest, the Great Stone Face.

Just how badly Burns wanted Brown to win was indicated through a statement by the then house speaker, Elmer Cravalho.

Before the election, Cravalho—dutifully pumping for Brown—warned that a divided Burns-Gill ticket would lose to Republican nominee Randolph Crossley and his part-Hawaiian running mate, Dr. George Mills. Burns responded by telling reporters he was inclined to agree with Cravalho's dire prediction.

This was strange politics, was particularly strange politics because Burns had made his stake as party chairman, whose role is to put the well-being of the Democratic party before personalities.

As the 1966 primary election day neared, Burns boarded a plane on a goodwill mission on behalf of President Johnson to represent America at the independence celebrations of a new African nation.

Burns was headed for a little known country named Botswana because of a little known word, antipode.

To explain: Botswana is Hawaii's antipode. It is on precisely the opposite side of the globe, which makes for something of a special relationship. If one dug a hole through the center of the earth, et cetera.

The antipode project originated from the inner recesses of the *Star-Bulletin,* and was promoted heavily as a matter of international goodwill.

It so happened that the date of Botswana's independence fell during Hawaii's campaign season.

And Burns took off, not to be seen for days.

The primary was on a Saturday. Very early Sunday a *Star-Bulletin* editor placed a call to Burns in Botswana. The telephone operator didn't know how to route the call, so the editor suggested she go through Europe to Capetown. Finally she made the connection.

"How did the election come out?" Burns asked from the other side of the world.

The governor was told that he had won but that Gill had beaten Brown.

Burns asked, "How many votes did I get?"

The answer was 86,000.

"How many votes did Gill get?"

The answer was 90,900.

There was a long pause, finally broken by a question from the editor. Burns interrupted, "Would you give me those figures again?"

Gill, running opposed by Burns and the top people of the Democratic establishment, had won more votes than the governor himself. Burns' token opponent, George Fontes, had received a surprising 22,000 protest votes.

The primary was on October the first.

Burns did not come back to Hawaii until ten days later—this, with only a scant month of campaign time between the primary and general elections.

In all, he spent two weeks in Africa, dropped by New York, and then spent two days in Washington for State Department debriefings and talks with Senator Inouye.

Interviewed on the Mainland, Burns shrugged off the Fontes vote by saying, "You didn't expect everybody to vote for me, did you?" Then, informed that Republican Crossley already was making much of Burns and Gill not seeing eye to eye, Burns said:

"Only one guy's eye matters. The one who has to make the decisions and take responsibility for them."

Finally a plane carrying the governor descended on Honolulu airport. Standing in the glare of TV camera lights, Gill waited at the bottom of the plane's off-ramp. Burns shook Gill's hand, then moved past him quickly, leaving his unwanted running mate hovering in the backdrop.

Facing the cameras, Burns was asked if he was happy to have Gill on the ticket. The governor said he was "happy to have any Democrat as a running mate."

Gill was one of a cluster of people behind Burns, his face pasted into a weak grin. It was not until two weeks after the primary election that Burns and Gill appeared together on the same platform, and they subsequently almost lost the general election. Each camp privately claimed the victory while blaming the other for the close margin of 5,000 votes.

After the election, Gill went to Burns for a clarification of his role in the state administration.

The only thing he knew of was a food price study, assigned by Burns when food prices had become an issue in the campaign.

Gill recalled proposing two jobs: One, that he handle the administration's legislative lobby and, two, that he work on coordinating federal programs.

Burns vetoed the first, carefully guarding his prerogative of negotiating with legislators, but agreed to the second.

From then on the trend apparently went from a state of limited, uneasy cooperation to close to none. There were rare exceptions, such as when the two worked together on preserving the Big Island's Kealakekua Bay.

Gill for his part would claim that he never was invited to a cabinet meeting, and was convinced that Burns had discontinued the meetings because of his—Gill's—presence in the government.

In 1967, Burns' new administrative director, Myron Thompson, was in Gill's office discussing several federal-state questions.

Thompson remarked that he and Gill could deal more effectively with the federal government if Gill would give some assurance that he would not run for governor in 1970.

Gill shrugged. "Who can say?"

They departed with radically different interpretations of the exchange. Thompson said he was sounding out Gill on his own initiative, "trying to find a way of bringing things together, so we could really get swinging on programs."

Gill later was to charge, "I was early given to understand that I could not work within the administration unless I pledged not to run for governor in 1970."

The gap was widening rapidly. As it did, Gill became more and more outspoken in his own views, and more and more critical of the direction of the Burns administration.

One of the cappers in the story of deteriorating Burns-Gill relations was Burns' hiring of Kenneth Brown as a $1-a-year assistant. And even though Gill had been assigned state-federal coordination, Brown was given the job of launching Hawaii into the new federal Model Cities antipoverty program, Gill's specialty.

When the legislature met in 1967, the organization of the senate was delayed for weeks by another factional fight which echoed the Burns-Gill primary battle. One side was led by Sen. Nadao Yoshinaga, the top strategist of the combined Burns-ILWU forces; the other side by Nelson Doi, an independent and a staunch Gill man. A settlement was reached only after a bitter round of charges and countercharges, the positions of power in the senate finally being divided into roughly equal halves between the contenders.

Throughout 1967, Gill, with little else to do, was on a heavy speaking schedule, often implicitly, and occasionally explicitly, critical of administration policies. These he did not nail specifically to the door of the governor, but the point was clear enough. Policy flows from the office of governor.

This was a ludicrous situation. The two men were not only of the same political party, but together they had won the election. Had they been president and vice president, such a situation would have upset the entire nation. This merely upset Hawaii, particularly in the early months, when it was not yet altogether clear that Burns and Gill were parting ways for good.

If there was any doubt in people's minds, it was dispelled in January of 1968, when Gill drew the perimeter of the battle lines.

Gill portrayed the Democratic party as having grown complacent from long years in office, as being dominated by a power center that "may grow narrower and narrower, to the point where it would not include more than Hall, Matsy Takabuki, Chinn Ho, and Clarence Ching." The Hall was the ILWU's Jack Hall; and both Ho and Ching were entrepreneurs and developers. All were close to the real object of the barb, Governor Burns.

Gill, looking back, dismissed the Democratic sweep of 1954 as "run by a bunch of would-be Babbitts who were not trying to overturn the system. They just wanted in, because they had been kept out. Now they have a slice of the pie, and some of them are getting fat.

"The people coming in now have different attitudes. I don't see many joining the party because they want a job. They join because they want to make a difference in society."

He ascribed his own problem to purity: ". . . the so-called inner group . . . cannot control me and my close political friends. There are absolutely no special deals, and they know it."

In Gill's view, Hawaii had gone full circle, from the closed society of the plantation days to a new closed society, this run by the Burns clique. The interview amounted to a warmup for the party's spring conventions, in which Gill's lieutenants came within a hair's breadth of recapturing control of the Oahu county committee. For months Gill's young organizers circulated among the burgeoning crowd of Gill's admirers, securing new signatures to party cards, explaining precinct boundaries, explaining the arcane art of organizing a precinct. From the outside it seems mysterious, but once done it is outrageously simple. One need only round up two or three family clans and cue them on how to vote.

The Burns organization was slow to perceive the threat, slow to react, but late in the day Dan Aoki assembled the Burns troops and turned back the Gill people at the county convention. By the time of the subsequent 1968 state Democratic convention, Burns was again secure. His vastly superior strength among the Neighbor Island delegations, long his strong areas, guaranteed him the undisputed control of the party apparatus to which he had grown accustomed.

Burns welcomed the delegates with a benign talk, praising the retiring chairman, Robert Oshiro, saying that the party's strength lay in its diversity of opinion, and concluding: "May you freely exchange your opinions and forge a party platform for the years ahead."

Gill, in defeat, took his pound of flesh with an attack on the proxy vote system, under which individual politicians carried anywhere from several to dozens of delegate votes signed over by absentee delegates. "It is essential that our precinct and district organizations be real. This means that our precinct and district officers must live in and be identified with the area they supposedly represent. A rotten borough is a rotten borough regardless of who carries the proxies to a convention."

The game was being played for keeps.

5

1969: No Consensus

By early 1969, all the signs pointed toward Lieutenant Governor Gill challenging the incumbent Burns, even though Gill contended that he had not reached a decision.

When David McClung, as the pro-Burns Democratic party chairman, proposed the harmony slate of Burns for governor and Gill for the U.S. Senate, Gill revived his booster club theory: "They would love to boost me out of town." He issued a public statement wryly suggesting just such a boost for Burns, or even for McClung.

"While it is very flattering to be promoted to the exalted seat of U.S. Senate," Gill said, "it does grave injustice to other potential candidates, one of which is Governor Burns. The other is McClung himself."

In weighing whether to run for governor, Gill was aware that he faced formidable opposition—from the tourist, sugar, and pineapple industries; from contractors and developers; from the ILWU and lesser unions; and from the majority bloc of the formal party structure.

Yet he was deeply impressed by the climate of unrest, the proliferation of activist groups, the new awareness and social conscience of the young, the new concern over the destruction of the environment, and by the disillusionment with established institutions which was rife in Hawaii as it was throughout the country.

Above all, Gill believed that the public was swayed not so much by the influential interest groups as by issues, and Gill had cultivated certain potent issues as his own, with the utmost care and energy. The essence of Gill's thinking was to control the wild growth which had swept Hawaii in the decade of the sixties. On a cerebral level, Gill had been far ahead of his time, had anticipated the problems of rapid growth when these problems had been only dimly perceived by others or not at all. As a state legislator, just after statehood, Gill had played a leading role in formulating legislation controlling the use of land, the precious resource on which Island politics turn. For its time, Gill's thinking was radical and socialistic, asserting a larger right of the society over and above property rights, so that the concept of land ownership would gradually be modified to a new concept of land stewardship.

One legislative act sponsored by Gill secured for the state the right to condemn land for the development of housing. Burns had never used the law, although he did not dispute the concept, and this was one of the sore points between him and Gill. A second and far more significant piece of legislation had been the State Land Use Law, which created the land use commission. In effect this was a statewide zoning board which at the time was the only one of its kind in the nation. Through this law, the concept of zoning in metropolitan areas was extended to the entire land mass of the Island chain, facilitating a statewide policy on land use. It was intended primarily to preserve the green belts of agricultural land and to guarantee the orderly and tightly knit development of urban areas.

In his 1966 inaugural address, Gill called for a "broad assault on the wildly proliferating problems of urban life," citing pollution, traffic, shrinking recreation space, the cost of food and housing, and inadequate public planning.

To this he added, "Finally we must be concerned that government is above reproach. We must be better than Caesar's wife."

Gill was constantly on the speaking circuit expanding on his inaugural address.

From speech after speech, Gill was gradually rounding out a campaign platform: Gimmicks such as trading stamps were costing consumers two cents on the dollar; legislation to require an optional cash credit could solve the problem.

Standard Oil, Gill charged, had a de facto monopoly on gasoline and oil distribution in Hawaii and should be sued (Burns subsequently filed an antitrust suit). A nuclear reactor could cut power costs and, consequently, attract diversified industry to Hawaii.

Gill contended it also could provide cheap electric power to propel a commuter train for Oahu, which in turn would work several wonders. Mass transit would provide a pollution-free alternative to cars, would cut personal auto costs, and would determine development patterns. The state, he insisted, had to play an aggressive role in shaping a new transit system for the city of Honolulu.

Generally the state government had been lax in enforcing its own pollution laws and slow to implement new federal laws.

The state had poured money into tourist development, but had overlooked housing. Gill pointed out repeatedly that his 1959 law to condemn private land for housing had never been used. What the people needed was a "second housing market," either on state land or state-condemned land. Such projects should be mainly multiple-unit constructions, not "tickey-tack subdivisions," both to save space for parks and save as much agricultural land as possible. The state could either rent, lease, or sell the new housing, but if it was sold there should be prohibitions against quick-profit resales.

The land use commission wasn't working out as intended, as Gill saw it. It was allowing land to be rezoned for urban use, then lie idle, awaiting higher speculative profits. The commission should rezone land in increments as a pressure on developers to deliver on promised construction. In major rezonings, Gill argued that developers should donate part of their land to the public for parks, school sites, and state-sponsored housing—a rebate to the public for the resulting increased value of the land.

Gill repeatedly attacked mass tourism as a mixed blessing, warning against shoddy tourist development. A moratorium on hotel construction in Waikiki would be a good idea, he thought. And to prevent further deterioration of tourist service, hotels should be graded and tour guides trained and licensed. Perhaps airline landing fees should be higher. A two-dollar-a-day tax on every hotel room was a must. The tax revenue should be poured into a special fund for improving beaches, parks, museums, and historic and scenic sites. The end result should be a slowdown on growth and an emphasis on quality, not quantity.

So it went. If it sometimes became too complicated for public consumption, Gill might boil down his thinking to a declaration that Hawaii "must not become another Los Angeles."

If inclined to be professorial, Gill on occasion could show a spark for dramatization.

He permanently parked his state limousine and drove around town in compact cars, first a Volkswagen, then a Toyota. He bounced through Volcanoes Park on the Big Island in a Land Rover, agitating for the park's expansion; and he trudged up Mauna Loa to inspect the conserved remnants of a sandalwood forest. When kids complained that a beach-widening project would destroy the surf, Gill donned swimming trunks and dived into the water to check their arguments on ocean currents.

Hammering away in speech after speech, Gill opened up a long head start on the issues, constantly making headlines.

By contrast, Burns, in his 1969 "subtle inferiority of spirit" address to the legislature, typically brushed past specifics: "The problems of housing and labor shortages, of rising prices, of environmental decay, of public services lagging behind public demand, of the education of our children, of crime, of land and its use—all these continue to warrant our fullest attention today. They are neither new nor insoluble."

Rather, "They simply require good men and women, great men and women, who will accept the challenge they offer."

Beyond a growing public awareness of problems such as housing, pollution, and urban congestion, several episodes at the Capitol seemed to play into Gill's hands.

Three stemmed from critical reports issued by the state's legislative auditor, Clinton Tanimura.

The first came in the 1968 legislative session, in which Tanimura disclosed fiscal mismanagement in the Hawaii Visitors Bureau, the tourism promotion agency which operated on state contract and with heavy state subsidies.

The second and third reports came in the 1969 session, a session that was remarkably bad for Burns' public image. One auditor's report charged mismanagement of both money and state personnel policies in Burns' Department of Personnel Services, a report which eventually led to the hiring of a new department director. Another alleged that the government was losing over $2 million a year in interest to banks, where vast sums lay idle in state checking accounts.

Near the end of the session, the State Ethics Commission chastened two Burns-allied senators, David C. McClung and John Ushijima, for representing developers on the Big Island's Kona Coast, Burns' priority development project.

While Burns could not reasonably be held responsible for the conduct of the two senators, the incident reinforced the impression of strange doings on the part of well-placed members of the Burns apparatus, particularly in this case because land use and large corporate interests were involved.

McClung was the chairman of Burns' party, and also was president of the pro-Burns senate. John Ushijima was the pro-Burns power in the senate from the Big Island, chairing both the Senate Judiciary Committee (the senate's second most important committee), and also the Big Island Select Committee, which lines up public construction projects.

Further, when the ethics commission made its ruling, it knew only the half of it—the rest would appear later in the *Star-Bulletin.* McClung, for his part, would be recorded as unapologetically telling a group of Hilo students that he had lobbied in the Big Island county administration on behalf of Signal Oil.

John Ushijima, for his part, had pushed through the state senate an intricate bill drafted by Boise Cascade Corporation's California attorneys. The effect of the bill, if one cut through its many pages of rhetoric and technical provisos, would have been to turn over to a private developer the power to levy taxes and to provide governmental services—a sort of a new plantation, in which the company was king.

The Boise Cascade Corporation bill had died in the house, but this particularly insensitive corporation had provided a case study of how the land development drive had run amok.

From the allure of Hawaii, the land developers had been mining vast fortunes during the middle and late 1960s, and Boise Cascade happened to be the biggest. Initially the Idaho-based corporation had planned to subdivide and sell 30,000 acres of the Big Island's famous Parker Ranch. When the planners pressured the land use commission rezoning downward to a mere 2,300 acres, there still were left $60 million in houselots—these to be sold by high-pressure tactics and by intensive television advertising.

The fact was that Hawaii did not need more houselots, but more houses. The Big Island alone already had 75,000 vacant houselots because of the craze for land speculation.

ʻWhile the Kona Coast project of Boise Cascade perhaps did not hurt Burns' cause much, if any, another incident at the close of the 1969 Legislature hurt him badly.

This was Magic Island.

Oahu's Magic Island had been conceived as a grandiose plan in the 1950s, when all such things were considered visionary and therefore good. The idea had been to fill the off-shore coral reef around central Honolulu's Ala Moana Park, bold men thereby creating dry land from the ocean. It was to have been done in three increments, one paying for another by using parts of the newly created land for construction of hotels. By the time Burns had become governor in 1963, a peninsula of thirty-five acres had been built off the Waikiki end of Ala Moana Park, and to Burns' credit he halted further land-fills.

There the matter hung suspended until 1969, when the Dillingham Corporation cast its eyes on a second prong of the submerged coral reef, thinking to create new land and to build towering and plush condominium apartments. This would be done under state terms of a new non-bid developer's law which had been sponsored by the Burns administration.

For this additional Magic Island development a legislative resolution was needed, and the ensuing battle would show how the times were changing. If at the top, the view of land-as-commodity prevailed, Honolulu—pressured by urbanization and tourism— had changed vastly since the 1950s. Some legislators had begun to respond to the new situation, a few of them noting, for example, that the Waikiki beaches largely had been taken over by tourists, that Honolulu's resident population also had greatly increased, that Ala Moana beach now was the only big "local" beach left between Diamond Head and faraway Ewa Beach in Leeward Oahu, and that on weekends the beach park was brimming over with people—many being people of modest income who lived in the central city.

The Dillingham condominiums might, some contended, have the same effect as the Waikiki hotels—that is, to further crowd the air bubble and to make the surrounding area an alien turf for residents.

Burns lobbied vigorously for the development plan, abandoning his attitude of keeping hands off the legislature, an attitude which he so often had attributed to the Jeffersonian concept of separation of powers.

In the private offices of legislators, Burns argued for the idea, and on occasion also displayed a legislative roll-call sheet, in effect tallying whether lawmakers intended to vote with him or against him.

Burns' chief political lieutenant, Dan Aoki, also patrolled the Capitol corridors, and so did the Dillingham lobbyists. (Dillingham proved itself particularly influential with Republican legislators, incidentally.)

Also lobbying was the ILWU's Eddie DeMello, who pursued the matter as if plush condominium apartments somehow would benefit the ILWU's members.

Until the last moment, it appeared that despite all this pressure the resolution would die in house committee, but on the 1969 Legislature's last day, as the clock neared midnight, there was a fast shuffle. The resolution first passed the house on a chaotic and hurried voice vote, and then at the stroke of midnight—or shortly thereafter—it passed the senate.

Among the dissident forces, Magic Island became a symbol, a rallying point. At once it brought into play the issues of the environment, the quality of urban life, land, suspect legislative proceedings, and the questionable dimension of the consensus: Burns, the largest of the developers, and the great industrial ILWU union had worked hand-in-glove on Magic Island, as if the interests of business and the state and the union were one.

Politically the damage was done, although Burns for his part contended that he wanted the development resolution merely as a contingency resolution, and that his primary intent was to keep the construction industry moving. Subsequently he executed a roll-back, saying the resolution was not necessary to the health of the construction industry, as patently it was not. He agreed to the project being shelved.*

After the 1969 legislative session, Burns' political stock seemed to have hit rock bottom. His marginal political allies talked privately of abandoning him, and some of the government's patronage employees were wondering aloud where they could find jobs after November 1970.

Gill was noticeably jaunty.

When pollution was particularly visible from the commuter traffic and from the smokestacks of Leeward Oahu, he might greet a visitor with a wave of the hand and quip, "Don't breathe too deeply."

In 1968 he had taken a poll which looked favorable.

A second poll in 1969 looked equally good, and Gill was in a confident mood. He made a critical decision. In June, shortly after the legislature adjourned, Gill leaked his poll to the press, showing a lead over Burns of more than 10 percentage points among Democratic voters.

Gill later would say that reporters were birddogging the poll so much that he could not have kept it secret, that there were twenty

---

*Burns seemed to have gotten the message. He ordered that the existing thirty-five-acre Magic Island peninsula be made into a park, which it was—in time for Burns to plant a ceremonial tree by the ocean before November of 1970.

to thirty people who knew something about it, that the press was bound to write something, so the facts might as well be straight.

In fact, it appeared that in his reckoning he was overly confident; he was thinking of creating a stampede in his direction, and thought that such favorable publicity would make it easier for him to raise a campaign war chest. This, next to his sharp tongue, always had been his most serious problem.

Nothing good came of it. On the contrary, the effect was to tell the Burns camp, in case there were any doubts, that they must shake themselves from the doldrums and get moving.

6
The Believer

There would be in the campaign, in addition to the candidates, several people who played pivotal roles, people who out of the thousands participating would single-handedly influence the course of events. Of these none was more important than Robert C. Oshiro, and none was more symbolic of Burns' unique political appeal, for while Burns, as the two-term incumbent and the architect of consensus politics, depended heavily on a coalition of interest groups, his political fortunes also rested on a strain of quiet idealism which reached beyond the scope of given interests, and this strain of idealism was indispensable. It flowed from the past, from the politics of first-class citizenship, and in 1970 Oshiro would redirect it, give it a new turn.

In the bleak days following the 1969 legislative session, when morale among the Burns forces was plunging downward, Robert Oshiro took it upon himself to strike the spark of a reelection campaign. To say that Oshiro was doggedly loyal, that he appreciated Burns' contribution to Hawaii, would be to understate the case: He well-nigh revered Jack Burns.

And this was infectious, because Oshiro was not defensive about Burns as many in Burns' entourage had become, but rather he talked of Burns the idealist.

Oshiro was forty-four, short and lithe, looking something like an AJA Tony Curtis. He was quiet, but had a quick grin. He was to devote nearly two years of his life to the campaign, drive himself mercilessly, and collapse in the hospital before election day.

Interestingly, Oshiro was not one of the old guard. Oshiro had been too young for World War II. He hadn't met Jack Burns until 1958, and hadn't himself become a politician until 1959, when he heard the announcement of the congressional vote on statehood for Hawaii. He equated statehood with equality, and the announcement gave him an indescribable thrill. As he recalled it, "I broke out in a cold sweat." In the first statehood election, he won a seat in the house.

He was a country lawyer representing the rural Oahu plantation towns of Wahiawa and Waialua, and in this sense he was in close touch with the spiritual home of the early Burns movement, even though a majority of those who had made their way from the feudal plantation structure into the wider society now lived in the Honolulu metropolis.

After three years as a state legislator, Oshiro was in 1962 elected chairman of the Democratic party, the post Burns had held in the crucial election of 1954. Oshiro was an effective chairman, but not a flashy chairman, not being given to strongly worded partisan statements. Tom Gill would be among those who privately criticized Oshiro for not providing the party with a strong public voice.

As chairman, Oshiro was aware that the Democratic party had arrived, that it now was overflowing with people who possessed leadership credentials, and that good young people seeking expression now had to wait their turn, as they had not in the old days.

So, to minimize the ill effects of this, he kept in his mind a record of all public officeholders, their ages, their possible desires to step aside, the possibility of vacancies, and this information he would relay to younger people who were looking for a way into the structure, so that the system would be supplied with new blood.

In 1962, the immediate problem had been a much more concrete one: the party was in a minority status in the senate, and it had failed to win in 1959 the prize of statehood, the office of governor. Further, because of a growing population, Hawaii in 1962 was given another seat in the U.S. House, so that now it had two seats. A coalition of the factions within the Democratic party was essential, and Robert Oshiro patiently worked toward that end, absorbing the flights of temper and the backbiting from the factions, and he succeeded. The year 1962 was the year of the winning unity slate: John Burns for governor, Tom Gill for the second seat in the U.S. House.

At the time Oshiro's effectiveness no doubt was enhanced by the fact that he was not a straight-line Burns man. He had, in fact, been in Washington after the 1959 election when Burns was closing out his delegate's office, and he had berated Burns for his poor showing in the 1959 governor's race, which was something that a good many disappointed Democrats had done, some of them publicly.

But 1962 was a different story for Burns, and it was a different story for Oshiro. Oshiro was now the chairman of a party which held the governorship, and a governor is not only the titular head of his party but also the dominant power—a party chairman is almost always an agent of the governor. So because Oshiro had not been a straight-line Burns man, had in fact carped at Burns for the defeat of 1959, he went to the new governor-elect and offered to step aside in favor of someone of Burns' personal choosing.

Burns suggested to Oshiro that he was merely worn out by the campaign, and that he needed time to rest and rethink his position. Burns argued that now the Democratic party held power, controlling the governorship and both houses of the legislature, the real task lay ahead, and that Oshiro could be particularly effective because he was also a legislator and hence could serve there as a liaison. After a rest of several months Oshiro concurred. For his trouble, at times when good will between Burns and some powerful legislators dwindled, Oshiro would be accused of being Burns' spy. Oshiro would say that in his years as Burns' man in the state house he came to see Burns' true genius for bringing together divergent forces for the common good.

At the acrimonious 1968 state Democratic convention, when it was clear that Gill would have overturned the Burns organization had that been within his power, Oshiro finally withdrew as state chairman (being replaced by the outwardly neutral David C. McClung, who was in truth pro-Burns).

Oshiro's let-up from organizational politics was brief.

In the early days of 1969, during the legislative session which was so harmful to Burns' cause, Oshiro already was thoroughly preoccupied with 1970, and he would sit back in his chair and gaze at the ceiling of the House chamber, puffing cigarettes through a white holder which he clenched in his teeth.

There had always been in him a certain flexibility, an awareness of the need to constantly adjust to new situations, to bring in new people and new ideas. In one of his rare public statements he had pointed to Aristotle as knowing that "nothing is more certain than change," and had added, "In my party we recognize that nothing is more certain than change."

In the legislature, he had fostered a program called the student intern program, which had brought hundreds of high school students to the Capitol for a week-long study of the legislature. This was not a mere walk-through put-on. The students were attached to the staffs of legislators or agencies of the legislature, genuinely involved, and even the most jaded Capitol politicians were touched by this.

By the time of the 1969 Legislature, Oshiro was satisfied that the student program had taken root, and so he turned all of his attention to formulating a new strategy which, he hoped, would salvage the career of John Burns.

In February, after months of sorting through Hawaii's numerous ad agencies, Oshiro made a crucial decision. Oshiro settled on the Lennen and Newell Pacific agency, knowing that as the local office of a national agency it could bring to bear the latest in political campaign techniques and the best of the new breed of political strategists.

This was a departure from the past. Once before in 1962 Burns had imported a Mainland publicist, who incidentally had stayed on in Hawaii in a small agency, but by and large both Burns and the Democratic party had been more wary than the Republicans of paid public relations. The Democratic party since 1954 had been strong at the grass roots, was in direct touch, and those people not reached by the party or by the feifdoms of legislators were reached by the Democratic-allied unions. When Burns was a penniless but nearly successful candidate for delegate in 1954, he had spent exactly $54.80 on a bill from the local agency of Beam and Milici. In the ensuing years the party had relied heavily on the agency of Carlos Rivas, who had done a reasonably good job, was practically one of the boys, but Rivas had no special sophistication in campaigning in the sense that Mainland agencies in the 1960s had developed sophistication.

From his faraway vantage point in Hawaii, Oshiro was aware that on the Mainland there had been a revolution in the image-making dimension of campaigning.

But while turning to the new politics of polling and electronic technology he remained deeply committed to the old-fashioned and unglamorous grind of organizing.

After the legislature adjourned, Oshiro was on the road day and night, searching for a first-hand feel of what was driving the voters, particularly what was on the minds of those who traditionally had supported Burns and were now wavering. And he passed by word of mouth the message that the old drive of the Burns movement was alive, and that Burns again would lead it. Always on these forays Oshiro looked for new faces, particularly young faces, and nothing delighted him more than when a young person would write either him or the governor a supportive letter, or even make a favorable remark. Oshiro would say that not all the young people were with Tom Gill, although he was one of the few in Burns' crowd who understood Gill's appeal. Oshiro would say that the young people were beginning to recognize that Gill had no corner on idealism.

For the paid core of the campaign staff Oshiro soon would hire five people, and all of them would be under the mysterious generational line, under thirty.

Oshiro set a hard pace, and by July the strain already was showing: He was a gaunt 130 pounds, 15 pounds off his normal weight. During this period there took place a telling exchange when a reporter questioned him one hot summer day in his office in the Capitol. Something extraordinary, beyond the usual political motives, seemed to be driving him. It seemed, to the reporter, that for Oshiro Burns' cause was an obsession, that his life revolved around it, and he was asked about this.

Pent-up, Oshiro responded on a tangential line, and at first it was not apparent that he would say anything of significance, because he broke into talking about his concern for his children, which is a rather hackneyed political line. But this was genuine. He was worried particularly over his children's sense of themselves and their sense of their cultural heritage. Pacing to a blackboard which he kept behind him, he wrote on it in foot-high letters the word WASP, a bit hesitantly, sensitive to the fact that the reporter was a White Anglo-Saxon Protestant born on the Mainland. From the word WASP Oshiro drew an arrow on the blackboard pointing to the west, where he drew a large circle which represented the Islands.

Coming at this time, and in such large numbers, Oshiro said, the WASP wave might altogether engulf Hawaii, so that his children and others would lose the sense of diversity which was unique to Hawaii. At a minimum, Oshiro argued, there needed to be time to reaffirm what was good and workable in the ethnic cultures, so the young would have a renewed sense of both their ethnic and Island heritages, and so they would not be overwhelmed by the new migration. In time Oshiro hoped that the new immigrants could be won over to respect Island ways, but he looked on this as a slow process.

From there Oshiro launched immediately into the description of Burns as the conciliator, the harmonizer of conflicting forces, and the point was made.

What Oshiro said that hot summer day was no less vague than the connotations of Burns' nickname, Great White Father.

Oshiro added in the conversation that in his grass-roots forays he found that one of Burns' main political liabilities was student unrest at the University of Hawaii, where Mainland students were widely blamed for infecting Island youngsters with the new dogma of confrontation. And this was compounded by the governor's having resisted a higher tuition for out-of-state students. The visionary utopian strain in Burns which saw Hawaii as an education for all of America, and which believed that every able student should be given an education regardless of economic status, had compelled him to veto two out-of-state tuition bills. The first was in 1967, the second in 1968. This had been one of his rare exercises of the executive veto power. Finally in 1969 Burns, under heavy legislative pressure, had allowed an out-of-state tuition bill to become law, but even then it was without the blessing of his signature, a strategem which connotes grudging acceptance.

The nisei, Oshiro said, could see the wisdom of Burns' Open Society position on out-of-state tuition after being reminded of the discrimination which they themselves had suffered during World War II.

That same month, July, Oshiro mass-mailed an appeal for a Burns campaign fund.

At the time, he hoped that after his initial push someone else would take over the campaign. But in a subsequent mass-mailing, he announced to the constituents of his legislative district that he was retiring from elective office because ". . . I can serve you more effectively in assisting with the 1970 campaign of the man I believe more responsible than any other for the vast and progressive changes in Hawaii in recent years, Governor John A. Burns."

The letter cited economic development, improved education, labor-management balance, and Hawaii's emergence as meeting ground of East and West. It conceded new problems in Hawaii, but "most of them actually [are] the result of our growth and prosperity."

Oshiro was in so deep, and so early, that he was carried along by events of his own making to fill the role of Burns' manager.

Among the under-thirties Robert Oshiro hired for the campaign staff, the most strategically placed was a shy student named Rick Egged.

Egged had gone to Waipahu High School, where he had sensed a rift between the haoles and nonhaoles. Although he was a Caucasian, he remembered seeking—and finding—acceptance among the nonhaoles in his high school. Before graduating he joined VISTA, Volunteers in Service to America, and worked on a Blackfoot Indian reservation in Montana. On the reservation, he met a touring politician who also was deeply concerned about the plight of the Indians, U.S. Sen. Robert F. Kennedy. Kennedy soon plunged into the 1968 presidential campaign to unseat President Johnson, and Egged joined Kennedy's staff.

For an eighteen-year-old, Rick Egged was handed an extraordinary political education. He now and then came into contact with Robert Kennedy, and he also worked as liaison to one of Kennedy's pollsters, John Kraft, organizing students to work in Kraft's polling apparatus.

In 1968 Egged also returned to Hawaii—"just carrying the bags," as he put it—for the Hawaii Democratic convention, traveling with Pierre Salinger, who had been President John Kennedy's press secretary and now in 1968 was working for Robert. As it happened Egged and Salinger landed in the midst of the Burns-Gill convention turmoil, which hopelessly complicated their position, although it was bad to start with because Burns was committed to Hubert Humphrey, even though personally Burns was no particular admirer of Humphrey.

Gill at the convention, as a dove on the Vietnam war, was riding a coalition of Kennedy and Eugene McCarthy forces. Actually he was for Kennedy, but did not say so publicly. While Egged was aware that Gill favored Kennedy, he nonetheless soured on Gill as a result of the convention. Both Egged and Salinger were under the impression that had Gill not pushed so hard for his own cause, Burns would have yielded a few votes for Kennedy as a concession to pro-Kennedy sentiment. In fact, this probably was a misinterpretation, because the chance of Kennedy's salvaging anything rested solely on Gill's taking over the party, and that was beyond Gill's reach. U.S. Rep. Patsy T. Mink likewise wanted Kennedy, but was not fighting Burns; nonetheless Patsy Mink was iced out of the Hawaii delegation when she refused to pledge herself to Humphrey. At any rate, Egged believed Gill had fouled the works for RFK, and when Egged reported Gill's behavior an irritated Robert Kennedy remarked, "That's characteristic of Gill."

Soon it no longer mattered, nor was Egged any longer involved in the heady business of presidential politics, because on the night of the 1968 California primary Robert Kennedy was murdered.

Egged came home to Hawaii and waited for the shock to wear off, marking time for the better part of a year until he began to take an interest in the mounting tension which attended the gubernatorial race. Because of his memory of the 1968 Democratic convention Egged ruled out the idea of working for Gill. Briefly he worked for Republican Sam King—in fact he briefly researched material critical of Burns—but wasn't enthusiastic about King. Then he talked to State Sen. George Ariyoshi, who turned him over to Robert Oshiro. Egged at first was skeptical of the Burns crowd, seeing Burns as the prototype old-line politician Kennedy had fought against, and Egged expected the Burns organization to be a closed book.

To Egged's surprise, Oshiro greeted him with open arms, talked to him for hours about Hawaii, and Egged got a new picture of John Burns.

Robert Oshiro, after talking to Mainland consultants, assigned Egged to Lennen and Newell Pacific to operate a weekly poll which would be one of the campaign's best-kept secrets. Egged, the Waipahu boy, started with a small crew which he eventually expanded to about two hundred pro-Burns youngsters who acted as interviewers, and these were a different breed from the kids who were so highly visible and vocal in their support of Tom Gill.

After the fact Rick Egged would describe them this way: "Ninety-nine per cent of them were local kids, the quiet kind. And you had to ask them to help. We got a lot of leads through their parents —you see, the rebellion syndrome is overestimated as far as the local kids are concerned. Their mothers and fathers would be for Burns so the kids would say, 'Well, I like Burns too.' "

Egged would concede that Burns got the "B" students, in the sense that "they were less active, but not less intelligent," while Gill got the "A" and the "F" students, the brainy young activists and the badly disillusioned. The Burns kids performed spectacularly. Egged started with weekly samples of 400 people and climbed to huge samples of 2,800. From his research Egged could brief the Burns organization on subsurface trends which other campaigns would only guess at, in particular ethnic trends which lent insight into the election's final outcome. Egged would call the primary election results within 4 percentage points, and he would be even more precisely on target in the general election, so that even sophisticated politicians would mumble stories about Egged as if he were a seer.

7

The Image-Makers

Lennen and Newell Pacific first had caught the eye of Robert Oshiro in 1968 with a polished TV campaign for Democratic State Senator John Hulten, who initially had been in trouble in his Windward district but had won handily. Of greater importance, Oshiro knew that Lennen and Newell's parent office in New York City had handled part of the 1968 Humphrey presidential campaign, and therefore it had a line on some of the best for-hire political talent in the country. Oshiro also liked Jack Seigle, the thirty-seven-year-old president of the Honolulu office, because Seigle wasn't a know-it-all, had a knack for listening, and, like Burns, "wasn't someone who shoots off his mouth," as Oshiro would put it. Seigle was reflective, and this was a quality Oshiro valued. When Seigle talked he had something to say, and his self-assurance was unafflicted by the gushy and wheeler-dealer style so common to the ad trade.

His spacious suite of offices on the twelfth floor of the new Financial Plaza of the Pacific housed a staff of thirty-six people, a talent bank of account executives, researchers, marketers, artists, designers, copywriters, and media space and time buyers. Seigle had come to Honolulu in 1962, building the Pacific office from scratch into a $3.5 million business, which made it a bigger business than sister offices in such places as London, Paris, Los Angeles, and Portland. His accounts were usually more simply saleable than politicians, commodities such as whiskey, cement, macadamia nuts, candy, paper, soft drinks, cosmetics, and guava juice.

Seigle's general policy was to turn down political campaign accounts. Only twice had he broken this rule. Once was for U.S. Rep. Spark Matsunaga in 1964, and the second was for John Hulten. In Hulten's instance, Seigle had thought the campaign budget was nickel-and-dime, although in fact Hulten had reported spending $42,000 on an office which pays a mere $12,000 annually. This was a record for a state legislative race, several times over the usual cost of a state senate race, and also a faint hint of things to come.

When Oshiro approached Seigle in early 1969, Seigle was unacquainted with Burns. Not unlike the average voter, Seigle had only seen Burns on TV, read about him in the press, and shaken his hand going through reception lines. Nonetheless, Seigle agreed to pursue the possibility of taking the Burns account.

Oshiro arranged a meeting over breakfast at the Washington Place mansion for Burns and three of Seigle's staff, including Seigle's director of marketing and research, Dr. Edmond Faison, who has a Ph.D. in mass communications from George Washington University. Burns, although at this point officially undecided on whether to wade into the 1970 campaign, spent most of his morning with Seigle's people, outlining his views on the state of government and politics.

From that starting point, Seigle's staff undertook a detailed analysis of voter attitudes and the strong and weak points of Burns and those who were expected to oppose him. This research alone cost $27,000.

Although details were never divulged, Seigle later summarized the outlook in 1969 as dismal, with some "king-sized problems to overcome." Seigle also concluded that Gill. was seemingly more with-it, as Seigle put it, and that Burns might only suffer from the face-to-face encounters of traditional campaigning. Burns' main liability, as Seigle interpreted the research data, was that most people didn't know what he had been doing as governor.

But Burns' image had several potent assets: He looked and acted like a governor ("... the stature and presence of a chief executive"), and there was "a strong, across-the-board acknowledgment that the governor had been the most influential, dynamic person in Hawaii, going back to statehood and pre-statehood."

This was of course true.

Burns also showed a strong plus on working harmoniously with the legislature, and even those who were pro-Gill were critical of Gill as a maverick.

Despite all this, Burns looked even shakier in Lennen and Newell's precampaign trial heat than he had in Gill's early 1969 poll. Lennen and Newell found their candidate trailing in the Democratic primary by more than 20 percentage points on Oahu.

Interestingly, Burns lagged behind Gill in every major ethnic bloc, including the AJAs.

It was this sort of finding by polls which had led a good many serious politicians to conclude that Burns was all but unelectable. He was the incumbent and had dominated Hawaii politics for years, and a great volume of research into American politics had found that voters are strongly inclined to favor an incumbent, unless in their eyes something is badly awry. Therefore at this point in the game Burns would have been expected to be leading the polls even if serious opposition were at hand. It was doubly interesting that even among AJAs, who had been the backbone of his support in past years, he showed no particular strength. Small wonder then that Burns had been heard to remark, "I may have outworn my welcome."

Seigle, after committing himself, had no option but to go to work and try to turn the situation around. By autumn of 1969 he was thoroughly enmeshed, so much so that the campaign became his compelling personal interest. Although Seigle had several million dollars worth of other customers to worry over, he would spend more than half of his time during the next year on the account of John Burns. Once his basic research was in hand, Seigle began organizing his media assault. And judging from the attention which other professional hucksters would eventually lavish on it, it would be one of the best on the globe in 1970.

It would be one of six American political campaigns studied later in a New York workshop of the American Association of Political Consultants. Then subsequently it would be one of two campaigns, and the only American campaign, to be reviewed in London by the International Association of Political Consultants. And one of the Burns ads would win top honors for a political production in competition involving thirty countries at an international film festival in Atlanta.

Yet in 1969 none of this could be foreseen, and only the fact that John Burns was in dire straits was of interest.

From the Honolulu office, Seigle assigned two of his top staff members to work full time on the Burns account, one was Chuck Heinrich, who functioned as Seigle's chief lieutenant and worked on interpreting the research findings. Although a political novice —Heinrich had specialized in industrial advertising in San Francisco—he was a man who did his homework, poring over the rash of Mainland campaign studies of the 1960s.

Heinrich was most impressed by three books. One was *The People Machine,* an exploration of television; the second was *The New Politics,* a case-by-case rundown on new campaign techniques; and the third was Theodore White's best-selling *Making of the President 1968.*

It was probably more than incidental to the 1970 Hawaii story that White's book dwelt heavily on Richard Nixon's controlled use of television and on Nixon's successful tactic of screening himself from a day-to-day interchange with the working press.

Seigle's other full-time staff member on the Burns account was Luann Burmann, a radio-TV producer from the broadcast department, assigned to birddog the electronics campaign.

After gearing up his Honolulu staff, Seigle embarked on a Mainland talent search, as Oshiro had expected. He first flew to New York to consult with Campaign Planners Inc., a Lennen and Newell subsidiary organized in 1968 for the Humphrey campaign. Then on the recommendation of Campaign Planners Inc., Seigle turned to the Washington-based firm of Joseph Napolitan.

Although Seigle later would refer to Napolitan as merely a "sound second judgment," Napolitan's history suggests that he had a strong hand in shaping Seigle's course.

Napolitan, an ex-reporter, had started dabbling in campaign management in Massachusetts in 1957, then teamed up with Larry O'Brien in 1959 to promote a local charter reform referendum— this was the same O'Brien who later served as a Kennedy manager, presidential aide, postmaster general, and national chairman of the Democratic party.

Napolitan's fortunes likewise rose with the Kennedys and survived their deaths.

He worked successively on the campaigns of U.S. Sen. Ted Kennedy, U.S. Sen. George McGovern, President Johnson (1964), Humphrey, and then—going international—hired out to Pierre Elliot Trudeau, prime minister of Canada, and to Ferdinand Marcos, president of the Philippines.

Napolitan particularly had developed a reputation for emotionally charged TV campaigning.

He ridiculed the old-fashioned TV talk to the voters, contending, "You lose them when you put your guy in front of a camera, the kind, you know, where he starts out 'Good evening, ladies and gentlemen, my name is Joe Blow and I want to talk to you tonight about taxes.' When you do that you can hear the click of sets being switched or turned off all over the state. That sort of program is just radio with a light to read by."

In the 1968 presidential race, Napolitan reputedly commissioned the film of Hubert Humphrey playing with his mentally retarded grandchild. In the film, an emotionally wrought presidential candidate confided to America that through his grandchild's disability, he had learned the power of human love.

In 1966, Napolitan had started going in big for half-hour campaign films while working for millionaire Milton Shapp, who aspired to govern Pennsylvania.

For Shapp, Napolitan collaborated with Charles Guggenheim, who had won an Oscar for documentary filmmaking.

Napolitan called the Shapp film *The Man against the Machine,* blitzing Pennsylvania with thirty-five TV showings throughout the state. In that particular race Shapp made history as the first man in Pennsylvania politics to upset the candidate of the state's regular Democratic party organization, although he lost the general election to a Republican. Two years later, in 1968, Napolitan brought home a winner in Alaska with Mike Gravel who ousted long-time incumbent U.S. Sen. Ernest Gruening. Although the polls on the Alaskan race seemed incredible, *Time* magazine reported as follows:

"On a Saturday a week before the voting, a poll showed Gruening ahead 2 to 1. On Sunday, a heavily promoted film, prepared by . . . Napolitan, ran on television. On Monday, a new poll showed Gravel ahead, 55 to 45. He then won by that margin."

Seigle signed on Napolitan as a consultant. After their initial talks, Napolitan flew into Hawaii for a series of four two-day working sessions with Seigle and his staff, always unbeknown to the public and the press.

After securing Napolitan's services, Seigle's second acquisition on the Mainland was a documentary film firm in San Francisco called Medion Inc., which had learned many of its techniques from the renowned Guggenheim. Medion was hired on the recommendation of Joseph Napolitan, who reputedly thought that Medion was just as good as Guggenheim technically and was even more desirable than Guggenheim from the standpoint of flexibility: Guggenheim supposedly was making such a bundle of money on one-minute spot announcements that he was reluctant to get into half-hour films. (Guggenheim, incidentally, prior to becoming a huckster had enjoyed a fine reputation as an artistic filmmaker, but a reputation for artistry apparently had not been that reward-ing financially.)

Napolitan's judgment on Medion would prove to be sound, would enhance Joe Napolitan's international reputation. Medion not only would deliver, but it would do so when it counted most. In the darkest moments of the Burns campaign, when Burns was to be staggered by the disclosure of scandal in his administration, Medion would release a heart-rending documentary on the life and times of John Burns.

Somewhere during this early period a Robert Squier also played a role, analyzing the research data and also coaching Burns on his television appearance (there was, in Burns' office, a TV monitor on hand, which gave an instant feedback and thereby facilitated ad-justments of TV style). Like Napolitan and the Lennen and Newell agency, Squier had acquired a national reputation for campaign management during the affluent 1960s.

In Honolulu, Seigle's office busied itself with putting together a variety of brochures and booklets. Also it produced the prelimi-nary battery of one-minute spot ads which, in Seigle's words, were designed to convince people that Hawaii after all wasn't such a bad place to live. *Wasn't such a bad place to live.* To those who conceived of Hawaii as the envy of the rest of the nation, this may sound absurd, but politically in 1970 it was not. On the contrary, it cut to the heart of the matter—to the sense of despair which had been generated by the invasion of Waikiki, by the visible pollution of the air, the noise, the traffic jams, by the soaring cost of living.

In Seigle's first battery of ads, a narrator invariably guided the TV viewer through sixty pleasant seconds of the scenic and un-spoiled parts of Hawaii—after all, it *wasn't such a bad place to live.*

One spot ad noted that unemployment had dropped sharply during the Burns years,* and that, despite the high cost of living, real income was up 40 per cent. "Things are better, but we've got some tough problems ahead."

Another pointed to the economic benefits of tourism, and to the growth of research and development employment. "Of course, we can't let tourism get out of hand."

---

*By 1971, unemployment would double, going over the 6 per cent mark, owing to an ILWU dock strike and the national recession—events no more subject to Burns' influence than was the national boom which largely accounted for Hawaii's low unemployment rate during the Kennedy and Johnson years.

One showed new beaches and parks, and another mentioned new government programs for the little guy—the Office of Consumer Protection, the Progressive Neighborhoods Act, and temporary disability insurance (all originally initiated by legislators). In pidgin, a voice was audible over the soft strum of a ukulele: "With Jack Burns running things, a guy really has a place in the big picture."

The tag line was a simple "Think about it," soft-sell, repeated over and over.

As Seigle would later explain to other professionals gathered in London from thirteen nations, "If our voters were to remain unhappy with the New Hawaii, they would surely not be inclined to vote again for its governor."

On May 12, 1970, *Think about it* first beamed through the TV tube, nearly six months before the final vote. It was by far the earliest media start in Hawaii's campaign history.

8

The ILWU

Although Joseph Napolitan and his ilk of new professionals had become accepted as a major asset in Mainland campaigns, indeed an absolutely necessary part of a national campaign, Napolitan et al. were untested in Hawaii prior to 1970. In fact many Islanders argued that anyone from the Mainland was a liability, because they thought Hawaii was so different from the Mainland—one could not possibly understand Hawaii politics without long exposure. Further, there remained a tinge of the interloper role on anyone from the Mainland, and this was thought to be politically significant, particularly if word of a Mainlander's influence was widely circulated among the voters. If anything, this feeling reflected the insularity and chauvinism which persisted in Hawaii, but it was genuine. Tom Gill for one, who was regarded by most people as a political sophisticate, would scoff at the idea of Mainland professionals.

But if there was some doubt about the effectiveness of the new professionals, there was little doubt about the effectiveness of Hawaii's largest labor union, the ILWU.

John Burns once had said that although the ILWU could not by itself elect a man to office, it could effectively thwart someone in a statewide race whom it vigorously opposed. Burns also would talk of the ILWU as the original guarantor of basic democracy in Hawaii, which meant that Burns held the union in high regard for its part in overturning the feudal economic system which had prevailed in Hawaii before World War II.

The initials, ILWU, stand for International Longshoremen's and Warehousemen's Union, but as with many unions the ILWU had outgrown its name. Its component of waterfront stevedores was but a small part of a membership which spanned the entire sugar and pineapple industries and the tourism industry on the Neighbor Islands. In political circles and in the rural areas, if one said *the union* that was enough to identify it—the union *was* the ILWU, all other unions being of secondary status. In times past, the planters in the search for labor had recruited workers first from China, then mainly from Japan, and then from the Philippines. Accordingly the first attempts to unionize the plantations were as if the planters had written the script—each ethnic group proceeded on its own, suspicious of other ethnics, and each failed. The ILWU had seen the tragedy of this and had effectively preached multiracialism and class interests. And immediately after World War II its membership shot up phenomenally to 30,000 members.

Its political influence had expanded accordingly, although there often was controversy. Even John Burns had fought the union when it had attempted to take over the Democratic party in the early years following the war, but once it had been established that the party belonged to the politicians then an alliance was worked out.

Through the years the ILWU would not always support Burns in elections, nor would it always support Democrats for that matter, but it would back Burns throughout the 1960s, and almost always the relationship was friendly. In fact the fortunes of Burns and the ILWU had risen on an approximately parallel course, and their overriding causes were the same—overturning the haole oligarchy in favor of a new multiracial order. Burns had been quick to recognize the potential effectiveness of union power, and even his first small political group in the mid-1940s had included Jack Kawano, a controversial ILWU official who collaborated with Burns on precinct organization.

When during the early 1950s many politicians in Hawaii had viciously attacked the ILWU as un-American, Burns had held his tongue. In fact he had lent his moral support to ILWU figures who suffered the outrages of the Joseph McCarthy era, an era which in some ways inflicted wounds in Hawaii even more severe than on American society generally. For one thing, a case can be made that the Red hysteria delayed statehood—at least the old territory's pro-statehood propaganda implicitly suggests this, because one of its main aims was exploding the idea of the domestic Communist menace. Further, McCarthyism destroyed some men and women in Hawaii, and it made life-long cynics of others.

But many among its victims endured admirably, recouped, and were eventually recognized for their contributions to modern Hawaii.

This was long after 1952, when the ILWU's legendary Jack Hall was tried along with six other people—the Hawaii Seven, they were called—on Smith Act charges of conspiring against the federal government.

At that time FBI agents appealed to Burns to testify in the trial against Jack Hall, and Burns said, "Sure, but I want you to know I'll say I've known Jack Hall to be a loyal American."

Immediately the FBI dropped Burns, and subsequently Burns told Jack Hall that he would testify as a character witness on Hall's behalf. Hall, while no doubt appreciating the gesture, said no, that Burns would only succeed in destroying himself politically.

Hall and the other six defendants were convicted and sentenced to federal penitentiary, but while the sentence was on appeal the Smith Act was ruled unconstitutional.

The ultimate irony of the story was that the ILWU succeeded so well in securing a better life for its members that none would be interested in Marxism; ILWU agricultural workers reputedly became the best-paid fieldworkers in the nation.

The economic benefits of unionism were basic to the influence of the ILWU leadership over its members on other matters, particularly political matters. So an ILWU statewide endorsement mattered, and in 1962 when the ILWU had thrown its support behind John Burns he had won the governorship.

In this office, Burns had promoted a new era of stability between labor and management, and ILWU prestige was even further enhanced. Some businessmen, recognizing that unionization was inevitable, were eager to be a part of the ILWU, so to speak, because Jack Hall had a reputation as an honest bargainer, and because the ILWU was looked on with special favor by the governor.

In effect, the ILWU became the cornerstone of the consensus. During the 1960s the ILWU was known to lobby in the legislature or the administration for business interests when labor-business economics overlapped, and also sometimes when there was no apparent overlap, as in the Magic Island controversy.

As governor, Burns also frequently assigned his first attorney general, Bert Kobayashi, to act as mediator in contract negotiations, not only with the ILWU but also other unions. And it was generally agreed that Kobayashi wielded more influence at the bargaining table than did professional men assigned by the Federal Mediation Service.

Burns also freely passed out appointments on key state policy boards to union people. At one point there were two ILWU officials on the State Land Board, for example. And Eddie Tangen, the union's hotel organizer, was an influential member of the State Land Use Commission, which in the late 1960s was rezoning major land tracts for hotel development in the ILWU's Neighbor Island strongholds. This was but a sample of the bonds which existed between Burns and the union.

Looming in the year 1970 as the alternative to John Burns was of course Tom Gill, and the union was well aware that if Gill ascended to the office of governor its influence there would be nil —Gill had said as much.

The ILWU had had a fling with Gill in 1954, helping him win the Oahu county chairmanship. But, as Lawrence Fuchs saw it in his book *Hawaii Pono,* when Gill refused to bend to union direction, he was written off as a phony liberal.

The union also fought Tom Gill in the 1959 house organization battle, successfully opposed his 1964 bid to unseat Republican Hiram Fong from the U.S. Senate, and unsuccessfully opposed him in Gill's 1966 primary battle with Kenneth Brown.

As 1970 approached, the union's long-standing animosity toward Gill was aggravated by several factors. One was Gill's stress on solving urban problems, which implicitly meant a lower priority for the ILWU-dominated Neighbor Islands.

Gill was also criticizing the pace of tourism expansion at a time when the union was organizing Neighbor Island hotels—bolstering its membership to offset losses incurred by mechanization in the sugar and pineapple industries. And always behind Gill loomed Art Rutledge, boss of the competing Hotel Workers' Union.

A third factor was Gill's hard-line support for the environmental movement, and the union feared that Gill would nail the sugar industry—a principal water polluter—to the wall. The sugar industry was already in dire trouble financially.

During the 1969 Legislature, for example, the union had joined forces with the sugar lobby to oppose a bill which would have allowed the state to impose heavier fines against polluters. For his part Burns had never resorted to even the light fines allowed by the existing law, but nonetheless the bill was killed. In the corridors of the Capitol both the sugar and labor lobbyists argued that if Gill were to become governor he would actually levy fines—relentlessly, they contended. The union never made this argument publicly, of course, because it might have struck some people as an excellent reason to vote for Gill in the next election.

To the Gill forces this instance of political hand-holding on the pollution bill was but further evidence of the gap between the public interest and the Burns consensus—pollution, after all, was a serious problem.

Throughout the Gill camp there was a feeling that the ILWU leadership not only had accumulated too much power but also had abused it. This sentiment was a binding sentiment among independent Democrats, even though most of them were sympathetic to the aims of organized labor. One state senator in the Gill wing of the party would complain bitterly, "It's not enough with the ILWU for me to support unions. What they want is guys who can't think for themselves, but I'll be damned if I'll go along with them on every move." Another senator would derisively refer to the ILWU headquarters on the edge of Waikiki as the Kremlin, not so much because of the old Red issue as for a feeling that the union was Machiavellian and dictatorial. The fact was that the ILWU leaders tended to be tough disciplinarians, having learned the hard way in the 1940s and 1950s that it was necessary to deal from a position of strength.

More alarming were signs that elements of the ILWU had abandoned their early idealism in favor of their newly found prestige and their Establishment political connections. For example, although vehemently opposed to the Vietnam war, the ILWU would again endorse the hawkish Republican, U.S. Sen. Hiram L. Fong, for reelection in 1970 even though the war entirely dominated national politics at the time. Or, to take another example, a key union politician in the 1968 session of the legislature had helped stall an increase in the minimum wage, thereby guaranteeing that 5,000 or so workers in Hawaii not covered by the federal wage law would continue laboring for a year at the poverty wage of $1.25 an hour. The reasons given were largely technical.

Such instances as these provoked the liberals of the Gill camp into a rigid anti-ILWU position, blinding them to the fact that the ILWU continued to be the main force propelling many of the progressive policies of the new state: In 1969, after years of research and lobbying, the ILWU secured a new state plan for temporary disability insurance. This was an important addition to the workmen's compensation program, which already was considered the best in the country. In 1970, to take a second example, the union played a critical supporting role in passage of a measure which almost unconditionally legalized abortion of unwanted pregnancies.

John Burns in this case, although himself a devout Catholic who started each day by attending mass, had allowed the abortion bill to become law, despite his misgivings and despite strong pressure from the church.

While Burns was trying to make his decision extremists were practically accusing him of complicity in mass murder, and proponents likewise were harassing him, although after talking with Burns they were impressed by the depth of his research into the questions and eased off. On the last day of his constitutional deadline for vetoing the bill, Burns had asked a reporter his feeling about the bill, and the reporter said that from a standpoint of social justice he believed it was a good bill—the well-to-do flew to Japan for abortions while those not well-heeled either sought out con artists or reluctantly gave birth. The reporter, thinking of his own child, added that nonetheless he was plagued by a belief that unique life began not at the time a fetus could live outside a mother's womb but at the moment of conception. Tears clouded Burns' eyes, and he thanked the newsman for understanding his moral dilemma.

Burns' own son, his youngest, had been born after his wife's crippling bout with polio and despite warnings by physicians that if the pregnancy were not aborted Mrs. Burns might die.

On the night of his deadline Burns further pondered two statements which his staff had prepared for him, one a veto message, the second containing his reasons for acceding to the legislature's majority vote. While Burns sat alone in the Washington Place mansion the bill became law at the stroke of midnight.

For this and other reasons the ILWU was not about to abandon John Burns when he was in trouble politically. And in fact such union officials as Robert McElrath detected in the abortion issue the first signs of Burns regaining lost favor with the public, even though more than 200,000 people in Hawaii are Catholic—the attacks of the Catholic hierarchy were so severe as to possibly create a flow of sympathy for the embattled governor. On the other hand the abortion measure had reaffirmed the union's view of Gill as a phony liberal: Gill, although supporting the reform, had not wanted to comment on it publicly, preferring that Burns take the heat alone, but a reporter had pressed him and finally Gill had made a terse statement supporting the bill.

Like Robert Oshiro, the ILWU was acutely aware of Burns' political plight and likewise made an early start in its drive for Burns for 1970. In a pointed move, Jack Hall endorsed all incumbent officeholders, meaning Burns for governor, Tom Gill for lieutenant governor, and the Republican Fong for the United States Senate. In effect this was a warning to Tom Gill to sit tight in his powerless office.

At the union's ensuing statewide convention in September of 1969, Hall went to work gearing up the union's rank-and-file.

The Burns administration, Hall predicted, would be attacked in the coming campaign as a combination of "buddha-heads (AJAs) and the ILWU, and there's going to be a vigorous campaign to try to unseat the present administration and replace it with one that has a lot of beautiful ideas.

"But if they were all put into effect," Hall told the delegates, "I don't know how we'd eat."

Hall argued that the union had taken a balanced approach toward conservation and expanding tourism.

And he disclaimed dictatorial control over Burns, but added, "we have a voice in the highest council. And I think we should all stop for a minute and think out what would happen if there were a new administration, and where the ILWU would stand in all of this."

Burns himself was introduced to the convention by the union's lobbyist, Brother Eddie DeMello—union members still call each other brother and sister.

Taking the podium, Burns turned to DeMello and quipped that perhaps DeMello had been chosen to make the introduction because DeMello spent so much time in the governor's office.

After Burns' remarks, every convention delegate stood to endorse a resolution to back Burns again for the office of governor. Yoshito Takamine, who was both a state representative and an ILWU business agent on the Big Island's Hamakua Coast, followed through with a talk urging convention delegates to "now polish up our machinery."

Takamine meant rank-and-file union members, who would hear the virtues of Jack Burns preached at stopwork rallies wherever there was a sugar or pineapple plantation, a mill, or a canning plant.

The ILWU machinery, from that base, extended in several other directions—all crucial to Burns' campaign.

It had, for example, carefully cultivated alliances in factions of other unions, alliances which in some instances would succeed in securing a Burns endorsement.

It also had working control of the state senate through a coalition with Burns proteges, and a strong minority voice in the house —all of this adding up to strategic clout in the coming push in the 1970 Legislature.

And it had a voice with the old enemy, the big business houses.

Two months after the union's convention, the ILWU's Robert McElrath appeared before a meeting of the Hawaiian Sugar Planters' Association. While making a point of insisting on his own radicalism, McElrath warned the planters against abandoning the alliance, against abandoning the Burns consensus in favor of a Republican.

"The next governor of Hawaii will be elected in the primary," McElrath said, "and that governor will be a Democrat. I do not see a single Republican in the state . . . who can defeat the Democratic nominee in next year's general election."

McElrath described the Burns administration as "many things to many people, but not all things to all people.

"The Burns administration has been called a consensus administration, an administration where all sections of our society have been invited to participate in and benefit therefrom. . . .

"The other choice is Tom Gill. Need I say more?"

The idea, as McElrath later put it, was this: "I was trying to lay down a policy for the Big Five."

9

The Legislature

By the time the state legislature convened at the State Capitol in January of 1970, the conflict on the Capitol's fifth floor between John Burns and Tom Gill had come to dominate Island politics almost totally. And the Democratic majority of the legislature was but a reflection of larger events—there was on one hand a dominant Burns camp and on the other an aggressive minority who favored Gill. If Burns could not be reelected, then inevitably in a period of years the Burns-ILWU faction in the legislature would deteriorate and its power would decline accordingly. So while issues would be legislated in 1970, the broader agenda was future power over the political establishment of the state of Hawaii.

From the standpoint of Burns' political popularity the prior year's legislative session had been a fiasco, but 1970 would be a different story. This was because Burns would succeed in establishing some credibility on new issues which Gill had made his own, such as housing and the environment. Previously Burns had uttered some typically vague generalizations on these issues, but had not exerted much leadership—on the contrary, several incidents had earned him a reputation in some quarters of being allied with developers who polluted the environment and returned nothing to the people in the way of modest-priced housing. In a landmark controversy in 1966 the Burns-appointed State Land Board had voted to fill in Oahu's Salt Lake for development's sake. This was Hawaii's only natural lake and one of the few salt water lakes in the world, so the State Land Board decision naturally offended conservationists, to put it mildly.

Their disenchantment was the more intense because the lake was to be filled in at the request of a development concern headed by entrepreneur Clarence Ching, who in 1966 had served as the treasurer of the Burns campaign and was a long-time Burns cohort.

Beyond the Salt Lake question, both Burns' first land board chairman, Jim P. Ferry, who had left the government following a controversial real estate transaction, and Burns' second chairman, Sunao Kido, publicly described themselves as "developer-oriented." And this orientation had been apparent in several land department positions, including Kido's role in the Magic Island controversy in 1969.

So it was not merely because of criticism from Gill, as many Burns camp followers would contend, that Burns needed to improve his position on issues such as the environment during the 1970 legislative session.

The legislature likewise was awakening to new public demands as the election neared. While the 1969 session had passed such important social measures as temporary disability insurance and a range of consumer protection laws, not until 1970 did the legislature catch up to the more contemporary trends current in the electorate.

Historically the legislature had played an exalted role in Hawaii. In its territorial years under an appointed governor the legislature was looked upon as the legitimate expression of popular democracy. The young Democratic warriors who in 1954 had captured the legislature were not only politicians but popular heroes. And even after statehood the legislature, under the influence of such legislators as Nadao Yoshinaga, Tom Gill, Nelson Doi, and Elmer Cravalho, had continued to play an inordinate role in comparison to the Executive branch. By 1970 most of the early leadership had departed except for Yoshinaga, and neither Tadao Beppu as house speaker nor David McClung as senate president was in the strong position which past leaders had enjoyed.

Further, there seemed to be a less confident mood among legislators as problems became more complex, although some would bolster themselves on a rating as the nation's seventh most effective legislature by the national Citizens' Conference on State Legislatures.

Myron Thompson, the governor's administrative director after 1967, detected in this situation an opening for an assertion of Executive leadership, and in context of gubernatorial politics Thompson planned to close the gap between Burns and Gill on the popular issues.

Because of the rift between Burns and his lieutenant governor, Thompson as administrative director had assumed extra importance in the government—he was, during his three years under Burns, the de facto assistant governor. Among the many people around Burns, Thompson was ideally suited to spearhead a legislative program, because he was as nonpolitical as anyone in his position could be—his motivation would not be suspect. Thompson would say that the best politics was simply doing a good job for the people and, although this is a standard political cliche, Thompson believed it and acted accordingly. By profession he was a social worker and by instinct an idealist, devoted to the aspirations of the dispossessed.

Thompson was of mainly Hawaiian ancestry and, even though he had done well and was genuinely cosmopolitan, he was still aware that in their native land the Hawaiian people were disproportionately represented among the poor, the unemployed, the school drop-outs, in delinquency and crime statistics, and in the wards of the state hospital; conversely Hawaiians were underrepresented in the legislature, the professions, the universities, and all those institutions which in both Western and Asian societies had meant respect and special privilege. Thompson, several years in advance of younger and more militant Hawaiians, had begun preaching recognition of the strengths of the old Polynesian culture.

Thompson was particularly drawn to the culture's emphasis on healthy personal dealings—its proclivity for collaboration rather than competition, its base in the extended family as opposed to the nuclear family, and its systematic techniques for resolving personality tensions—all of which seemed worthy of attention in the Western urban rat race of 1970.

Myron Thompson saw John Burns as many had seen Burns in past days, as the champion of the underprivileged. He also respected Tom Gill for his work on behalf of the dispossessed and for Gill's special reverence for the land—Thompson in 1963 had chaired for Burns the first State Land Use Commission, which Gill had devised as a legislator. But Thompson considered Gill to be too prone to confrontation and by instinct he preferred consensus politics: Consensus was the Hawaiian way. Younger militants, many of them trained in the antipoverty movement or inspired by the example of blacks and chicanos on the Mainland, would not agree. Many would embrace Tom Gill, while a large remnant of the Hawaiian people would cling to a Republican party which Delegate Jonah Kuhio had drawn them into many decades earlier. The effect of this would be a hopelessly divided Polynesian vote, although in the new militance and stress on the Polynesian culture the year 1970 suggested a future cohesion—it appeared that at last Hawaiians were preparing to drive a harder bargain.*

As administrative director, Myron Thompson was not only Burns' chief lobbyist but also was in charge of riding herd on all of the governmental departments, and his view of the Executive agencies was not altogether unlike Tom Gill's. Thompson perceived many of the departments as having grown sluggish, as reacting to problems rather than anticipating public problems, and he was saying as much privately. No sooner had the 1969 Legislature adjourned than Thompson began pressing department heads for a coordinated and meaty legislative program to open the year in 1970. The housing issue which Gill had so successfully preempted was assigned to a new aide to the governor, Bill S. Cook. Cook had been a pioneering planning reporter; he knew little about the details of housing, but he understood broad planning concepts and of greater importance was adept at putting the best face on things. He came to Burns by way of a public relations agency which he had joined after giving up reporting. Cook unofficially doubled as a second press secretary and so far as possible helped heal the growing breach between Burns and the working press. On Cook's entry into the governor's office, Burns simultaneously appointed a housing task force and announced an all-out attack on the housing crisis: "A man's home is his castle, but there is no reason it should cost so much." For Burns this was a rare bit of dramatization.

By the opening of the legislature in January 1970, ten months before the election, Burns, Cook, and Thompson had readied a comprehensive housing proposal, packages on the environment and oceanography, and other politically important measures. The public relations angle improved markedly. In past years administration proposals often had dribbled into the hands of newsmen and legislators directly from the governmental departments, on occasion one department's position conflicting with another's. This time the package was indexed, integrated, and came directly from the office of the governor.

*The forty-six-year-old Myron Thompson, while being both an early and effective advocate of the Hawaiian cultural revival, was rapidly losing his position of ethnic leadership to younger grass-roots leaders such as Pae Galdeira, Darrow Aiona, Larry Kamakawiwoole, Randy Kalahiki, and Rose Victorino. The day would come when The Hawaiians, led by Pae Galdeira, would expressly oppose Thompson's directing the Hawaiian Homes program—such, for Thompson, was the price of working for the Establishment.

It included a modest tax break for renters, restrictions on resale of state-sponsored housing projects, a second mortgage fund, a fund for mortgage assistance, provisions for experimental waiver of building and zoning codes, and a variety of financial aids to housing developers.

A new Office of Environmental Quality Control was proposed to cope with environmental issues, as well as with proposals for pesticide control, auto emission controls, prevention of construction on the shoreline of the beach (an administration bill that had been before the legislature for two years), money for a master open-space plan, and a half million dollars in aid to the city of Honolulu for mass transit.

The oceanography package, drawn from a study panel which Burns had organized, proposed an office of marine affairs and a series of marine laboratories, research centers, and marine parks—in effect, a stimulus to diversification from the state's increasing dependence on tourism.

Burns, with Thompson as his chief lobbyist, would succeed in securing its passage despite much in-fighting during the session. Despite balky elements in a divided House of Representatives, Burns got everything he needed and more, the Burns-ILWU faction of the senate prevailing in negotiations between house and senate. Toward the session's end, the ILWU took the lead in lobbying a pay raise and a collective bargaining law for public workers, who flexed their muscles in the Islands' first strike of public workers—a probable taste of things to come. In the carnival something-for-everyone atmosphere of election-year legislating, the session dragged on a month past its normal sixty days; but if the process was messy, the product was impressive.

Some of the pro-Gill legislators, catching the drift, wanted to make a show of the weak spots in the Burns administration, but Gill advised against it, arguing that such a tactic would do little good and would only tie up the legislative process.

The lieutenant governor was quiet throughout the session, observing with seeming unconcern, apparently skeptical that Burns' eleventh-hour attention to issues which he had been talking about for years could make much difference in a campaign. Gill in fact was eager for much of the legislation to pass, thinking that he as governor could use it to accomplish his own ends—such was his mood of confidence in early 1970.

By this time, Gill's plans were altogether apparent to those who knew him well, but still there were many attempts made to forestall him from confronting John Burns. At one point, Robert Oshiro and the big Democratic bank-roller, Clarence Ching, conferred with Gill's backer, Arthur Rutledge.

Subsequently, at a somewhat boozey celebration marking the end of the 1970 Legislature, State Sen. John J. Hulten's son, John Hulten, Jr., made an informal pitch for the Burns forces to provide organization and money to Gill if Gill would run for the U.S. Senate. Hulten, encouraged by the response of party chairman David C. McClung and several other senators, then contacted Gill, saying that perhaps $500,000 could be raised for a U.S. Senate campaign.

Gill, for his part, responded by issuing a darkly worded press release alleging that the Burns faction was trying to buy him off— a much overblown contention, it appeared, given the fact that Hulten was not a major political operative, and also given the fact that Hulten's only apparent motivation was his hope of avoiding a Democratic party blood-bath.

This was the hyper-suspicious dimension of Gill, the Tom Gill who peered so critically at the motives of others. Through the years, Gill had made many enemies because of this quality. But in political terms of the moment, the Hulten incident suggested an element of panic current in the opposition.

Gill also was aware that Governor Burns, during this period, had told several people that Gill was in a formidable position. Burns had told one of Gill's runners, "Tom's got me backed against a wall."

Burns perhaps was particularly aware that polls showed Gill as a stronger Democratic gubernatorial nominee than himself—that is, polls taken in early spring of 1970 suggested that Gill more so than Burns could hold in line Hawaii's vast Democratic vote against whomever the Republicans would run.

But if the polls were not encouraging for Burns, the primary election was still five months away.

And Burns was deeply pleased and much heartened by the support of the 1970 Legislature for his program.

Long after the session adjourned Burns would contend that the support given him by the 1970 Legislature determined him un-equivocally to run for a third term. In his words: "After the legislative session I didn't have anywhere else to go. It was a *fait accompli.*

"The legislature had gone all out to make the legislature and the executive into one package. After that kind of effort, not running would be to deny the house and senate an integral part of their package." An integral part of the Burns campaign, the unprecedented media assault planned by Jack Seigle, immediately and predictably began drumming into the public such phrases as "the governor's hundred million dollar housing program," even though Burns had asked for only $32 million from the legislature. Harmony was the central theme of the Burns campaign, and such details were readily brushed aside.

10
Okage Sama De

In the late spring of 1970, the successful legislative session behind him, Governor Burns busied himself with a series of public bill-signing ceremonies, flanked by legislators, dramatizing the joint accomplishments of the administration and the legislature. Burns' lieutenant, Robert Oshiro, and Oshiro's acquisition, Jack Seigle, already had a year of work invested in campaign preparations, and television already was beaming the Burns message.

The ILWU was heavily committed, and pro-Burns elements of other unions were lining up support for Burns. A struggle for power was underway, predictably, for the conglomeration of trade and craft unions in the State Federation of Labor, AFL-CIO. An endorsement for Burns by the 15,000-member Hawaii Government Employees' Association was practically a foregone conclusion. But the smaller, better-organized, and more militant United Public Workers was divided, the dominant faction on Oahu inclining strongly toward Gill. The United Public Workers first had been sponsored by the ILWU, but in the mid-1960s a breach had occurred which seemed to be ever-widening. By 1970 the ties between the Hawaii Government Employees and the ILWU were stronger than was the old ILWU-UPW alliance.

All this was in motion.

Then, on May 18, 1970, yet another element was injected which would have a far-reaching effect on the course of events.

George Ariyoshi, a 1954 Democrat who now sat in the state senate, announced as a candidate for the office of lieutenant governor. In his initial announcement Ariyoshi said only that he wanted to be a team player with John Burns, revealing nothing of the emotional· charge that would soon be introduced into the campaign.

This opening move was as low-key as would be expected from a man of Ariyoshi's reputation.

Ariyoshi, during his sixteen years in the legislature, had almost never been controversial, had seldom asserted himself, and had been among the least influential of the legislators. In the running dispute during the 1960s between Senators Nadao Yoshinaga and Nelson Doi, Ariyoshi had not taken sides; and neither faction thought highly of him. There also had been a dispute in the late 1950s over an ILWU bill, and following that the union had tried to beat Ariyoshi at the polls but had failed. In 1963, the only year Ariyoshi had received much publicity, the senate had split—twelve votes to twelve votes—on the so-called Maryland land law bill.

This bill would have given a person who lived on leasehold land the right to buy the land, and thus was an assault on a system under which land ownership was concentrated in the hands of a privileged few.

The Maryland bill was a Democratic party measure, but Ariyoshi had equivocated, not committing himself to either side. And then it became apparent that his vote was the tie-breaking vote. Ariyoshi came down against the bill, killing the bill, and it was not until 1967 that a land reform bill passed the legislature, a much less radical bill. No one in politics would accuse Ariyoshi of radicalism, even though within the Democratic party a tinge of old-time radicalism was something which by 1970 enhanced a person's prestige. In fact there were such people as Koji Ariyoshi, a friend of many influential political figures, who thought that George Ariyoshi had gone far out of his way to be respectable. In 1952 Koji Ariyoshi had been prosecuted along with the ILWU's Jack Hall on Smith Act charges and had not forgotten George's early-day habit of telling political crowds, "I'm George Ariyoshi. I want you to know I'm no relation to Koji Ariyoshi." If this sometimes had been good for a laugh, Koji Ariyoshi himself had never been amused.

Because of such things George Ariyoshi had earned a reputation for being noncommittal, and it was not well known in early 1970 that he felt strongly about John Burns.

In private life Ariyoshi was doing well, so that a full-time political career would mean a financial sacrifice. He was on the board of directors of Honolulu Gas Company and was also a director of First Hawaiian Bank. These board positions were in addition to his law firm, which was located on the twelfth floor of the bank building, just down the hall from another bank director, Republican

Sen. D. Hebden Porteus, who was proud of his friendship with Ariyoshi: Porteus occasionally would mention that he had been instrumental in getting Ariyoshi onto the bank's board of directors.

Ariyoshi was forty-four years old, had an attractive wife and three well-scrubbed children. He was lean, as some cross-country runners are lean, tall, and also handsome. This was not so apparent on television, which exaggerated the craggy cut of his features, as it was in person. In his childhood Ariyoshi had suffered from a speech defect, but with special help from a sympathetic teacher he had overcome this. The result was he spoke in a clipped, rhythmic way somewhat reminiscent of the Kennedys.

Because of such assets Ariyoshi was an attractive candidate, but until 1970 he never had been promoted as a possibility for higher office, probably owing to his relatively anonymous role in the legislature.

Burns for his part maintained that he was staying clear of the lieutenant governor's race, saying that he had been duly chastened by his unsuccessful intervention in 1966 on behalf of Kenneth Brown. Nonetheless word spread throughout the Burns organization that George Ariyoshi was to be the organization's candidate for the state's second-highest office. Ariyoshi, even before his announcement, had made a public stand-in appearance for the governor. And the pro-Burns majority in the senate Democratic caucus, picking up the signal, had given Ariyoshi the job of managing Burns' legislative program in the 1970 session—this role, as it had turned out, had been more in name than in fact.

It was not until July 8, as the tempo of gubernatorial politics was rapidly picking up, that the highly emotional voltage of the Ariyoshi campaign was set loose.

From beneath the well-groomed and comfortable exterior of George Ariyoshi there was to emerge a passion which dated to a bleaker time for AJAs in Hawaii.

On the night of July 8, about a thousand people gathered at a hundred-dollar-a-plate dinner in Waikiki's Hilton Hawaiian Village, a crowd that was sprinkled heavily with Burns appointees and pro-Burns legislators. Burns himself mingled in the crowd during the cocktail hour, shaking hands and doing some personal campaigning, but Burns circumspectly departed before dinner was served, maintaining his posture of noninvolvement. Once people were seated, and once the usual lavish dinner of high-priced fundraisers had been consumed, party chairman David C. McClung—

who in 1968 had won the post as a nominal neutral in intraparty disputes—raised his glass in a toast and endorsed Ariyoshi's candidacy.

Next Burns' administrative director, Myron Thompson, begged the endorsement question by saying that while the governor could bless none of the candidates for lieutenant governor, for the Democratic party's sake Ariyoshi's competition—if there was to be any —should declare shortly. The part-Hawaiian Thompson also noted that Ariyoshi was thought of favorably by many Hawaiians for his Maryland land position—this, because Hawaiians regarded the Maryland land bill as a threat to the Bishop Estate and to other trusts intended to help the Hawaiian people. In this instance, Thompson was talking mainly to himself, there being few Hawaiians who could afford a $100 dinner—and fewer still who would spend it on a business-oriented politician such as Ariyoshi.

When George Ariyoshi took the podium, he opened by thanking his friends in Japanese: *"Okage sama de,"* meaning, I am what I am because of you. He also said that this was a new experience for him, that he wanted to speak from the heart, and he instructed the press corps that he would depart from his prepared text. For someone who was portraying himself as a novice at big-time campaigning, Ariyoshi was proceeding masterfully. Following his greeting of *"Okage sama de,"* Ariyoshi wove his way from the glitter of the moment back to the darkness of the old days.

"Having been born on the corner of Smith and Pauahi streets [a corner in the central city which in 1970 was dominated by tense black faces which spoke of truly intense discrimination], I am, literally, a product of the slums," Ariyoshi said. "In reality, I am your product, for it's been said that no man lives in a vacuum. And what little measure of success I have attained has been the result of the help and efforts of so many of you."

Ariyoshi's voice broke, and he was silent for several seconds, and then he composed himself and recalled that as a child in grade school he had decided to become a lawyer. He had confided this ambition to his father, who had come from Japan and was a sumo wrestler and the operator of a laundry. And his father had told him that to realize this dream of becoming an attorney, "I could have the shirt off his back."

Ariyoshi settled his eyes on his three children, the grandchildren of the sumo wrestler Ryozo Ariyoshi. The candidate for the second-highest office in Hawaii, addressing his children by name, told them they were lucky to live in America, particularly lucky to live in a state "where government places its emphasis on people and human dignity, where your education and your enjoyment of life is given such high priority, where there is equality of opportunity, and where you can dream, and dreams become real if we work for them.

"But Hawaii was not always like this, for we didn't always have equality of opportunities, and people were not always advanced in business on the basis of their abilities. Better job opportunities were not always available to all.

"If any man in Hawaii is to be given credit for this change, it is your present governor," Ariyoshi told his children, "our dear friend, John A. Burns."

The assembled crowd cheered spontaneously, wildly—Ariyoshi had succeeded in spanning the years of affluence, had succeeded in reminding them of the sweet taste of equality following the several decades of second-class citizenship. And in this context John Burns was not merely a two-term governor but a champion of entire races who had felt the weight of discrimination.

In the psychological flavor of George Ariyoshi's appeal, the past, the battles of 1941 and 1954, was anything but a long-ago past. It was real, immediate, only yesterday.

From that night forward, wherever Ariyoshi would go throughout the campaign, he would bring to life the past, telling and retelling the story of 1954, of how as a young graduate of law school he had found the path of opportunity closed, and of how John Burns, then a struggling and controversial ex-cop, had told him to get involved in politics and to help build a new order, one in which each man could rise according to his own ability.

Ariyoshi was running as the personification of a dream come true.

11

The First Image-Maker

During the spring of 1970, Tom Gill's commanding edge in the trial heat polls predictably began to give way. By July, three months before the primary election, several polls were showing Gill and John Burns running even: Gill's percentage being in the low forties, Burns' in the low forties, and the balance of 15 or so per cent undecided. Much of Gill's cocksure way had evaporated, as had the aura that the man was almost certain to be governor. Gill and some of his chief lieutenants, concerned that the campaign force still was gripped by the confident mood of winter and spring, began spreading the word that the campaign would be a close thing. But while Gill was worried, he was by no means pessimistic, and for good reason. He would say, "Maybe Jack has taken his best shot."

The fact was that although Burns had not yet declared himself a candidate, the Burns campaign already had taken several of its best shots and had merely drawn even.

Burns had resorted to six weeks of television ads, the "Think about It" series; had milked considerable publicity from the 1970 Legislature with the prolonged series of bill-signing ceremonies; and had run a heavily promoted housing fair for a month on each of the four major islands. This fair was a display of low-cost experimental housing, drawing an estimated 50,000 people with its implication that modest-priced housing for a family of average income lay in the not-too-distant future.

And by mid-summer it was altogether apparent that Burns would be a candidate for a third term, a factor which is generally thought to fatten a politicians's poll showing by several percentage points.

Gill, on the other hand, had been relatively quiet during the spring. And even though it was commonly believed in political circles that he would run, many ordinary voters were not aware of this. So in no way had Gill's campaign for the office of governor formally surfaced.

Further, while Gill faced formidably organized opposition, Gill was idolized by dissidents imbued with an infectious fervor, verve, and confidence in the rightness of their cause. Within the Gill camp there was a substantial cadre of experienced veterans, but many Gill people were heading into their first political campaign: students, educators, conservationists and ecologists, the newly active poor, Vietnam war doves, and newly arrived haoles who cared nothing for the old days.

The 1960s, inflated by the idealism of Kennedy and Johnson and then tortured by assassinations and a tragic war, had been a decade of expanding political participation—scrambling great hopes with anger and despair. If this was not so acutely felt in Hawaii as on the Mainland, it still was true that in Hawaii Tom Gill was both the main beneficiary and leading proponent of the new politics.

Gill himself seemed to be coolly angry by instinct, as if he lived too close to an awareness of society's ills to ever be wholly comfortable. In the sense that he was capable of this without giving way to despair, Gill engendered confidence and hope in many people. But Gill did not make people feel comfortable, nor was he otherwise adept at many of the things which endear one to people. Once as a legislator Gill had been congratulated by an admirer on a particular bill, and Gill in response had merely nodded. Observing this, one of Gill's colleagues had berated him by saying: "Tom, you don't know how to say please and you don't know how to say thank you." And if he was quick-witted, eloquent, and straightforward, many who were less articulate than Gill regarded him as having an unduly sharp tongue.

In fact this problem ran far deeper. From the outset of his career, Gill had shown a streak of self-destructiveness, a capacity for pointlessly alienating people. Gill had dismissed much of the postwar Democratic movement as a generation of Babbitts. And once, in a prepared speech, he had suggested that many of his fellow legislators had not understood the land use law when it was passed—while no doubt there was some truth in this, there was no point in saying it. There were those in his own camp who were not only appalled by such things in political terms, but also had felt personally the burn of acid from Gill's tongue.

One of Gill's most devoted campaign workers would complain,

"Tom tells us something about what is going on. And what he says I agree with, but in the process he makes me feel stupid—like he thinks nobody knows anything except Tom Gill."

If analyzed in terms of the effect on people's egos (an enormously complicated subject), it was perhaps generally true that Gill made many people uneasy, while John Burns had just the opposite effect, that is, Burns had an ego-building effect in his role as the lofty yet humble father figure, even as the Great Stone Face.* There was in all this no single nugget of compelling fact, but merely a repetitious echo, a pattern of sorts. There was Burns' ease of communication with people of humble origin. As pointed comedy, there was his Dan Aoki supposedly fuming, "If the Old Man is stupid, what does that make me?"

There was Burns' durable patience, his habit of absorbing criticism without response, his willingness to lose face rather than force another to lose face. Burns had his own image problem, owing to the impression he would make on occasion of being hard-bitten and cold. But this was a relatively small matter when weighed against the issue of Gill's personality. While Gill was aware that his style of dealing with people loomed significantly in the public mind, he seemed little inclined to reflect creatively on the question. In 1968, when he had led the Hawaii campaign against Richard Nixon, Gill often had contended that "old leopards don't change their spots," perhaps thinking also of himself.

Given all this, during the early spring of 1970 Tom Gill seemed more relaxed. He seemed more at peace with himself after a long inner struggle over the question of running for governor. His aides would contend that at last Tom Gill was mellowing.

Edward Joesting sensed this in Gill, and it was for this and many other reasons that Joesting approached the campaign season optimistically.

Joesting had met Tom Gill at a party in 1965, the two standing in a cluster of people, and the talk had turned to Gill's political image, particularly to Gill's reputation for being snappish and bellicose. Joesting could speak to this problem as a professional. He had spent thirteen years in public relations, and in 1965 he was director of public relations for First Hawaiian Bank, the same bank

*This bit of speculation revolves around the distant impression of the men—that is, a voter's impression. In dealings with their respective staffs, Gill of the two seemed the more courteous and appreciative. Burns on occasion would belittle staff members, displaying impatience or tossing off uncomplimentary nicknames, "Runt," "Fatso," and so forth.

which included George Ariyoshi and the Republican Hebden Porteus on its board of directors. The result of the conversation was that Joesting had volunteered to advise Gill on questions of image, and Gill had accepted.

The next year's campaign, 1966, had been easy enough. After studying surveys taken by volunteers from the University of Hawaii faculty, Joesting coaxed Gill into gearing down, cautioning specifically against making cutting attacks on the opposition. For newspaper ads that year, Joesting deleted most of the verbiage on issues, choosing instead to feature a smiling Tom Gill with a jacket slung over his shoulder. Those few words which Joesting did use stressed the themes of experience and compassion, attributes which according to Joesting's research the voters most admired in Gill. The idea merely was to reinforce Gill's best qualities, and for this the 1966 slogan was ideal: "Tom Gill Cares."

Gill, of course, had won handily, and as a result Joesting enjoyed a reputation as something of a wonder-worker, although he was quick to say he only was helping to facilitate "Tom's potential for greatness." Even though unpaid, Ed Joesting was probably the first of the modern political image-makers in Hawaii, tying research on image and issues together with advertising and tutoring of the candidate.

Following the 1966 campaign, Joesting had quit his job to pursue his boyhood dream of writing, and he was well into his fourth book on Hawaii. During this time Joesting also consulted frequently with his friend, the lieutenant governor of Hawaii.

In February 1970, while Gill was still far ahead in the polls, Joesting predictably was not so interested in trial heat polls as with research on image and issues. Aided by a university political scientist, Joesting again secured a basic research file, as had been done for Gill in 1966 and already had been done for Burns by Lennen and Newell Pacific in 1970.

Then, one night early in the spring of the campaign year, sitting on the lanai of his Woodlawn house overlooking Manoa Valley, Joesting fed the research to Gill. At the time Joesting sensed that Gill, although he had behaved according to script in 1966, was not altogether sold on the validity of image research. And later events would indicate that Gill did not really absorb some of the crucial lessons of this night's session in Woodlawn. For openers, Joesting was acutely aware, as he would put it, "that Tom is terrifically issue-oriented. So are a lot of people around him. The problem is that normally the people who are issue-oriented are with him anyway." The survey found that several issues dominated the public, none a surprise: traffic, the environment, housing, the high cost of living, and education, in descending order of importance. But two salient points emerged. One was that no single issue pervaded —that is, no single issue was cited by a majority of the voters as a vital concern. The second was that, as an issue, corruption in government scarcely registered; fewer than two of every hundred voters expressed themselves as worried over impropriety at the Capitol. (Given this, Gill still would make much of Burns' "alarming friends.")

The research also employed a semantic differential technique that by 1970 was standard for major candidacies. In essence, the technique tells a candidate how the voters look at him, and also how they look at an opponent. For example, on a calm/excitable scale of one to five, both Burns and Gill scored 3.5. The survey found that people saw the two men as equally strong personalities, Burns slightly more dependable, Gill a bit more "real." Interestingly, perhaps not unexpectedly, neither rated as highly lovable. The strangest finding resulted from a clever/dull question. On this, Gill scored as far more clever than Burns, 3.1 to 2.2, but there was a perplexing hitch: When people were asked how clever a governor should be, the result was no higher than Gill's score. Since Gill's was an average score, this meant that Tom Gill was regarded as more "clever" than half the voters wanted a chief executive to be.

On balance Joesting was pleased with the findings: As he interpreted them, Gill's image assets were roughly on a par with Burns', and Gill had the issues locked up.

As before, Joesting was opposed to Gill taking the attack in the campaign; on the contrary, he hoped that the Burns organization again would lash out at Gill, making Gill "the long-suffering underdog."

On the positive side, Joesting was bent on portraying Gill as a strong, young, and energetic public servant and, of course, a good family man. He thought that while he lacked Jack Seigle's budget, and also lacked Seigle's thirty-six-man staff, Seigle's consultants and Seigle's film-makers, the Gill campaign might hold its own in media advertising, and if so that the highly articulate Gill could carry the election.

12

Kids, Haoles, and Warriors

If Tom Gill did not have a monopoly on the young, as the Burns organization contended, it still was true that the young people who supported Gill were the most visible, vocal, and energetic in Hawaii. Accordingly the campaign of 1970 was to be in part a test of how much influence the new generation could exert on the older one—this, at a time when the entire country supposedly was experiencing a breach between the generations.

One of the most prominent of the Gill kids was Cindy Yokono, whose story told the story of many. Cindy Yokono in 1970 still wore braces on her teeth, and she remembered the great Democratic year of 1954 as a good year for rock and roll, for Elvis Presley. She had a strangely bigoted notion that there was something special about her generation—they were more into music.

When Cindy Yokono, the daughter of a mechanic from Kalihi's Gulick Avenue, started college, she was not initially into politics, but in 1968 she began taking an interest while sharing a room with two Mainland girls. Her roommates, Cindy thought, looked at things differently, were more radical, were more critical of the established order. By the spring of 1969 Cindy Yokono had herself begun to follow events critically, and the legislative fight over Magic Island particularly caught her eye. She began wondering what the score was with Governor Burns, and why he had backed the ILWU and the Dillingham Corporation to "push Waikiki into Ala Moana park," as she put it.

In 1969 she also figured out what some people had known for seventeen years: "Jesus, Tom Gill and Governor Burns don't seem to get along. And Tom is speaking up."

Cindy called Tom Gill's house and talked to Gill's wife Lois, who told her to see Arthur Park, the lieutenant governor's young administrative assistant. Park, of Korean ancestry, functioned as the down-the-line Gill loyalist much as Dan Aoki was the down-the-line loyalist in the Burns organization, but Park also was developing a sensitivity to social issues. In high school he had been a tough kid on the streets, but in the Air Force he had taken hold of himself, gone on to study political science at the University of Hawaii, and to campaign for Gill. In Gill's office, although resented by many older men in the Gill organization, he had administered elections and also run most of Gill's polls. Park therefore was no starry-eyed child, but nonetheless was impressed by the boundless energy and enthusiasm of people even younger than he.

On Gill's small office staff Cindy Yokono also could find such other young people as Lloyd Asato, who kept an eye on state public works and land deals, and stayed in close touch with the press corps; or Yen Lew, a researcher who was influential in the reform Democratic Action Group and in the American Civil Liberties Union; or Tim Leedom, who, with his athletic looks and trusting manner, might have glided smoothly into the world of corporate board rooms, but had not chosen that route. Leedom had been stunned by the death of John Kennedy, then by the death of Martin King. Subsequently in 1968 Tim Leedom had flown to California to help his presidential candidate, and he had been there when it was flashed on the news that Robert Kennedy also was dead. Tim Leedom was wondering what was happening. The Burns organization, through its political man at the university, Dr. Ralph Miwa, initially had channeled Tim Leedom into Governor Burns' office as a student intern, and Leedom there had listened to all the anti-Gill arguments and then had joined Gill. So too had many of the other student interns, and the pattern had become so familiar that among the politically hip young it was a joke.

Cindy Yokono was one who had not passed through Burns' office, nor collected the student subsidy, but had gone directly to Arthur Park in Gill's office, and Park had given her all of Gill's speeches to read—this was indoctrination, the thoughts of Tom Gill. Cindy was what Park was looking for. Park had already ruled out as political poison an alliance with the hard-core leftists in the university's faltering little chapter of Students for a Democratic Society, telling them: "If you want to help us, tell people you're for Governor Burns." As had Gene McCarthy in his 1968 presidential campaign, Park wanted the Gill kids to stay neat and clean—and generally they complied. Cindy would tell other students that Tom

Gill was worth it, Tom Gill could be trusted, Tom Gill was better than throwing rocks or carrying placards in the streets.

By July of 1969 Cindy Yokono had teamed up with a second university student, Barbara Tabrah, and together they organized their first Tom Gill coffee hour, which for Cindy was the first of more than a dozen such sessions. When she heard Gill talk informally, where he was at his best, she was sure he made more sense than any professor she had heard in school, meshing together one event in Hawaii with another. The format always was the same. Gill talked, then answered questions and listened to others, always in search of support and yet another campaign worker. Cindy Yokono particularly had been impressed when Gill had told her, "You can't grab people at a gut level. All you can do is tell them about issues, and let them decide," an attitude which no doubt exasperated people like Arthur Park and Edward Joesting.

Because Cindy Yokono had quickly made many friends as an organizer, she was elected by her peers along with Barbara Tabrah as chairman of Youth for Gill, and this organization ultimately pulled around five hundred student campaigners from the university and from the urban high schools. Alone among the political youth networks in 1970, Youth for Gill had a semblance of autonomy, deciding how and where it would do its work: dances, booths at fairs, recruiting tables, voter registration, Tom Gill jackets, endless legwork, and the production of brochures which were among Gill's best material. Cindy Yokono and Barbara Tabrah also sat in the inner sanctum of Gill's strategy committee, trusted—although volunteers—as only the salaried young staff of the Burns organization were trusted. In the process, Cindy Yokono, even though a third generation AJA, absorbed Gill's skeptical view of the Democratic revolt of 1954 from which all contemporary politics flowed. She thought: "Those cats around Burns really believe it was a revolution—it was an ethnic revolution, but the power structure hasn't changed that much. If you go back to the little guy on the totem pole, you see we still have the Big Five syndrome. The poor people and middle-class people are still being pushed out, like out of the housing market, for instance." And while she acknowledged that the early movement had favorably affected her life, had in fact provided her a good education, and while she personally fretted over the destruction of ethnic identity, she saw in Gill the promise of a more cosmopolitan era. She thought: "Tom looks at people and he says, 'Hell, what is it? Let's take care of human needs.' Race didn't matter."

In this irregular entourage around Tom Gill who called them-selves Democrats, who indeed thought the Democratic party was just as much theirs as it was Burns' or Aoki's, there were other symbolic people in addition to Cindy Yokono, people such as Allen Trubitt, who was one of the many new Mainland immigrants flocking in the late 1960s to the door of the lieutenant governor. Trubitt at the opening of the gubernatorial campaign year was thirty-eight, and he had amassed a wealth of experience in tilting at windmills. By 1970 he knew, as the nation knew, that when enough people join the assault, a windmill will topple. Trubitt four years prior had been marching in the streets protesting the in-humanity of the Vietnam war, and now America even under Rich-ard Nixon was slowly withdrawing. In the 1966 campaign, Trubitt had promoted peace candidates who had won only small fractions of the vote but nonetheless had made their point. Placing a heavy strain on his own work in the university's music department, Tru-bitt next organized a forum of forty or so people, mostly Mainland haoles like himself, into something called Volunteers for Indepen-dent Politics. Trubitt's forum group met monthly to review issues, to piece together a political platform, and to deal with their own wide-eyed naivete. Trubitt would say, "We were amazed. We dis-covered the simple fact that all you have to do is get your people to the right place on the right night for precinct elections." When in 1968 Eugene McCarthy set out to topple Lyndon Johnson from the presidency, the forum was transformed into Volunteers for McCarthy, and expanded: Trubitt built a card file, passed petitions, organized coffee and cocktail hours, distributed bumper stickers, and collected $12,000 in nickels and dimes for the national McCarthy movement. Trubitt also signed up enough novice pre-cinct politicians as party members to control a small bloc of votes in the 1968 state Democratic convention, taking a beating at the hands of the Burns-Humphrey forces along with Gill and the Kennedy people. When McCarthy in due time fell by the way, Trubitt nonetheless predicted that the movement was the wave of the future. The truth was that its strength, although expanding, was confined almost totally to the university area of Oahu's Manoa Valley, and to some of the wealthy residential suburbs toward Hawaii Kai and on the island's windward side. There was a considerable chasm between the McCarthy movement and the great mass of Democratic voters—this was intellectual and privileged class liberalism, but nonetheless highly spiced. At a funeral luau for the McCarthy campaign, labor boss Arthur Rutledge—no doubt with Hawaii's immediate future in mind—told a crowd of 300 people, "You have a mission for this state. It's to disestablish the Establishment. This group is imbued with that certain something that labor had before we got fat and affluent." Tom Gill, as the movement's favorite local son and most prominent dove on the war, also addressed the crowd, calling on Trubitt and the others to stay in the Democratic party and turn it around. The crowd roared its approval.

Subsequently Trubitt picked up the pieces and organized yet another reform movement, the Democratic Action Group, which as with its two predecessor organizations was preoccupied with national politics, as well as Island matters. While some Gill insiders resented the national emphasis, in the broader spectrum of 1970 the Democratic Action Group generally was regarded as yet another Tom Gill front organization. The fact was that most of its members were preparing to support Gill. To Mainland haoles, Gill was the interpreter of the mysteries of Island politics, the link forged by time to the non-Caucasian mass of Democratic voters. Trubitt himself would be liaison between the Gill campaign and DAG, and also would be one of Gill's principal coordinators on Oahu, thinking that for once the possibility of victory was real, was immediate, was only as far off as November 1970.

For many people in Hawaii the 1970 campaign would be an intensely personal venture, and for Arthur Rutledge this was doubly so. Naturally the well-being of Rutledge's union fiefdom would be affected—it always is good for a union to be strongly allied with the governor's office. But there was more to it than that, because Rutledge was devoted to Tom Gill as many men are devoted to their sons, and with the advent of old age such a relationship takes on an even more loaded meaning.

Further, Rutledge always had been at odds with the Burns-allied ILWU, and in the early 1950s even had played a bit role in a Red-baiting Hollywood production. The star was none other than John Wayne, playing an FBI agent chasing dangerous subversives around the Honolulu waterfront. Arthur Rutledge, looking then as he looked in 1970, like a bullfrog, was cast as the earthy and staunchly American (and therefore legitimate) leader of organized labor, collaborating with John Wayne to destroy the Communist cell. For those who knew anything about Hawaii, the plot was only too thinly disguised.

Art Rutledge went about his union work with equal flair, building his Unity House alliance of Teamsters and Hotel Workers to around 10,000 members, a distant but substantial second in size to the estimated 22,000-member ILWU, excepting the Hawaiian Government Employees, at around 15,000, which with the onset of public collective bargaining was only just beginning to function as a real labor union.

Over the years, Rutledge's Unity House unions and the ILWU were constantly engaged in jurisdictional battles, and on the side played tug-of-war for political influence among the smaller unions of the AFL-CIO. As Neighbor Island tourism began to mushroom in the late 1960s, Rutledge also was fighting the ILWU to organize the new hotels. And although he had sewed up Waikiki, he was losing the Neighbor Islands with only one exception, the Big Island's Kona Hilton. Rutledge nonetheless thought his day was coming, partly because of Tom Gill.

His ties with Gill dated back to 1952 when Arnold Wills of the National Labor Relations Board introduced the two, telling Rutledge, "If you're half as smart as you think you are, you'll hire him." Gill subsequently handled Unity House legal affairs for seven years, until 1959, when Rutledge helped Gill win his first election to the Hawaii House of Representatives.

In 1962, Rutledge also played a part in working out the Democratic-labor unity slate before Gill's successful campaign for the U.S. House. So, like Gill, Rutledge had been a long-time political force, but peripheral to the center of power—the State Capitol. No doubt also goading Rutledge in 1970 was the memory of a secret meeting of labor bosses which was held to distribute the spoils of victory derived from the 1962 campaign. According to Rutledge, the ILWU's Jack Hall presented himself at the meeting as an emissary of the then Governor-elect John Burns, who wanted to know if they could not agree on a slate of appointees to the key state boards and commissions of interest to the labor movement. Jack Hall then asked for names. Taken aback, one of the influential marine union leaders said he had none. In turn a strategically placed leader in the construction trades said he had not thought the matter over. And Rutledge was in the same bind, thinking,

"Dammit, I don't know what half of those commissions do." Jack Hall, obviously having made a careful study of the power structure of state agencies, then produced an extensive list of names, read them, and asked if there were any objections. Accordingly Hall left the meeting well pleased, and with his operatives soon to be well placed in the government.

For the next two years, from 1962 to 1964, Rutledge's principal consolation was young Tom Gill in the U.S. House, and Rutledge was most unhappy when in the 1964 campaign the ILWU backed the incumbent Republican Hiram Fong for the U.S. Senate rather than Tom Gill. The fact was that Gill and many of his followers such as Rutledge had believed that the ILWU looked with favor on Gill as a national legislator. On this score two stories were told repeatedly. The first was that Harry Bridges, the controversial ILWU international president, had walked into a U.S. House Labor Committee hearing, listened to Representative Gill examine witnesses in a very pro-labor vein, and said, "That is a good young man." Another story had it that State Sen. Nadao Yoshinaga, the darling of the ILWU, had been in Washington only months before the 1964 campaign and had pronounced Gill to be the bright star of Hawaii's congressional delegation. Nonetheless Yoshinaga had run against Gill in the Democratic primary and, although Yoshinaga was trounced, this was interpreted by the Gill people as a tactic for weakening Gill in the general election race against Fong, which Gill had lost.

For these and many other reasons Rutledge thought that the ILWU could not be trusted, which was precisely what the ILWU thought of Rutledge.

Gill himself, believing that his politics lay to the left of John Burns, certainly to the left of Hiram Fong, once had professed not to know why the supposedly radical ILWU did not like him, "Unless it's because I want them to knock before they walk in the door, just like anybody else."*

---

*As noted in chapter 8, by 1954 the ILWU had written Gill off as a phony liberal. Regarding phoniness and other things—the bipartisan consensus, the Gill-Burns clash, and the ILWU's having embraced the hawkish Hiram L. Fong while passionately opposing the Vietnam war—a startling paragraph from *Hawaii Pono* on the ILWU's Jack Hall is worth quoting extensively. "From Hall's point of view there were four kinds of legislators. The best were the half-dozen from Maui and Kauai who did not dare buck the union on any issue. Next were the political spokesmen for big capital . . . symbols of the old regime, of a capitalism that could not be modified or ameliorated, but only destroyed, in the long run, and it was important from Hall's viewpoint to keep those symbols alive. The Burns faction and some of the young Democrats comprised the third group. Their own militant rejection of the past made them sympathetic to

Following the 1966 victory, Rutledge could only fret through Gill's four-year term in the constitutionally powerless office of lieutenant governor in anticipation of 1970, when all the chips would be down. Rutledge, for instance, had told the McCarthy crowd their job was to "disestablish the Establishment." And in a subsequent verbal assault he contended that the economic power structure of Hawaii had not really changed since the old plantation days. The corporate business empires still got what they wanted from the Capitol, Rutledge argued, while many an ordinary worker simply had traded the stoop labor of sugar and pineapple for low-paying mop-and-maid jobs in the sprawling tourism industry.

So no doubt Rutledge was disillusioned with the status quo, but also as the 1970 campaign approached Rutledge gave the impression that this was his last big political ride. Rutledge was past sixty, was increasingly overweight, his eyes were going bad, and there were signs that he was preparing for his retirement. Jack Hall, his long-time adversary, already had largely withdrawn from Island politics in accord with the terms of his new position in San Francisco as international vice president. And Hall would be dead within the year—a giant fallen. Time also was claiming others among the labor pioneers, and time was pressing Rutledge too.

Known only to a few—interestingly, to John Burns, for one— was Rutledge's frustration in the role of Big Daddy even as he played it with such abandon. Rutledge would muse, after eighteen years with Gill, "Sometimes Tom can't even talk to me, and people think we're so goddamned close. He's a loner, a funny guy. He's cold and he's not cold. He'll listen so far, but he gets irked. He doesn't have much patience with anyone who hasn't done his homework. He's honest, but a little too goddamned suspicious. He can't accept a little hanky-panky, but this is the system. Sometimes

ILWU goals. More important to Hall, Burns and his group were tough. Their deals were based on self-interest, and in that sense, Burns could be trusted. The only group of politicians despised at union headquarters were the so-called independents in each major party, who, because of a liberal, prolabor record, believed they were entitled to union support without being obliged to take 'advice' from the ILWU offices on Atkinson Drive. The Democratic independents, especially, came in for abuse. . . . In Jack Hall's opinion, there was no room for independence or party loyalty if it interfered with ILWU aims." Hall praised Fuchs' book as incisive. The attitude toward politicians which Fuchs described survived Hall's death, although by 1970 the rating system had changed slightly. Second only to the union's legislative runners, Burns of course had become the union's ideal of an officeholder. In the capitalist category, it should be noted that the 1970 endorsement of reelecting Fong to the U.S. Senate embarrassed several ILWU people. They said nothing publicly—the union never washed its linen in public. Solidarity, etc. But, in private, several people who were part of the ILWU's heroic days described themselves as dismayed. At least one was heartbroken. Small wonder that by 1970, only hold-over cranks from the McCarthy era saw the ILWU as a threat to the political system.

I think I hear him saying, 'I am the way, I am the light; if you don't like it then goodby.' "

Yet it was perhaps for some of these same reasons that Arthur Rutledge so admired Gill, and would also say: "I can take nothing away from Tom—he decides on what he thinks is right."

If by 1970 only the politically naive and quixotic, only the Cindy Yokonos and the Allen Trubitts, had been disenchanted with the established order, then John Burns likely would not have been in serious trouble. But disenchantment also ran to the political center, to long-time party people who had helped make Burns what he was. And no one was such a painful reminder of this as Sakae Takahashi. While Burns in 1970 would hold in line the majority of the fifty-five incumbent Democratic legislators, as the performance of the 1970 Legislature already had suggested, Sakae Takahashi and others would bolt. And in Takahashi's case there was particular significance, because Takahashi was in many ways the archetypal Burns man.

Sakae Takahashi had been born on a Kauai plantation, had been educated to teach school, and then had fought in the 100th Battalion and 442nd Regimental Combat Team, from which Burns after World War II had drawn his closest comrades (under Dan Aoki's presidency of the 442nd Club, Burns had become an honorary member).*

Badly wounded in battle, Takahashi had been hospitalized in Atlantic City with Daniel Inouye, whose autobiography has recorded Takahashi as saying: "I want to know why all those nisei in California were locked up. And most of all I want to know why there has to be a limit to our hopes."

Inouye: "Who says there is?"

Takahashi: "Suppose you want to join the Pacific Club?"

Inouye: "Big deal."

*From a distance, the distinction between the 100th Battalion and the 442nd blurs. Indeed, the two eventually merged into a single fighting unit. But in many ways their experiences were not the same, either in war or peace. And even in 1970 this would be reflected in gubernatorial politics. The 100th never had been so close to Burns as the 442nd, and in 1970 such prominent members of the 100th as Takahashi and Howard Y. Miyake would back Gill. One 100th man suggested this reason: Their outfit only saw Burns as the police captain who participated in the December 7 Pearl Harbor roundup of AJAs. Then the 100th Battalion departed for army training. The 442nd had to wait longer for the right to bear arms, thereby having time to see Burns in his subsequent role as moral supporter of the AJA community. One 442nd argument, on the other hand, has it that 100th members were older, more conservative, and therefore less inclined to identify with the early postwar political militance in which Burns played such a large role. Who knows.

Takahashi: "Suppose you want to be territorial governor of Hawaii?"

Inouye: "We ought to have that right."

Takahashi: "We ought to have every single right that every single other American has. Man, we shed a lot of blood in this war. What was that all about?"

Takahashi, no longer content to be a teacher, had earned a law degree, and had been the first of the nisei veterans to rise in politics, winning a seat on the Board of Supervisors in 1950, then appointment in 1951 as treasurer of the territory. In 1954, he first won his legislative seat, and after that had been a fixture in the senate. He also had helped lay the economic foundation for AJAs as a founder, like Dan Inouye, of the Central Pacific Bank, and in 1970 he was chairman of the board. Bushy-browed, overweight, by now well-heeled, Takahashi looked the part of the political fat-cat, but was plagued by the disparity between the early fire and things as he found them in the late 1960s. He would say of Burns, "In the old days he did a good job, a wonderful job. We were very idealistic then. But somewhere around 1966 I had the feeling that Burns was mellowing, and that a lot of people around him were mellowing. I was getting the feeling that he had fallen under the influence of very powerful forces in the community, and I sensed that he had lost the idealism that he taught us was so important in politics." In 1967, after a period of equivocation, Sakae Takahashi had sided with the Democratic independents, led by Nelson Doi, in the battle against Nadao Yoshinaga. And from there the breach had widened, although many in Gill's inner circle would be slow to recognize it—for a time, Takahashi was among the loneliest of men in politics. During the 1969 legislative session, as chairman of the public employment committee, Takahashi drifted further from Burns when he reviewed the legislative auditor's allegations of mismanagement in the State Personnel Department. After hearing testimony from all sides, Sakae Takahashi issued a committee report which declared the auditor's findings to be valid and just. Takahashi also was aware that during this period the department was in chaos, because its director, Edna Taufaasau, had been put uncomfortably on ice in favor of her deputy, David K. Trask, an ex-senator. In Takahashi's eyes Mrs. Taufaasau was taking the gaff for policies in part devised by Burns, and so Takahashi was also questioning the interpretation which Burns placed on loyalty (Burns later would give Mrs. Taufaasau another high-paying post in the administration).

Perhaps the dying moments of the 1969 legislative session were the last straw for Takahashi. While Burns and ILWU lobbyist Eddie DeMello watched from the side of the gallery, Takahashi held the floor of the senate arguing against the Magic Island reef-land development in an attempt to run out the legislative clock— it was only seconds until the stroke of midnight. David C. McClung, presiding, pounded his gavel and ruled Takahashi out of order, then declared the development resolution as having validly passed on a hurried voice vote. Takahashi was further incensed when McClung suggested that Takahashi's real interest was in preserving a view of the ocean from a single nearby apartment. If not a low blow this was at most a feeble one, in light of Takahashi's considerable wealth, and also in light of the fact that McClung himself was defiantly proud of the fact that in Hawaii County he had lobbied on behalf of his client, Signal Oil developers. For his part, Takahashi was among those old-line Democrats, such as Duke T. Kawasaki in the senate and house majority leader Howard Y. Miyake, who would charge that Magic Island was a railroad job, and likewise would stump for Tom Gill in 1970. But before the campaign, yet another unusual moment in contemporary Island politics was to unfold at Takahashi's feet. During the 1970 legislative session, Takahashi maneuvered a modest ethics bill through the senate, no doubt aided by the pressures of the election year.

When the bill also was approved by the house, this ethics measure lay on the governor's desk for consideration, and it was widely assumed that John Burns would approve it. Apparently on that assumption, Burns' housing committee—which had played such a crucial role in gaining credibility for Burns on the housing issue— abruptly disbanded, sprinkled as it was with bankers, developers, and construction suppliers who seemingly feared they would be found in a conflict-of-interest situation under the new bill.

Then, on July 2, 1970, with the election only three months away, and just as he was pulling even with Tom Gill in the polls, Burns surprised everyone by vetoing the bill. In his veto message, Burns argued the bill was so vaguely worded that a public official might be prosecuted for an undefined crime: that is, for securing "undue advantage" for a client. From a civil liberties standpoint, in a state where the civil liberties of many people had been violated in the recent past, this was a heavy argument. Takahashi, however, countered by disclosing that he had borrowed the "undue advantage" phrasing from a bill previously cleared by Burns' own attorney general, whose duty is to advise the governor on constitutional questions. Takahashi also contended that he had purposely used the Administration-sanctioned language to enhance the bill's chances, and he wryly suggested that in any event Burns might have left the question of constitutionality to those better qualified, to the justices of the supreme court.

By this time it was no real surprise that only days later Sakae Takahashi would figure prominently in the campaign kick-off dinner of Tom Gill, who in his 1966 inaugural speech had admonished, "We must be concerned that government is above reproach. We must be better than Caesar's wife."

13

Alarming Friends

On July 9, 1970, seven days after the governor's veto of the ethics bill, and only a day after George Ariyoshi's testimonial dinner, Tom Gill gathered his own faithful, nearly 3,000 people, packing the Honolulu International Center. Because the event had been so long awaited, it was not a surprise but rather a catharsis for the Gill people. Over a paper-plate dinner, Gill's old ally from the 1959 house organizational fight, O. Vincent Esposito, played emcee; then, in quick succession, came the warm-up speakers: Cindy Yokono, Duke Kawasaki, Sakae Takahashi (predictably, and pointedly, mourning the dead ethics bill), and then the manager of the posh Kahala Hilton Hotel, Bob Burns, a recent Gill convert who was prominently displayed to allay fears that Gill—because of his long-standing proposal for a tourism tax—was antitourist. Finally the lights dimmed. The legendary keeper of Hawaiiana, Iolani Luahine, appeared on stage, and the audience hushed as she chanted and danced a traditional hula. The effect was nearly religious and, once finished, she called Tom Gill forward and draped over his shoulders a maile lei, like a primitive blessing—adding the artist's touch to Gill's politics of purity. Gill took the podium beneath his equally pure slogan, "You Can Trust Tom Gill," which to many bore a double entendre reflecting on Burns.

And Gill, always quotable, was on July 9 especially quotable. Like Ariyoshi's speech the night before, this was one of the few memorable exercises in oratory during the campaign.

Gill started: The 1960s had begun with great promise, with the idealism of the civil rights movement and the national crusade against poverty. "Then it slowly turned sour under the crushing weight of Vietnam. Social programs died for lack of funds. The President (Johnson) lost credibility. The campuses fell into disorder, and the ghettos convulsed with despair."

The 1960s in Hawaii had echoed the Mainland, "but in a distinctly local way.

"The long period of plantation colonialism was over.

"Our legislature, filled with bright and feisty young men, had turned out a mountain of new and innovative legislation. Finally in 1962 our party also gained the executive power, and the ability to make things happen.

"Growth burst out all over. Development was progress and progress was good.

"Some of our people became rich beyond their every expectation; most of us gained more income and more things than we ever had before. Most agreed—and still would today—that having been both poor and rich that 'rich is better.'

"But things began to happen to us," Gill said. And here Gill painted strokes of blackness.

"Some of our poor and struggling public servants became less poor and struggled less. Some of the crusaders for change decided that change wasn't so important after all. The result was a slow and insidious loss of momentum. We became more interested in the form of social innovation, not the substance.

"There was talk of planning and proper land use, but action on variances and zoning giveaways. There was refusal to recognize the growing crises of housing and pollution until this election was almost upon us.

"Those who sold tourism spoke of the 'golden people of Hawaii,' but turned Waikiki into an overbuilt human bog.

"Belatedly, as the smog begins to blind our view of the mountains, some verbalize the need for pollution control, but then fail to fill necessary positions in the control agencies and hardly move to enforce existing laws and regulations. . . .

"There is a flutter of concern as the election approaches, a great deal of expensive public relations, but no real answers.

"In Hawaii the sixties came in with a shout and crept out with an ominous shudder.

"It seems clear: The seventies are a watershed."

Gill injected a superficially kind, but essentially cutting word for the man of the sixties: "I think Jack Burns is a very decent human being and personally an honest man.

"He has a deep sense of duty and loyalty to his friends. But here lies the rub: Jack has some most alarming friends." At this point Gill's crowd applauded wildly.

"Too many of them are doing too well to risk the uncertain winds of change. [More applause.] Even if the governor had no personal desire to serve a third term, I doubt very much if his associates would allow him to retire."

Gill then described his isolation from Burns' administration, then pointedly took note of the high-priced image-making at work for Burns.

Scouting for the Burns camp, Jack Seigle, Luann Burman, Chuck Heinrich, and Rick Egged sat on the fringe of the crowd, sizing up the style of their opponent.

"Dear friends," Gill said, "an effort of this sort is not financed by selling sweet bread. Nor is it likely that this kind of money can be collected without obligation.

"What is it the hangers-on fear?

"Can it be that I have alarmed them by saying that government should be run without influence or favor; that all citizens of this state are entitled to fair and equal treatment; that the government should belong equally to all of our people, both the humble and the mighty; that these fair islands are ours to treat with reverence and pass on to our children, and they are not to be destroyed by greedy and thoughtless men?"

Gill skimmed over his platform again: A mass housing program; reinforcing free price competition on food, gasoline, and housing; rethinking the education system; broadening the economic base; mass transit.

"Through all of this we must find ways to weave the thread of our humanity, and our respect and tolerance for one another. Through all of this we must keep a reverence for our land, for our multitude of cultures, for the history of this place and this people."

Distinctly in the Kennedy style, Gill plunged to a dramatic closing.

"If, my friends, we must pledge these things, then I must also make a pledge to you.

"I will struggle with all the fiber of my being, against whatever odds fortune seeks to impose, to make these things come to pass.

"The time has now come, at this time and this place, to commit ourselves to the stormy task ahead."

Gill stepped down into the press of an electrified throng, their new day as close as the grasp of Tom Gill's hand.

The election was a mere three months away.

14

One Republican

Once it had come close, but Hawaii's Republican party had never truly recovered from the disaster of the 1954 Democratic sweep.

Periodically there would be a surge of new blood, new organizing drives, the drawing of more progressive platforms designed to break the grip of the Democratic party on Hawaii's electorate.

But success at the polls—or the prospect of success at the polls—seemed to hinge largely on factional disputes among top Democrats.

When the Democrats swept the 1954 legislative elections, the Republicans were left with only two positions of significant power. One was the territorial delegateship to Congress, held by Elizabeth Farrington, who had defeated Burns. The second was the mayor's office of the city and county of Honolulu, held by Neal S. Blaisdell, who had defeated Frank F. Fasi.

In both instances, Burns and Fasi lost those 1954 elections by razor-thin margins which could be attributed to the refusal of one to help the other.

When Burns subsequently won the delegateship in 1956, the Republicans then were left with only Blaisdell—who hung on until his 1968 retirement by virtue of his personal flair, a cooperative attitude toward the Democratic council, and by minimizing his Republican identity.

The closest the Republicans had come to actually recovering their past power was in the 1959 statehood election, a time of intense Democratic factionalism displayed publicly in the organization battle that took place in the state house. Appointed Republican incumbent William F. Quinn won the first governor's race in the 1959 statehood election. Republican candidates also won a slim margin in the state senate, and Hiram L. Fong won a U.S.

Senate seat (one of Hawaii's three congressional slots open at the time).

But the 1962 Democratic unity ticket headed by Burns had unseated Bill Quinn. Democrats also recaptured control of the senate. And Gill won Hawaii's newly apportioned U.S. House seat —making the lineup in Washington three Democrats and Republican Fong.

The Brown-Gill primary fight of 1966 again had revived Republican hopes, but in the general election Randolph Crossley fell 5,000 votes short of defeating Burns.

Heading into the 1968 elections, the Republicans set their sights on recapturing the faction-ridden state senate.

But when Mayor Blaisdell shocked the party with a surprise announcement of his retirement, Republicans shifted most of their resources to retaining Blaisdell's office. Young D. G. Anderson, the favorite of the senate minority, was chosen to wage the Honolulu mayoral battle, the party again counting on a hotly contested Democratic primary between the lone-wolf Frank Fasi and council chairman Herman Lemke, who was supported by the Burns faction. The third Democrat out was Kekoa Kaapu, a young and relatively inexperienced Burns protege whose ambitions far outweighed any realistic chance of victory. Fasi, of course, swamped both of his Democratic opponents, then D. G. Anderson.

Still the Republicans looked ahead to the 1970 gubernatorial race with a special sense of anticipation, despite their fourteen-year history of frustration. This was so because a battle between Jack Burns and Tom Gill promised the most clear-cut and bitter public display of Democratic in-fighting since the Democrats first had risen to power. By comparison, past warfare among Democrats seemed fuzzy and ill defined.

This time around, 1970, the Democrats seemed so thoroughly polarized, so deeply divided, that the losing faction would surely either sit out the general election or bolt to the Republican candidate, that is, if the Republicans could just find the right man.

The problem naturally was the same as 1966, and the same as 1968. The Republicans had no candidate, that is, they had no one possessing anything close to the stature and mass following of either Burns or Gill. Either Democratic faction, taken alone, was more vigorous than the Republican party, and this suggested to many observers that in Hawaii the two-party system had all but collapsed. The only possible strongman was Hiram Fong, but Fong was firmly committed to running for reelection to the U.S. Senate. For him, that race was made even more attractive because a Republican was in the White House, and because the national Republican party hoped—to no avail, as things turned out—to parlay social unrest into majority control of the U.S. Senate. So if the Hawaii gubernatorial situation was pregnant with possibilities, the Republican situation still came down to this: the party in 1969 had no candidate for governor. No sooner had the 1969 Legislature convened than a handful of Republican state senators set out to solve the problem. The intricate play that followed revolved around Senators D. G. Anderson, Fred Rohlfing, and, to a lesser extent, the Island caretaker of Fong's business and political empires, State Sen. Wadsworth Yee. Outwardly all three traveled the same road. They were relatively young, progressive, and bent on shaking the plantation hangover—the ghostly image of the Big Five and the haole oligarchy which had haunted the party through all the years of Democratic domination.

Following the disastrous 1962 elections, these three constituted the liveliest new-look leadership available to the Republican party.

In 1963, Rohlfing took over as floor leader of the tiny Republican minority in the house. In 1965, he and Anderson jointly ousted their seniors—Rohlfing emerging as house minority leader and Anderson as floor leader. In the 1966 elections, both Anderson and Rohlfing made the jump to the senate, as did Yee.

Then, slowly, their paths diverged. So gradually as to be publicly imperceptible, Anderson and Rohlfing drifted off on separate courses within the lofty senate club. Anderson won the job of floor leader, while veteran Republican Sen. Hebden Porteus, wrapped in the cloak of senior statesman, retained the top post of minority leader. Rohlfing took a back seat as minority whip (later retitled minority policy leader). Of the two, Anderson was the more charismatic and engaging, Rohlfing the more biting and analytical.

Anderson, taking counsel from the veteran Porteus, became the senate's Republican wheelhorse—making a mark on state fiscal and education policy, while delicately balancing Republican partisanship against shrewd dealings with Democrats.

During the 1967 and 1968 sessions Anderson proved himself particularly adept in dealing simultaneously with the Democratic factions of Nelson Doi and Nadao Yoshinaga. For example, collaborating with Nelson Doi, D. G. Anderson in 1968 devised Hawaii's progressive early childhood education program, wherein three teachers were pooled into a double-sized class. The idea was to greatly increase the attention paid to a given child, so that a child might work more nearly at his given individual pace. During the same session, in a complex maneuver, Anderson collaborated with Yoshinaga's faction on a bill to reduce Hawaii's regressive and pyramiding 4 per cent excise tax. While this tax was a great money-maker for the state government, it was undemocratic in its application. Proportionately it took the most from those who could least afford it, and the pyramiding affect also discouraged small businesses while hurting the large corporations relatively little.

As a social statement, the 4 per cent excise tax scarcely lived up to Democratic party rhetoric. But because it was the state's largest source of revenue, much of it being poured into education and social welfare, it had become sacrosanct as an article of Democratic party faith. When the Anderson bill came to the floor, Nelson Doi had played the fall guy, defending the 4 per cent tax on many technical grounds, but Yoshinaga's votes had combined with Anderson's to pass the bill out of the senate and into the state house. There it finally died, but not before bending out of shape many house members—all facing reelection.

Thus Anderson and the Republicans in effect had often determined the balance of power in the senate during the period of intense factional in-fighting between Doi and Yoshinaga.*

Rohlfing, by contrast, was not so influential as Anderson within the senate, inclining more toward rigid partisanship, toward playing devil's advocate and molder of public opinion. Not unlike Tom Gill, Rohlfing stressed such broad issues as housing, planned urban development, transit, and land use.

Rohlfing in a 1968 speech made a splash by condemning the Burns-style consensus as "government by hui," meaning a new closed system ruled by an elite clique. And Rohlfing also became increasingly skeptical of the senate as a bipartisan club—for good or ill, it was that in many ways. Fred Rohlfing, in effect, thought the comforts of the senate's clubbish life-style paled in comparison

---

*Anderson's stock among Yoshinaga Democrats would dip sharply in the 1970 session. The reason was this: Anderson initially supported a bill devised by Yoshinaga's faction to cut Mayor Frank F. Fasi's four-year term short by two years. Then, once the bill was in motion, Anderson reversed himself. Such were the passions which Frank Fasi aroused.

to the chance for the Republican party to become a vigorous opposition party—perhaps to one day become the majority party. To play that role of vigorous opposition was no easy thing.

For one thing, the Republicans were a small minority throughout the 1960s, and therefore were not inclined to be pushy—the beloved William H. "Doc" Hill had counseled, as senior statesman, that when a party has no substantial number of votes its legislators should behave accordingly.

Perhaps more basic to the situation, the Republican party lacked a cogent identity, a sense of self, perhaps lacked a soul.

One part of the party had its heart buried in the past, a second had its head buried under a wing of the Democratic party—often the Burns wing, although there were those such as Rohlfing who grudgingly admired Tom Gill, feeling that Gill was fulfilling the responsibility of a loyal opposition which the Republicans had largely abdicated. Wadsworth Yee, under these circumstances, kept his lines open in all directions, maintaining where he could Fong's Republican base and also Fong's alliance with the ILWU.

Such were the subtleties of the Republican caucus in early 1969 as the search for a gubernatorial candidate got underway. Various accounts indicate that several names bounced around informally among senate Republicans. Fong of course was to stay in Washington. Bill Quinn had quit politics for good, and was presiding over Dole Pineapple Company. Randolph Crossley, although he had run surprisingly well in 1966, had systematically alienated people thereafter, first by pressing a recount of votes to the point of seeming to be a sore loser, then by blaming his defeat on the sluggishness of party workers.

Neal Blaisdell was sixty-seven years old, and had ended his career on a sour note. He had abruptly retired from the mayor's office in 1968 only to shortly thereafter run a futile race for the U.S. House. Outwardly Blaisdell's shuffle was inexplicable, but there was more to it than met the eye. For many years Blaisdell and John Burns had drawn votes from an overlapping constituency, and the two men also had shared close in-supporters. For example, attorney Matsuo Takabuki, one of Burns' long-time intimates and also a city councilman from 1952 through 1968, had been an influential advisor of Mayor Blaisdell. And conversely, such people as Blaisdell's top political man, Angel Maehara, also had ardently supported John Burns, the partisan distinction between Burns and Blaisdell mattering for nothing. Nonetheless Blaisdell in 1966 was under heavy pressure from the Republican party to challenge Burns for the governorship, and because of Blaisdell's enormous popularity he no doubt was a potentially formidable opponent. Blaisdell considered a 1966 gubernatorial race down to the last possible moment, considered it clear down to the Republican party's spring convention, thereby precipitating a flurry of anguished caucuses among people who supported both himself and Governor Burns. At the Republican's 1966 convention, Blaisdell had dramatically withdrawn himself from contention for that year's governor's race, so that the Republicans in desperation had called the testy Randolph Crossley in from his country home to save the day—which subsequently Crossley very nearly did. Later it was learned, beyond any reasonable shadow of a doubt, that somewhere along the line Blaisdell had been led to believe that if he did the pleasant thing—that is, if he contented himself with the office of mayor—he could look forward to becoming a trustee of the Bishop Estate. Burns for his part would flatly deny being party to any such *quid pro quo,* noting that it is the state supreme court and not the governor who names trustees to the Estate. As it happened, an opening occurred in the Bishop Estate in 1968, two years after Blaisdell had declined the gubernatorial nomination, and also it so happened that Blaisdell abruptly announced he would not seek reelection as mayor, for personal and family reasons. Then the black-robed justices of the Hawaii Supreme Court, after giving the matter much thought, chose not Blaisdell but a long-time Democrat and financier, Hung Wo Ching.* Only then did Blaisdell launch his improbable candidacy for the U.S. House, conducting an uncharacteristically intemperate campaign against Hawaii's two popular incumbents, Spark M. Matsunaga and Patsy Takemoto Mink, and losing badly.

So it was that Blaisdell as 1970 approached was not quite the gubernatorial timber that he had been in 1966.

As for the other two possible standard-bearers of Republicanism in 1970, Family Court Judge Sam P. King seemed to many people to be an interesting possibility. But in this early 1969 period Sam

---

*Three years later, in 1971, Matsuo Takabuki himself would be appointed a Bishop Estate trustee, despite the opposition of an ad hoc committee which for a moment united almost the entire Hawaiian and part-Hawaiian community. Hung Wo Ching's 1968 appointment had gone virtually unchallenged by the Hawaiian people, but three years later would be a different story. Three years later many of the Hawaiian people would be on the move, would be more assertive, would serve notice that they like others wanted their share of things. The most vigorous leadership would be asserted by the young Hawaiians.

King was hoping by the grace of Richard Nixon via Hiram Fong to become a judge of the U.S. circuit court of appeals.

Hebden Porteus wasn't saying yes and wasn't saying no. Porteus was watching and listening attentively.

Among the senators, Anderson was pressing the hardest for an early decision, chafing to get a candidate into the field. Anderson's sense of urgency stemmed from his own defeat in the 1968 mayoral campaign, which he blamed on a late start and all that entailed: a dearth of planning, organization, and top managerial talent.

Anderson decided that Porteus had to be persuaded to run. And once having settled on a candidate, he threw himself into whipping up enough support to induce Porteus into the race. First Anderson quickly raised several thousand dollars and called the Los Angeles managerial firm of Spencer-Roberts.

Anderson also surveyed the senate Republicans and found that Maui's popular Sen. Toshi Ansai, a long-time friend of Porteus, was enthusiastic. The Big Island's venerable eccentric, Sen. William H. "Doc" Hill, also was agreeable.

Yee for his part stayed in constant touch with Fong, reporting on the search for a candidate, telling Fong that Porteus appeared to be the sole possibility, and that Porteus probably could secure the nomination uncontested. Fong subsequently talked with Porteus, urged him to get an early start, and assured him of his support. Thereafter Yee jumped in with Anderson to promote Porteus. While this was an impressive start for Porteus it was scarcely a bandwagon, because scores of Republican party people insisted on keeping their options open. And of course the most prominent skeptic was Anderson's long-time ally, Fred Rohlfing.

In the first place, Rohlfing didn't think Porteus had a prayer of winning, being convinced that the voters were in a mood for a substantial change, and that Porteus represented no real departure from the Burns years. In Rohlfing's eyes, Porteus had merely drifted along with consensus government, played senate politics close to the chest, and failed to provide the party with an aggressive alternative to the status quo. Without saying it in so many words, Rohlfing also considered Porteus a patsy for the Burns forces—"too close to Jack and his boys."

In fact this was no mere suspicion on Rohlfing's part, because Porteus long had enjoyed a close relationship with Burns. Porteus had confided to a fellow Republican that Burns was lending him some encouragement to run—this, on the apparent belief that Porteus was preferable to Tom Gill. Burns for his part did nothing to dispel the impression of kinship with Porteus. On the contrary, Burns spoke warmly of Porteus in private, and to a newsman he confided that of the potential candidates, Gill and Sam King were the least acceptable. Leaving Porteus. Further, an ILWU man, who worked hand-in-glove with Burns on large political questions, supposedly approached Porteus and quietly encouraged Porteus to run—or so Porteus told a *Star-Bulletin* reporter.*

Thus the strongly partisan Rohlfing felt that only as a last resort could he help Porteus. And therefore Anderson was left to proceed without him.

Anderson first organized a Friends of Porteus committee, while he talked continually with the prospective Republican nominee, confident that at last Porteus was in a frame of mind to run. Anderson's candidate for governor was fifty-eight years old, and if ever he was to make a bid for high office, the time was upon him.

Porteus had made the transition from a by-gone era, and he prided himself on some of the very qualities which appalled Rohlfing: Porteus viewed himself as a force for moderation, for progressive economic and social legislation when the time was ripe, and also for reconciliation of past and present.

Porteus first had been elected in 1940, and he now was serving out an unbroken string of thirty years in the legislature. The colorful Senator Hill was to die before the election, making Porteus the dean of the legislature and the last of the pre-World War II politicians.

His father, a distinguished psychologist, had emigrated from Australia when Porteus was a boy, had sent his son Hebden to Punahou, to the University of Hawaii and to Harvard Law School, where Porteus graduated as a Phi Beta Kappa. Hebden Porteus had married well (a daughter of the Dole family, as in Dole pineapple), joined the Republican party and the Pacific Club, and

*The official ILWU attitude, reported in chapter 8, was that whoever won the Democratic nomination—that is, either Burns or Gill—would ultimately win the governorship. In fact the ILWU by this time was finding it increasingly difficult to drag its members across party lines. In 1968, the ILWU endorsed Democrat Herman Lemke in the Honolulu mayoral race, then when Lemke lost to Frank Fasi, the ILWU endorsed Republican D. G. Anderson. Fasi nonetheless ran well against the ILWU-backed Republican in some ILWU precincts. Accordingly, a contention of Wadsworth Yee's seems credible—that the ILWU operative told Porteus the union likely would not endorse him if Burns lost to Gill, but that the ILWU probably would do what it could behind the scenes. While details are shrouded in silence, the pattern of a strong Burns-Porteus-ILWU relation is unmistakable.

managed the legal department of the Big Five's Alexander and Baldwin from 1942 to 1960. In addition to being a director of First Hawaiian Bank, where he enjoyed such a comfortable relationship with George Ariyoshi, Porteus also was a trustee of the Damon Estate. This was one of Hawaii's major estates, and in this capacity as trustee Porteus had done business with such people as Clarence Ching, Burns' leading fund-raiser. In one notable instance, Porteus had been a party to the Damon Estate's selling to Clarence Ching's interests the Salt Lake area which, through the Burns-appointed State Land Board, Ching arranged to fill and convert to a golf course. This was in the days before Porteus made much of himself as a conservationist.

Porteus was one of the few Republicans who had ridden out the storm of 1954, and he fondly recalled teaching the ropes of legislative procedure to the spirited but inexperienced young Democrats. Porteus also had the unique record of having served as both the majority leader and minority leader of his party in first the house and then the senate.

But never had he shown that gut-level yearning for great influence which is the mark of so many top political figures.

In the territorial house, although Porteus appeared to have had an edge, he had stepped aside to allow Hiram Fong the speakership; and he had yielded the senate's presidency to "Doc" Hill. In 1957, when Eisenhower's White House was looking for a new territorial governor, Porteus reputedly was on the list of possible appointees, but he wasn't interested, holing up on his ranch in West Hawaii until William Quinn was chosen. Following statehood, Porteus frequently had been urged to run for statewide office, but always had declined. After Randolph Crossley's near-miss in 1966, some Republicans speculated privately that the party would have won if Porteus had been the candidate rather than Crossley.

Finally, in the summer of 1968, Porteus broke this long-established pattern of shunning stage-center by waging a swift and unequivocating campaign for the presidency of the nonpartisan constitutional convention. He succeeded handily, organizing a coalition of Republicans and Burns-ILWU Democrats who were following signals called by Nadao Yoshinaga. During the convention, Porteus played his job low-key as good shepherd, advocating nothing more than the timely movement of committee reports and floor debate.

Generally the convention moved smoothly, and Porteus received good editorial reviews in the press. The political catch was that the state's constitution already was basically sound. The convention stirred a minimum of public interest and Porteus himself stirred even less.

Looking to 1970, Hebden Porteus could either regard the convention as the zenith of his public career or go for the office of governor.

During the first week in May 1969, beckoned by D. G. Anderson's telephone call, Bill Roberts of the political management firm of Spencer-Roberts arrived from Los Angeles for a look at the chances of electing Porteus governor. The Spencer-Roberts firm had a splashy reputation, based nationally on its 1966 role in electing Ronald Reagan governor of California. The eye-catching part of that was the fact that Reagan had been an actor, not a politician, and had won as a Republican in a marginally Democratic state.

The reputation of Spencer-Roberts was especially good for organizing balanced grass-roots campaign forces from scratch, something Porteus badly needed because he had no statewide organization. The owlish-looking Bill Roberts, after a week of scouting in Honolulu, was impressed by the climate of discontent with Burns and also the likelihood of a Burns-Gill primary fight. Even though not overwhelmed by Porteus, Bill Roberts thought that this silver-haired and well-spoken gentleman had possibilities. Roberts subsequently recommended a depth survey by Decision-Making Information, also of Los Angeles. And, one night in the early spring, he accompanied Porteus and D. G. Anderson to a meeting at the Pacific Club.

Like salmon which must return to their place of birth to spawn, Porteus and fifteen or so well-heeled and well-placed businessmen filed into the downtown club which had so symbolized the era of oligarchic Caucasian domination—which even in contemporary times evoked the memory of a planter-dominated economy. By the time of this 1969 meeting, the Pacific Club had recently opened its doors to non-Caucasians, but even now there was something self-conscious about the attempt to be a part of the New Hawaii. Its bar room walls were hung with dank-looking oil portraits of Pacific Club presidents dating back to the beginning of the century, and on entering the front portal, one saw a landscape by the now-dated Howard Hitchcock. But further on, there hung a painting by Tadashi Sato, a bright star among Hawaii's contemporary artists, best-known for his "Aquarius" mosaic, which fills the center court of the new State Capitol.

In fact this was one of Tadashi Sato's least-inspired works, so that a passerby might wonder whether the Club's buyer knew the difference between a good Sato and a mediocre Sato, or simply whether someone had thought a Sato—any Sato—would help things a bit.

But on this May night in 1969, thoughts ran not to art but to politics, and to the possibility of launching a candidacy for the next governor of Hawaii.

Millionaire contractor E. E. Black played the role of chairman.

Roberts presumably outlined a favorable picture for Porteus, then Porteus himself talked and fielded questions.

Eventually the meeting got down to its real agenda, which was bankrolling the campaign.

Apparently impressed, the businessmen pledged sizeable sums of money, and D. G. Anderson left the meeting confident that Porteus could open a campaign with over $100,000. In fact one account of the Pacific Club meeting put the figure at close to $200,000, but whatever the figure was, judging from Porteus' ensuing finance problems, many of the promises made that night must have been overblown.

By early June of 1969, Porteus was into the race up to his neck, while publicly maintaining he was still merely weighing the possibility.

He soon had a full-time staff and had received the Decision-Making Information survey, which impressed Spencer-Roberts staffers on several points. One was that Hawaii Republican voters tended to be highly issue-oriented, as contrasted to Democrats, who tended to be more influenced by personalities. Second, Porteus was widely seen as being aloof and indecisive, while rating favorably on knowledge and experience.

Number three: a third of the voters had never heard of Porteus, despite his twenty-eight years in public life. Accordingly the Roberts staff soon would go to work on Porteus—presenting him as decisive, and as holding firm opinions on many important issues, while simultaneously trying to milk the media for exposure of the Porteus name. This would not always come off, as when a press release depicted Porteus as being greatly concerned that a large fish just caught in the Pacific be preserved for posterity.

On September 4, 1969, George Young, from the Roberts agency, a veteran of the Ronald Reagan campaign and also of Nelson Rockefeller's 1964 presidential campaign in California, arrived in Hawaii as overall director for the duration. Then came Jack Orr, a press secretary, and next a precinct organizer and a Girl Friday. One of the first things George Young learned on his arrival, contrary to all prior intelligence and planning, was that Hebden Porteus likely would face an opponent in the Republican primary election.

15

Two Republicans

Fred Rohlfing had not been idle. By late May of 1969, while D. G. Anderson was attempting to put a lock on the Republican nomination for Hebden Porteus, Fred Rohlfing had set his mind on drafting Samuel P. King, even though King had been out of the political limelight since 1954. First, Rohlfing had commissioned a poll. It had convinced Rohlfing that while his own chances were nil, King could be a viable candidate, potentially a far better candidate than Hebden Porteus. In trial-heat runoffs against John Burns and against Tom Gill, the part-Hawaiian King looked as strong as Porteus, even though King had been isolated on the court bench. The poll found that in the simulated runoffs, both King and Porteus got three votes to every four for John Burns, while neither Republican was within striking distance of Tom Gill. On a leap of logic, Rohlfing therefore assumed that Tom Gill would almost certainly win the Democratic nomination; also, that for a Republican candidate to have a chance against Tom Gill he would have to be extremely dynamic.

Rohlfing further reasoned that King could descend from the bench in the role of giant-killer while Porteus' reputation had set like Jello because of Porteus' three decades in the public arena. Rohlfing and King had served together in the Naval Reserve, and through this acquaintance Rohlfing had come to regard King as decisive and outspoken, guided by instincts for innovation and reform.

Rohlfing also saw in King a multicultural man who might exorcise the Republican party's old elitist Caucasian ghost and thereby transform the Republicans into the majority party. If this plantation syndrome was in many ways only myth by the late 1960s, there remained an element of fact. In 1968, the part-Hawaiian Anderson had been plagued during the mayoral campaign by Republicans who seemingly regarded him as too much the "local boy"—Anderson had quit high school just prior to graduation, and was both a self-made and self-educated man.

Early in the 1969 legislative session, Republican Sen. James K. Clark—a friend of both Anderson and Rohlfing—brought the issue into the open. Clark had grown up in the Hawaiian Homestead neighborhood of Papakolea, and had climbed to fame as a college football star and then a professional. Returning home, and being married to the daughter of Neal Blaisdell, Clark had easily won house and then senate races as a Republican. But he long had chafed at what he saw as paternalism or worse directed at non-Caucasian Republicans, and after Blaisdell's retirement Clark fled to more comfortable surroundings. At the outset of the 1969 Legislature, Clark announced that he had signed a Democratic party card. Clark would confide to friends that he no longer could tolerate being type-cast as "the big, dumb Hawaiian." And Clark also would bitterly recall that some conservative Caucasian Republicans had actually opposed Anderson in the 1968 mayoral race, to which Clark would add, "Look at me. I'm a lot more of a 'local boy' than Andy."

David McClung, as Democratic chairman, skillfully made much of the incident, reviving memories of plantation days and the Big Five. In return, the Republican chairman, Edward E. Johnston, released an ethnic breakdown of Republican and Democratic legislators. Johnston noted that the Republicans were more balanced than the Democrats, owing to the predominance of AJAs in Democratic ranks—at the time, there was not a single Caucasian in the Democratic majority of the state house.

Rohlfing, for his part, had grown up in Hawaii as a privileged Caucasian, but from school days had sought out James Clark's friendship, Rohlfing perhaps never quite shedding a certain self-consciousness about his own origins. In Clark, Rohlfing had found a comrade and also an open door to Papakolea. And so Clark's change of parties hit the blond Rohlfing especially hard, bruising a sensitive spot in his personality.

As the gubernatorial season approached, this still was working on him, but—ever the torn man—he located two wealthy haoles as his most influential draft-King cohorts. They were Phil Spalding, Jr., a kamaaina industrialist, and Edward Brennan, a Gold Bond trading stamp executive who had been a top man in campaigns for both William Quinn and Neal Blaisdell. This three-man draft group had come about when both Spalding and Brennan simultaneously began pursuing the party post of Republican national committeeman, and separately had sought out Rohlfing for his support.

Rohlfing had responded by saying that the national committeeman's job was relatively immaterial, what the Republican party really needed was a man who could win the governorship, and so Rohlfing had engaged both of them in drumming up support for a King candidacy. The trio circulated through party and business circles and, at various times, all of them reported to Judge Sam King that the response was encouraging.

King himself was intrigued but was making no commitments. He was approaching fifty-four, and although he had been a judge for thirteen years, his roots ran deep in politics. For one thing he was heir to a historic name. His father, Samuel Wilder King, had served as territorial delegate to Congress from 1934 until 1942, and had been appointed by President Eisenhower in 1953 as governor of the territory.

The senior King governed Hawaii through the years of the Democratic upheaval, making many a political enemy by frequently vetoing bills laid on his desk by the young Democratic lawmakers.

Finally, in 1957, rumors began circulating that changes might be in the making, and to check the political winds Republicans Arthur Woolaway and William Quinn journeyed to Washington. On arriving, Woolaway found that Eisenhower was looking for a younger and more liberal governor for the territory—that Eisenhower planned to replace the senior King. Statehood for Hawaii clearly was in the offing, and with it a public gubernatorial election. Therefore Eisenhower wanted a younger and perhaps more electable man, King by 1957 being seventy years old.

Woolaway met for more than two hours with Fred Seaton, Eisenhower's secretary of the interior, whose department controlled American territorial lands.

Because Woolaway revered Sam Wilder King almost as he would a father, he argued for Secretary Seaton to intercede with Eisenhower on King's behalf. The interior secretary countered by offering Woolaway the territory's second-highest appointed position, secretary of the territory, but Woolaway declined, saying, "That's not what I'm here for." Woolaway persisted on his original course, and finally Secretary Seaton replied, "Your points are well taken, but the man on the Hill," the president, "carries a burden greater than any man in the world." Meaning the decision had been made, and that the case was closed. Shortly thereafter the senior King gracefully submitted his resignation, making way for Woolaway's traveling companion, William Quinn.

While years later Woolaway along with others would think, "It was a hell of a way to treat a man," all in all Sam W. King's career had been long and productive. And even in 1969, as the new state's fourth gubernatorial election approached, the name King was still a household word in Hawaii.

Being very much his father's son, Sam P. King had many things going his way. He was, like Porteus, educated at Punahou; he then attended Yale and Yale Law School. And after navy service in World War II he had returned to the Republican-dominated territory and had followed his father into politics. First he tried for a house seat in 1950, won a nomination in the primary, but lost in the general election. The same year he made his way onto the party's central committee, establishing himself as a leader of a younger element, which included Phil Spalding, and the younger King won the party's chairmanship in 1953.

It happened that just as Sam King was stepping up in the political world, the tide of history knocked him down. He had won the party chairmanship in time to preside over the Republican debacle of 1954. In the precipitous plunge downward, Sam King had played out his part, ungracefully, as a Red-baiter.

King, in a celebrated incident of the 1954 campaign, had said, "No one is accusing all the Democrats of being Communists, but they are politically obligated to the Communists." King was a one-term chairman. If King's early political ventures scarcely qualified him as a gubernatorial contender, his reputation as a judge was another story.

King in 1956 started as a district magistrate, then Governor Quinn elevated him to the circuit court bench in 1961. Particularly after 1966, as a judge of the state's new and progressive family court, King came to be regarded as a social thinker, sympathetic to the plight of juvenile delinquents, critical of the penal system, and an advocate of sex education, abortion, and divorce reform. He also had spoken up for state support of family planning and for day-care centers for children of working mothers. Hawaii, at least in part because it had the nation's highest cost of living, and also because of very compelling status drives current among many people, was reputed to have the highest national percentage of working mothers. So this was one of several points which had enhanced King's reputation, and additionally King had developed more than ordinary sophistication about the world outside of Hawaii: He had traveled widely, and each summer had lectured on the faculty of the National College of State Trial Judges.

In 1969, as the pressure to enter the gubernatorial race became more intense, King listened with increasing interest. It had become clear that Hiram Fong would not support him in Washington for a federal judgeship. And, although King had been reappointed to the Hawaii bench in 1967 by Burns, he later would portray himself as profoundly disgusted with Burns' proclivity for appointing Democratic political allies. On July 29, 1969, King called Porteus, looking for a clarification of Porteus' intentions, and Porteus had suggested that they talk over lunch at the Pacific Club.

The gist of the meeting was this: King said he was under pressure to run, but wanted to know what Porteus planned to do.

King wanted to know if Porteus was for real, or if Porteus was merely thinking about it as he had so often in past years. Porteus replied that he most certainly intended to run, and that he was confident of widespread support. King said in that case, if Porteus was committed, he would defer. More than a little ambiguously, King amended his basic statement by telling Porteus that if he was really running, then Porteus should move fast.

And, King added, he was not yet ready to tell his own promoters to stop their work. Porteus, who regarded himself as very much on the move, left the lunch confident that he had King's word. Subsequently King, some two weeks later, over lunch with Phil Spalding, Ed Brennan, and Rohlfing, reported that he had deferred to Porteus.

The three men argued for King to change his mind, presumably contending that Porteus would be a pushover in the primary.

Rohlfing, for one, had been speculating aloud during this period that Porteus, given his past record of equivocating when the stakes were high, could be bluffed out of the race. King again wavered. Before departing from Rohlfing and the others, King promised to think over the matter further and to give them an expression of intent shortly. After two more weeks of agonizing, King arranged to meet Porteus, again at the Pacific Club, this time in late afternoon. Over coffee, King announced to Porteus, "I'm withdrawing my statement that I defer to you."

Accordingly the stage was set not only for a primary contest, but also an acrimonious one.

Without making a public issue of it, an obviously embittered Porteus let it be known to many people—including newsmen—in the ensuing months that King had gone back on his word. And King, when questioned by reporters, could only concede that indeed he had undergone a change of mind, then move on to another subject as quickly as possible.

When it was past history, King also would rationalize his turnabout by embracing the theory that Porteus was Burns' backstop candidate: "That's why I didn't have too much trouble changing my mind," King would say. Following the King-Porteus coffee talk, the King movement accelerated rapidly, but chaotically. With King still on the bench, draft-King meetings inside Brennan's Gold Bond building started regularly in October 1969, for organizing, fund-raising, and planning.

At one time or another, the meetings included some of the most experienced men in the party, such as Arthur Woolaway, a former party chairman; Ken Nakamura, also a former chairman and Anderson's 1968 manager; former legislator Ambrose Rosehill; and former Gov. William F. Quinn. But for months on end, King's campaign forces were in a constant sorting-out process. Attorney Clinton Ashford, political novice, was the initial spokesman of the draft-King committee, but quickly drifted to the sidelines. Phil Spalding, whom King credited as being the one to most influence him to enter the race, took the job of national committeeman. As such, Spalding felt obliged to sit out the primary, although he would reemerge in the general election in last-minute desperation negotiations with the White House.

Fred Rohlfing had his own state senate campaign to run, and he too drifted to the periphery of the King organization. Quinn became chairman of the King-for-Governor Committee, but his role turned out to be largely ceremonial. He was little involved in day-to-day work.

A *Honolulu Advertiser* reporter was hired as press secretary, then given his walking papers after two weeks. Whittaker-Baxter, the nation's oldest campaign management firm, was brought in during the fall of 1969 to draw up a strategy plan, but the draft-King group was dissatisfied with its preliminary work and dropped the firm. On this went. John Kraft of New York, one of the nation's leading campaign pollsters, conducted an extensive survey as a foundation for campaign strategy. While Kraft's findings remained a secret, King would dismiss Kraft's work as "not telling us anything we didn't already know." The McCann-Ericksen ad agency was initially involved, then replaced by the Fawcett-McDermott agency.

However, the brunt of the ad planning subsequently fell to a second Mainland import, Sanford Weiner and Co. of San Francisco, known throughout California for its handling of Republican U.S. Rep. Paul McCloskey, who had defeated the one-time child movie star, Shirley Temple Black, and also for its handling of Democratic U.S. Sen. Alan Cranston.

The real decision-making power of the campaign organization eventually settled in the hands of Ed Brennan, whom King had scarcely known before the campaign started.

Three others—all equally inexperienced in campaigning—fell into key staff positions. Stan Anderson, another Gold Bond executive, was put in charge of precinct organizing.

Bill Bachran, a public relations man, played press secretary, scheduler, and driver, or "keeper of the body" in Brennan's bubbly terminology. Attorney Marilyn Van Winkle, the first executive-secretary of the State Ethics Commission, headed a research group which eventually would include a tax researcher and two speech-writers.

While the King campaign was moving on this uneven course toward a formal kickoff, Hiram Fong returned to Honolulu for the Christmas holidays of 1969 and made an eleventh-hour attempt to head off a contested Republican primary.

Two days before Christmas, Fong granted an interview for the purpose of publicly warning that a primary battle would be a disaster. Fong reasoned that the party already was a small minority and that a contested primary inevitably would be divisive: "My advice to them is to get together."

Because Fong made it clear he was with Porteus, Fong was implicitly suggesting that King take the lieutenant governor's slot on the ticket, although Fong stopped short of saying this in so many words. So it was that by May 29, 1970, its primary election four months away, the Republican establishment had produced not one but two candidates. And to the further dismay of Hebden Porteus, radical right-winger David Watumull heard the call of destiny and made it a threesome.

The Republican nomination for lieutenant governor was another matter. Because while there had been so much concern over a contested gubernatorial primary, both the King and Porteus forces wanted to see a contest for the second spot on the ticket, for lieutenant governor.

The reason was Richard "Ike" Sutton, a perennial loser, who was given to wild flights of rhetoric which almost invariably left people wondering what he had said. When on occasion Sutton was understood, most of his line was so conservative as to be out of step with the times. Ike Sutton was the only announced candidate for the second slot on the Republican ticket.

In the Porteus camp Wadsworth Yee devised a plan to kill two birds with one stone: First, to defeat Sutton; second, to minimize the inherent problems of a King-Porteus fight.

Yee's plan hinged on Arthur Woolaway, a beloved figure in the party. As Yee envisioned it, Woolaway would run against Ike Sutton in the primary.

Immediately after beating Sutton, Arthur Woolaway would magnanimously resign his nomination, allowing the party to appoint a candidate for lieutenant governor. The appointee, of course, would be the loser in the gubernatorial primary, either Porteus or King.

Thus, in Yee's mind, the Republicans would be assured of having their two strongest men on the general election ticket. And, second, the plan would virtually guarantee that the King-Porteus contest would be a powder puff clash, since the interests of both King and Porteus would be bound inextricably through the general election.

Yee insisted that he was serious. He further insisted that the idea was taken seriously by the Porteus people, and that Woolaway was agreeable, although Woolaway would later dismiss the idea as outlandish.

At any rate, King's agents flatly rejected Yee's ploy.

A month later, King produced his own candidate, Ralph Kiyosaki, his neighbor, to knock down Sutton. As state superintendent of schools the preceding three years, Kiyosaki could lend some degree of prestige to the ticket. And, with Kiyosaki's entrance into the lieutenant governor's race, the Porteus camp was as relieved as King's; almost assuredly Ike Sutton was no longer a problem. So far, for all the sweat that had gone into Republican slate-making, for all the solemnity that only solid Republicans can conjure, this was political slapstick.

Disregarding Fong, on the third day of February 1970, Judge King called a press conference to announce his candidacy for governor, decrying "overcrowding, insufficient housing, inadequate help for our teachers, reckless exploitation of our land, and pollution of our air and water. These things are not future threats to Hawaii. They are here now."

The early glow was amazing. Shortly after the announcement, a variety of polls appeared showing King ahead of Porteus by as much as three-to-one and four-to-one. Porteus' financing was drying up and his scheduled staff build-up was being delayed. In short, Porteus looked like a sure loser, but he refused to back down.

In one utterly human moment, when some of his own early backers were suggesting that he withdraw, Porteus reputedly rapped the table and announced that by God, if he had to campaign in the streets alone, then he would do so.

On May 11, shortly before the end of the 1970 legislative session, Porteus formally announced as a candidate. Always the moderate, the conciliator, Porteus embarked on a strategy designed to arouse the conservative instincts of Republican voters and to isolate King as overly liberal: D. Hebden Porteus became Hawaii's first law-and-order candidate.

Skimming over the conventional issues, Porteus assaulted the dangers of prostitution, unwashed hippies (a menace to public health), disruptive student demonstrations, and the widespread use of drugs, marijuana in particular.*

This was a new Porteus: Terse, resolute, telling it like it was. He would say, "It's high time people took positions, spoke up for them, and then stood on them."

There was in this a potentially interesting commentary on Hawaii. In 1964, when the purist right-radical Barry Goldwater was the Republican nominee for president, he had won fewer than twenty-two of every hundred votes cast in Hawaii, his worst show-

*The importance of the "hippie" anxiety to 1970 should not be underestimated. Porteus led the way in opposing a World Peace Festival in Hawaii, a position shared by the four county governments and also by Governor Burns, his "Open Society" theme notwithstanding. Burns would say of the young immigrants, "Like everyone, they deserve all rights under the law. But they have sorely strained our Aloha spirit." Gill would tell a non-Caucasian audience to think twice before maligning the long-haired newcomers, reminding them that in past years many people had been maligned for being "different." Though sentiment ran strongly against hippies during this period, Gill was cheered by his listeners at Oahu's Leilehua High School.

ing in the nation with the exception of Rhode Island. In the 1968 presidential race, another sort of law-and-order candidate, the blatantly racist George Wallace, ran poorest in Hawaii among the fifty states, at only 1 per cent of the vote. While any comparison of Wallace to Porteus would have been enormously unfair to Porteus, the two like Goldwater worked variant dimensions of law and order. Nationally by the late 1960s law and order had taken root as a fundamental issue, and was therefore respectable, even though most proponents made little or no mention of justice—"the social issue," it was euphemistically called, a reaction to the many changes of the decade. Often it is theorized that in Hawaii national trends take hold in a delayed-action sequence; that is, several years in the wake of national trends. So now in 1970 Hebden Porteus was counting on a swing of the pendulum in an Island society which seemed to pride itself on its compassion, flexibility, tolerance, and indeed on its permissiveness. In context of the 1970 battle for the governorship, this was mostly of interest because of the presumed value of the Republican nomination, because Tom Gill was at the throat of John Burns.

16

The Tempest

Following his emotion-laden campaign kickoff on July 9, Tom Gill continued on the verbal offensive, scoring left and right. Over the next several weeks Gill again would pull out in front in the polls and again would carry with him the aura of a man who was about to become the governor of Hawaii. On the other side, a virtually silent John Burns, for his part, would counter with the most massive and sophisticated communications campaign in the history of Island politics.

If there had been any doubts about Burns' preference for remaining above the battle, which he had made into a political strategy, these doubts were dispelled the day after Tom Gill's biting attack of July 9 on the governor's alleged alarming friends. In the early morning of July 10, a reporter called the governor's press secretary, Don Horio, seeking a response from the governor. Horio, showing no interest in personally arranging comment, as would press liaison people in normal political operations, advised the reporter that Governor Burns might be reached after early mass, which Burns attended at the downtown Cathedral of Our Lady of Peace. At seven o'clock, the reporter then went to Washington Place, but was informed that Burns was out—a maid agreed to take a copy of Gill's speech and relay it to the governor. Mid-morning telephone calls to Washington Place and the Capitol yielded nothing. The governor was not available. Then finally in early afternoon, Burns dropped by the Capitol press room, sat down, and leafed through Gill's scathing speech, alternately pursing his mouth, raising an eyebrow, frowning, smiling to himself—bemused.

"What's new?" he asked.

Pressed on specifics, Burns took exception to Gill's having implied that he, Burns, was compromised by his financial backers: "I owe nothing to anyone, except to do the best possible job for the state. Anyone who contributes to my campaign does so knowing that." Otherwise he did not bother to make a point-by-point response, saying, "I'm not going to play yo-yo."

However, late that afternoon, Burns called a press conference, a notice that quickly assembled a dozen radio, TV, and newspaper reporters who swarmed into his ceremonial chambers on the top floor of the Capitol, expecting something further on the Gill speech.

Instead, Burns announced that he was sanctioning the merger of the two local airlines, Hawaiian and Aloha. With his prepared statement on the airline merger out of the way, reporters then asked him to take up political questions, Gill's speech in particular. But Burns shook his head, said no, and withdrew into his working office.

Reporters, keenly aware that the governor's race was the story of the year, trooped out wondering just what sort of campaign this was going to be, although two or three of the better informed were beginning to have a fairly clear idea.

Gill persisted in cutting away at Burns.

Starting his Big Island campaign on July 12, Gill attacked Burns' "massive and expensive effort to resurrect public confidence.

"If an administration has a good record and people know it, why do you have to spend half a million dollars to convince them?" (Gill was underestimating finances, as he would learn later.)

July 19, Maui: "The [Burns] administration has discovered the housing crisis. A tremendous amount of public relations time will be invested in proving that housing is on the way. It's not, really, but what people can be brought to think is happening is more important sometimes than what is really taking place."

On July 30, Gill, Hebden Porteus, and Sam King addressed several hundred members of the Honolulu Board of Realtors. The governor did not attend, and this was the first of eight platform appearances—the time-honored forum for campaigning—which Burns boycotted. Consequently the campaign platform became a sort of three-on-one traveling show, with Gill and the two Republicans running against the absentee. At this time there was only a presumption on the part of some people that Jack Seigle had concluded Gill seemed to be more "with it," a conclusion Seigle later would put on the record. Often in these platform appearances, the

crowd resented Burns' absence, and so there was an added tempta-
tion for Gill and the Republicans to lean hard on Burns. Inevitably
they seemed to be influenced by the sentiment of the audience, even
though the mass media effect was that of a gang-up attack on
Burns.

On this particular day, Hebden Porteus criticized Burns for
ineffective administration of the state's housing and pollution laws.
King took Burns to task for unplanned development, for the sprawl
of urban Honolulu across the sugar fields, and for the rezoning
record of the State Land Use Commission. Long before Gill himself had laid this out: In the previous six years, the land use commission had rezoned nearly 3,000 acres of prime green agricultural
land on Oahu, and much of this land still was idle, awaiting a ripe
time for a high-profit resale—that is, awaiting a time when the
general scarcity of land would drive values to even more as-
tronomical highs. Gill then took the podium, congratulating Sam
King for the speech, and saying the speech sounded as if he had
written it himself—in fact, Fred Rohlfing had written the original
draft.

Then Tom Gill uncorked.

He began: "We have had several examples lately of what might
be politely called 'puffing' on the question of housing."

Gill went on to describe the "puffing" in the most impolite
terms. Promotion of the Burns Housing Fair, he said, "borders on
fraud." Around the dining room people shifted uncomfortably in
their chairs.

Gill then singled out a widely distributed Housing Fair brochure which listed "prices for houses which are not the prices paid
—or promised to be paid—by the state for those same houses."

The sticky example was Durite Corporation, whose two model
houses had been listed in the thirteen- and fourteen-thousand-
dollar range. Subsequently Durite had filed for bankruptcy, and in
the bankruptcy proceeding had listed a bill to the state of about
$4,000 apiece above the brochure price of the two houses.

Gill also noted that all the list prices failed to mention the cost
of land, improvements, water, sewer, and electrical hookups. "Nor
does the brochure indicate whether the prices are supposed to be
for individual houses, or for production in volume. The net effect
is extremely misleading."

He closed with a call on Burns to "stop playing games with the
housing crisis."

Once again the press descended on the Capitol, but Burns' whereabouts was unknown.

Bill Cook, organizer of the Housing Fair, was on the Neighbor Islands, and while reporters milled about the chief executive's office, Cook's secretary finally reached Cook on Kauai. She subsequently sat down and typed out a garbled four-paragraph reply to the Gill assault.

That night, Burns surfaced at a campaign dinner for a legislative candidate, and was asked about Gill's speech. Burns dismissed it with a "No comment," and he added that the statement from Cook was unauthorized.

Burns' manager, Robert Oshiro, was unconcerned, was if anything pleased. That same night, when asked if it was wise for Burns to give away the platform to his opponent, Oshiro countered mysteriously by likening Burns' behavior to sound military strategy. Oshiro swept his arms in a circle towards himself: "You draw your opponent in—you let him come at you." Jack Seigle, probed on the same question, said he had found in his years in the advertising business, "Never answer your competitor."

July ended with the resignation of Burns' deputy director of the State Department of Social Services, Royce Higa, who defected to Gill. Royce Higa, although a veteran of the famed 442nd, never had been close to Burns' inner circle, but in 1962 had campaigned for Burns in the Pearl City district, and on the strength of this and his extensive experience in public health and social work had been awarded the departmental position. Higa initially had been perplexed by what he regarded as lax and indecisive direction of the department. And then, having many friends in the Gill apparatus, such as Nelson Doi and Togo Nakagawa (a one-time president of the 442nd Club), he had been embarrassed and put off by Burns' 1966 campaign for Kenneth Brown. In that instance, Royce Higa had supported Gill for lieutenant governor, despite pressure from such Burns insiders as Matsuo Takabuki and Robert Oshiro. Higa was not only unmoved but disgusted when told that his role with Burns was special owing to his being the only top-level Okinawan appointee.*

*Historically Japanese looked down on Okinawans, even though prior to World War II Okinawa was an integral part of Japan (and would be returned to Eisaku Sato's government by Richard Nixon). Japanese bias against Okinawans lingered into modern Hawaii, as did Japanese disdain for the *eta*—outcast tanners and skinners dehumanized by the Japanese culture, although not to the extent that America dehumanized the black slave.

Because a department-level appointee is expected to follow the political line of his employer, he no doubt was walking on thin ice in 1966, although Burns nonetheless had kept him on—as he had several others whose loyalty was known to lie with Tom Gill. Now in 1970, despite a last-moment attempt by Burns' administrative director, Myron Thompson, to head off the move—Myron Thompson was aware that all was not well in the department—Higa abandoned the Burns administration in favor of Tom Gill, as Ralph Kiyosaki also had abandoned it to go with King. Higa left behind many people who regarded him as an ingrate, particularly because he had been well paid for nearly eight years. Burns himself might also have thought this but was of too magnanimous a bent to say so publicly, or for that matter allow it to be said. Privately Burns more than once had expressed bewilderment that so many people in the social development and education fields did not support him, given what he had done for these fields, particularly for education. The greatly improved University of Hawaii was a monument to John Burns' dedication to education, and yet the professors lined up with Tom Gill. Burns no doubt wondered if it was more a matter of style than substantive performance, being neither eloquent like Gill nor capable of expressing himself in a high-flown intellectual way—John Burns had dropped out after one semester and was most articulate over his breakfast table, spicing his English with well-chosen phrases of pidgin. Professors could not understand that. So on occasion there could be seen in Burns the pain of a perceived betrayal. In his own value system Burns considered loyalty—the Japanese word is *on*—to be an essential virtue. Among some of Burns' cohorts, the interpretation of this value on loyalty was narrowly political and phobic. But Burns in many instances had extended the concept beyond personal loyalties to a generalized community loyalty—if Burns thought a person was dedicated to Hawaii's betterment, this might be all he asked. Royce Higa was a case in point. There was no other adequate explanation for his surviving in the administration after 1966, although the relationship had deteriorated, and in 1970 Higa cut the tie.

Royce Higa in fact was badly needed in the Gill organization, because Gill's campaign manager, Dr. Thomas Ige of the university, had been sidelined by an attack of tuberculosis. Higa moved in as campaign coordinator and, at peace because his political identity finally was resolved, he enjoyed himself: He particularly was delighted by Gill's young workers, and they in turn regarded him as a fellow traveler on the far side of the generational line.

Six days after Higa's resignation, Thomas Ige's wife provided Tom Gill with yet another publicity coup. For two and a half years Mrs. Fumi Ige had been the coordinator of the AFL-CIO's Committee on Political Education (COPE). But on August 6, following a chaotic meeting of COPE's endorsement committee for the Oahu division, Mrs. Ige resigned in anger. In her resignation statement, Mrs. Ige directed her fire at Walter Kupau, the pro-Burns AFL-CIO president. Kupau, she claimed, had packed the Oahu meeting in violation of the federation's constitution to bar her from participating in the screening of candidates. A second person boxed out by the maneuver was Bill Abbott, the AFL-CIO executive secretary, who likewise was pro-Gill, and likewise was destined to resign. Kupau retorted that Gill people characteristically, whenever they were outvoted, picked up their marbles and ran—in this case, to the press.

But whatever the merits of the situation it probably was true that no union boss can effectively wage public battle with an indignant woman. On leaving, Mrs. Ige proclaimed that she no longer wanted her name associated "with men who are bent on obtaining a COPE endorsement for Governor Burns even at the cost of ruining the state federation." The truth was that the fragile federation several times had wrecked itself over politics, and was doing so again.

Mrs. Ige subsequently set up shop in Tom Gill's campaign headquarters downtown on King Street, just a block from Burns' headquarters, and she proceeded as chairman of a Women for Gill committee.

On August 7, immediately following the Ige-Kupau blowup, Gill and Royce Higa huddled with fifteen AFL-CIO union bosses who had been called together by Art Rutledge. They emerged endorsing Gill for governor, adding a union blessing to Gill's candidacy beyond the highly personal attachment of Arthur Rutledge.

Later in the month, to the surprise of many people, the 7,000-member United Public Workers also came out for Gill, although many Neighbor Island segments would defiantly stay with Burns. Generally, while the giants were supporting Burns (the ILWU, the Hawaii Government Employees, and what was left of the AFL-CIO Federation), Tom Gill was showing that he also had substantial backing in the ranks of organized labor.

From a broader perspective what was happening was this: With the breach between John Burns and the independent Democrat Tom Gill now at last in the open, the labor movement was being torn asunder into two hostile camps. If this came as no surprise to people who followed politics closely, it may well have puzzled those who, through their ignorance of the labor scene, viewed the movement as monolithic.

By this time Tom Gill's instincts seemed to have gripped him completely: he kept on attacking. At a rally on Maui he accused Burns of trying to buy the election with his TV media campaign.

Gill further suggested that the money was coming from subdividers, land speculators, and outfits on contract to the state—architects, engineers, planners, and so forth. The Burns TV strategy, Gill asserted, "is to purify and 'can'—and use your money to push it out through the tube."

Burns, still officially unannounced, left town for five days to attend a national governors conference. And on his return, he said at planeside that he guessed he would have to do something soon, because the filing deadline was only six days away, on August 19. The election itself was only fifty-one days away.

On the 14th of August, Burns summoned the press to Washington Place for his only full-scale news conference of the campaign.

Burns formally entered the race with a pledge to continue working for an "open society," his favorite phrase, connoting as it did the politics of first-class citizenship. "We have worked to remove those barriers of the past which kept us from being the open society we are today. We will continue. . . ." He cited legislative cooperation of past years and added, "I am deeply obligated to see . . . that we remain united."

Although this was a live press conference, Burns' aides distributed TV tapes of a prerehearsed announcement statement by the governor; regardless of how the media played the announcement, this tape would be aired on paid time over the next week. Then Burns again went traveling, far from the political hustings, to Japan's international exposition, Expo '70, for ceremonies dedicating the Hawaii pavilion in the fair.

Behind him Burns left a scandal.

It resulted from the abuse of Burns' trust, and from the abuse of appointed office. Further—at least on the face of it—it could not have been a more loaded incident in light of what so far had been said in the campaign.

The story revolved around a member of the land use commission, recently resigned, a Shiro Nishimura of Kauai, known there as Sally Nishimura, a chicken farmer who also had gone into the business of speculating on land. As detailed on the front page of the *Honolulu Star-Bulletin,* which for weeks had been investigating the case, Nishimura had formed an investment hui (syndicate) and had bought a tract of land in the countryside district of Kalaheo on Kauai.

The story recounted how Shiro Nishimura then had successfully led a vote of the land use commission to rezone the land for urban development. Subsequently the Nishimura hui had resold the Kalaheo tract for a quick gain of $575,000, which among other things showed how valuable urban zoning was in a land-poor island state.

Gill leaped. An "alarming friend" had been unearthed. Better yet, Nishimura was a speculator and tied to Gill's choice issue of land use. "Nishimura, unfortunately, is another of the governor's most alarming friends," Gill said.

"We've just seen an example of a commission member with a sleazy sense of ethics."

Gill said the incident underscored a "need for a fresh look at ethics in government. A good place to start would have been the ethics bill the governor just vetoed."

All three challengers demanded an investigation, Porteus terming the Kauai case deplorable, and King saying it reflected a "developer-oriented sickness" at work in the administration.

Before leaving for Japan, Burns countered briefly by saying via a favored reporter that he already had investigated Nishimura because Nishimura had boasted that he "could get things done."

Nishimura had resigned the preceding September, citing health problems, but had continued to sit on the commission for three months—until he was replaced in January. Burns was quoted as saying the investigation had never been disclosed because it wasn't the state's job "to destroy a man's reputation." Spirits in the Gill camp soared.

Catching a late political fever, a popular Democratic state senator, Vincent Yano, announced on August 18 that he was running with Tom Gill for lieutenant governor.

If Vincent Yano was in the race far too late with no money and no organization, Gill at least had a counterpart to Burns' Ariyoshi —an AJA on the ticket and stumping for him.

On August 20, Burns returned from Japan and immediately issued a brief statement taking a new tack on the Nishimura case.

Conceding "improprieties or worse," Burns ordered an investigation by his attorney general, Bert Kanbara.

The same week the *Advertiser* added fuel to the land use commission controversy by focusing on the commission chairman, Wilbert Choi, who soon was to die of a heart attack. Choi, it turned out, had, like Nishimura, voted to rezone his own land. But in this instance, the land had been downzoned to conservation use from urban zoning. However, there was a hooker on which the *Advertiser* pegged its story: Choi's land was used for a nursery in open space, and he had a building on the land which violated the city government's zoning code. By transferring the land to a conservation zone, the land reverted to state zoning control, thereby solving Choi's violation of the city zoning ordinance.

A kind of scandal craze ensued.

One reporter grumbled that his employer had asked, "Can't you dig up one of these?"

KGMB-TV did come up with its own, disclosing that SIDA taxi drivers—who held an exclusive contract to handle airport traffic—had kicked back at least $15,000 into the Burns campaign fund.

By comparison to the Shiro Nishimura incident, the KGMB disclosure was innocuous enough—in fact, the newspapers after checking it out refused to touch it. But on film, the SIDA manager, Charles Kiaha, inadvertently managed to make SIDA's campaign fund sound sinister, and it was perhaps partly for this reason that his drivers subsequently deposed him as manager.

There was more to come. On September 2, a month before election day, the *Star-Bulletin* revealed that land use commissioner Alex Napier also had voted to rezone land in which he had a direct interest.

In this instance, the land was on the Big Island's Kahua Ranch, whose director, general manager, and vice president was—Alex Napier. After the urban rezoning, the tax department increased the land's assessed valuation 116 times over.

Gill for his part kept up an intense barrage of criticism and again overreached, telling a crowd in Hilo that $50,000 had been offered to him by a Mainland engineering firm in return for naming their agent as the next state director of transporation. While no doubt a compromised transportation director could be worth $50,000 to a large firm, on the face of it the story sounded as if it had been lifted from a bad novel, and certainly it required something further by way of detail. Challenged by Sam King to spell out the entire story, Gill did a rollback, professing not even to know the name of the firm.

In another late August speech, Gill likened the 1960s to rule "by the alley-cat morals of the fast-buck artist.

"This sleazy attitude has seemingly found its way into the edges and corners of the government. We are now paying the piper for this sad tune. Unless we clean house at once the price may be more than we can bear.

"When we destroy the people's confidence in the honesty and impartiality of our government, we destroy the guts of our society. We cannot afford such self-immolation in these times when the world moves in uncertain ways and our values are under serious question. No announcement of broad investigations will suffice to clear the air.

"This is a human tragedy.

"The governor, always loyal to his friends, has been betrayed by some of them.

"However honest and decent Jack may be personally, he can hardly escape the cloud cast ... by his most alarming friends."

Then Gill outlined his own remedy: A review of all regulatory agencies, a team of investigators in the attorney general's office for a running check on powerful state agencies, a review of all nonbid contracts for fairness and impartiality, enactment of a strict ethics code, an open list of government contractors, and a modification of the tax law to eliminate much of the speculative profiteering in land rezonings.

It was a wild month; for the Gill forces, a heady month. As August came to a close, it seemed the deadlock was broken, and that a victory for Gill was a solid bet, a view which Gill himself appeared to embrace temporarily.

Addressing his labor supporters on August 31, Gill wrote off Burns as too beholden to the developers and speculators to solve the housing crisis, then took a couple of verbal potshots at King. It was as if Gill was already looking past the October 3 primary to the November 3 general.

Just how much of a leap Gill had made in his August 31 speech was probably best understood at the time by Rick Egged, the resident boy pollster of the Burns organization.

Unknown to all but a few of the Burns strategists, Egged had taken a poll after the Nishimura scandal broke into the open. His question was, "Do you feel that something illegal was done by the land use commission, and who do you think is to blame?" Only seven of every hundred people blamed Burns and to Egged these were hard-core Gill people anyway.

Only 13 per cent mentioned Burns in any way. Simply put, scarcely anyone connected Burns with the commission he had appointed.

Egged also found that a large majority of the voters, well over 50 per cent, were unaware of the scandal, despite the barrage of publicity, and accordingly Egged concluded, "We felt the land use commission story wasn't breaking too hard on us."

In fact, Egged thought, "The more Gill swung at Burns, the deeper he sank. The people's image of the governor was that his administration may not be perfect, but he's a nice man, a good man, who's done a lot for Hawaii." The Nishimura incident, and Gill's attack, would prove to be one of the hidden ironies of the campaign.

While Egged had never seen the Gill poll taken in the long-ago spring of the year, he would not have been surprised at the finding that less than 2 per cent of the voters had expressed a concern over impropriety in government. A second poll run by Rick Egged on September 10 was to round out the story.

Along with the usual trial-heat question, Egged injected the question that was being hotly debated inside the Gill camp: Whether Gill was coming on too strong, hitting too hard. The Burns camp wanted to know, too. Was the governor's silence, outwardly so risky, the right tack to take? Burns, after all, was absorbing a verbal beating without fighting back, so Egged's pollsters asked: "Do you feel that Lieutenant Governor Tom Gill is justified in his accusations against Governor Burns?" Essentially, the answer was no. Of those polled, 72 per cent said no, only 28 per cent said yes.

Even more fascinating was the comparative reaction of the two biggest ethnic groups in the Democratic primary, the Caucasians and AJAs. Among Caucasians, four of ten approved, saying Gill was justified in his accusations. But the much larger AJA list was an entirely different story. Only 4.5 per cent—4.5%—saw Gill as justified in his attack on Burns.

Egged, highly sensitive to the subtleties of ethnicity, interpreted his poll as a matter of ethnic style: "The fact is that it's simply not Japanese—or Chinese—to say 'my opponent is a dirty, rotten, lousy guy.'"

In fact, from his poll results, Egged came to believe that Tom Gill was forcing undecided AJAs into the Burns column: "They might have thought, Governor Burns may be old, but he's done a lot for us."

In Egged's view, Gill was pushing many AJAs to the point of feeling they would be condemning Burns if they didn't vote for him.

"Further, he gave them a choice of saying that either Governor Burns is crooked or the people around Governor Burns are crooked, and a lot of those, incidentally, are Japanese. It was getting pretty close to home."

Burns himself analyzed the backlash in more personal terms: "Frankly, I know more people than [the other candidates]. And they've made their own judgment, and it means their own judgment is being attacked.

"They spread the word to their friends that this was contrary to everything they knew [about me]."

Gill later conceded he had "misgauged the land use thing badly. Most of the people who voted in the Democratic primary didn't react at all, or else they reacted the other way—that the guy who got the money was a hero." In fact there were perceptive people on Kauai who sensed that Shiro Nishimura's reputation was enhanced, and that he was widely regarded as a victim of the big city press, although no doubt it occurred to many others that the integrity of the government also had suffered.

17

I Am Hawaii

During the primary election campaign, John Burns broke silence only once to respond to Gill. The prelude to Burns' move was on September 3 at a Burns dinner organized by the ILWU, AFL-CIO, and the Hawaii Government Employees. The main speaker was the ILWU's Robert McElrath, who claimed, "This is the dirtiest campaign in Hawaii's history. The opposition says, 'Throw the rascals out.' The opposition hangs a halo over the head of their candidate and says, 'Vote for our boy and all of your problems will be solved.' " McElrath went on, "They lie in their teeth, and they lie deliberately. Their tactics include smear-and-run, innuendo, the big lie, guilt by association. The current smear by innuendo is Governor Burns' 'alarming friends.'

"If this gathering here tonight is any indication of the popularity of Governor Burns, I would say that he has an alarming number of friends. And the opposition has good reason to be alarmed."

"Julius Caesar had his Brutus; Jack Burns has his Tom Gill," McElrath concluded, being the only figure in the campaign other than Tom Gill to dabble in Shakespearean references. Governor Burns, surviving his many wounds, briefly followed Robert McElrath and remarked that it takes more than talk to run a government. If this was a commonplace, it also was a familiar and effective theme: That John Burns in his quiet way was a doer, that Tom Gill was *waha'a,* all mouth. The following day Governor Burns attended the funeral of Wilbert Choi, the land use commissioner who had been criticized for his rezoning vote and shortly thereafter had died. Already Burns had issued a testimonial salute to Wilbert Choi, and in it Burns had implied that the press stories had contributed to Choi's death. Burns had said: "In his actions as a commissioner, Mr. Choi even voted to downzone his own property into the conservation class. . . . While this resulted in a loss to him personally, it led to a misinformed news article which caused him strain."

Following Wilbert Choi's funeral, Burns then went to a campaign dinner at Honolulu International Center, where a crowd of around eight hundred people only partially filled the cavernous hall. Arriving late because of the funeral, Burns moved slowly through the crowd to the head table. As the white-haired governor moved along, the band struck the theme song from *The Hawaiians,* the Hollywood production based on the James Michener novel. Inevitably the lyrics ran through one's mind. "I am Hawaii. I am forever." In his speech, Burns made an attempt to be light, saying how pleased he was to see so many of his alarming friends. But he obviously was feeling anything but light. Discarding his prepared text, he related that he had just come from the funeral of a personal friend, and "I was terribly saddened." Alluding to the attacks on both himself and Wilbert Choi, Burns then said by way of contrast that he had been raised in the Polynesian tradition, and as a child had been taught that "if you can't say something good about someone, no say nothing." There had been, of course, the allegation by Robert McElrath just the night before that 1970 was the dirtiest campaign in the history of Hawaii. "That I don't know," Burns said. "I've seen some reasonably dirty ones before." There had been, for example, the 1959 gubernatorial campaign, in which the *Honolulu Star-Bulletin* gratuitously had featured a picture of him with Harry Bridges and Louis Goldblatt of the ILWU, and also James Hoffa of the Teamsters—as Burns described these men, "citizens who disturb some citizens." Having said all this, Burns followed with his most impassioned appeal of the campaign: Before his election in 1962, the Islands had been plagued by constant friction between the office of governor and the legislature. But now, "the things that unify us are far greater than the things that divide us. We have set the foundation for the kind of society where every human being can reach his full potential.

"We lead the nation in social legislation.

"We lead the nation in concern. I couldn't stay high and mighty in my office—unapproachable by the legislature—and have legislation like this enacted. We have cooperation between the executive and legislative branches of government. One is not running the other. There is mutual respect, with each of us conscious of his responsibilities.

"I am a candidate for reelection because I believe this must continue."

And, Burns went on, Hawaii must become a model for the Pacific and for the world as a multicultural and multiracial community.

"This is our challenge. This is our responsibility. This is our opportunity.

"This we can do. This we must do. This we will do with your help."

His was a positive campaign, he said.

"I am for Hawaii, the people of Hawaii, and everything that is good in Hawaii."

From the same platform, U.S. Sen. Daniel Inouye, back from Washington, in his turn laid on the largely nisei audience a heavy ethnic line.

John Burns, Inouye claimed in a colossal overstatement, was the "first and only person" who stood up for the AJAs in 1941, when others were playing on the community's hysteria. "When I see my dear friend and political father attacked, I get mad. When I see the godfather of my children attacked I get mad."

Whenever Burns "is involved in anything, it's a very personal matter for me."

Then Inouye turned his fire on the press in equally emotional terms. The land use commissioners, Inouye charged, had been found guilty "in a way that no democratic society can condone. They have been tried in the press." Further, as a United States senator, Dan Inouye wanted someone in the State Capitol with whom he could work closely. "I know I can work with Jack Burns. It is like working with your father."

Only later, when it no longer mattered politically, would the last word be said on the land use commission stories, and it would come not from a critic but rather from the governor's own attorney general.

Following this night, the night of September 4, Burns and his camp were virtually silent through the next month until the closing three days of the campaign. As Burns had done in July and August, he continued to avoid meeting Gill, King, and Porteus on the public platform, limiting himself to an occasional solo appearance. One of his classic performances was a talk at Hawaii Loa College before a roomful of students. Burns described the 1960s as a decade of sweeping change and promised that the 1970s would be likewise.

The new decade, he said, would bring more individualized education, better environmental planning, new transit systems, quality tourism, and "new housing—thousands of units—on all Islands."

"How shall change for the better come about?" Burns asked rhetorically. "In the same way it came about after we pledged change eight years ago—by old-fashioned hard work, by the cooperation of citizens who have seen the wonderful achievements possible by working together in harmony."

Generally, quiet was the word.

Disappointing the Gill camp, Burns strictly forbade attacks on Gill or anyone who had anything to do with Gill. Almost the sole exception was a September issue of his campaign house organ, the "Burns Family" newsletter, nailing Tom Gill, Royce Higa, and Sam King on the disloyalty question. The squib noted that each had once been appointed to a job by the governor, and now they had turned on him. Burns read this, picked up the phone and reprimanded the author. This never happened again.

At the coffee hours where Burns personally appeared, reporters were admitted only on an off-the-record basis—unlike those of the other candidates, who were eager to get the exposure—so what Burns said in these question-and-answer sessions went unrecorded.* And unlike Gill, King, and Porteus, who went out of their way to supply the press with campaign schedules, Burns' was a mystery.

On any given day, a reporter would call Burns' headquarters, where he might or might not reach one of three people—Bob Oshiro, Dan Aoki, or the Burns press secretary, Don Horio.

If a connection was made, it likely resulted in very little information or none at all. Burns may or may not be at such-and-such a place. One might try calling Mary Isa, Burns' personal secretary. Miss Isa was uncertain, because the governor was running late on his appointment schedule and had several people waiting to see him.

---

*A writer who covered Burns' 1962 campaign contended that Burns was at his best in small-group coffee hours. On the contrary, in a 1970 session at Washington Place he appeared somewhat ill-at-ease—indeed, given the fact that campaigns are an ordeal, Burns nonetheless seemed inordinately tense throughout, as if his sometimes capacity for charm and warmth were blocked. At this particular 1970 coffee hour, many of the people there fidgeted self-consciously —most perceptibly when Burns repeated his "subtle inferiority of spirit" theme. One of his brightest moments was at the low-income Kalihi Valley Housing, where as Grandfather Burns he warmly admonished the children to study hard and stay out of trouble—Burns as patriarch of the extended Burns family.

This was more than a put-off, although it was clear that Burns and his staff wanted as little contact at this point with the working press as possible. The simple fact was that nobody except Burns knew where he would be, except for major events. Burns' attitude toward the campaign extended beyond the press to his own campaign staff, who would sit in line outside his office waiting to find out what Burns thought on a given matter.

Burns himself would say he never attended a campaign committee meeting, a heresy of heresies, in that American political folklore demands late-night strategy sessions with the candidate surrounded by his advisors, arguing among themselves. But however unexciting, however little Burns had to say, the Burns campaign moved like a glacial force—combining as it did a massive organizational effort with elaborate electronics. Even though Burns avoided traditional stump oratory, the organizing capacity of his campaign work force brought him face to face with far more voters than reached by any of the other three candidates.

As early as the legislative session, Robert Oshiro had launched the first of a series of dinners to revive support in Burns' Democratic strongholds on Oahu. Tickets ran $3 apiece, and were spread by long-time Burns loyalists, party workers, patronage employees, union organizers, and the individual organizations of legislators.

Crowds for these dinners on Oahu ranged from four hundred to a thousand or so, and Burns made a point of trying to shake every hand, moving up and down the rows of tables, a word here, a word there.

Burns—as always erect and suited in dark blue—was a master of the politician's art, being at once charming, courteous, and humble. He had a memory for obscure, little people and once when a diminutive, shy lady wished him luck, he had said, "I'll need it, thank you," then asked, "Say, do you still have your hairdresser's shop?"

"Ah, Mister Governor, you remember that!"

In the endless round of campaign events, one reporter sometimes took with him his three-year-old son, and Burns never failed to take his hand. "How are you, young man?"

"Daddy, was that the governor?" This could not be the man who was being subjected to such harsh criticism.

The format of the Oahu dinners usually called for a brief testimonial talk by a politician of the district, followed by a tape-narrated slide show which pumped up the imagery of Burns as a contemporary visionary. Burns himself would say something brief and humble in tone, such as, "I'm a little bit embarrassed. Whatever I am today is because of you people." *Okage sama de.*

Oshiro's first Oahu dinner for Burns was in Wahiawa, followed by dinners in Waipahu, Kalihi, Aiea, Waianae, Moiliili, and Kaneohe, all of these areas being largely nonhaole neighborhoods, most in fact being heavily AJA neighborhoods.

Burns touched his Neighbor Island bases at Sunday meet-the-governor parties, a break in the tedium of rural and small-town life costarring the governor and a variety of Waikiki celebrities: Don Ho, Al Lopaka, and Zulu. A Neighbor Islander got this, and all the food he could eat, for only a dollar. The Kauai party drew several hundred people, the Big Island 1,500, and Maui an amazing total estimated at 6,000.

But the biggest audience, the TV audience, needed no organizing. After the warmup round of "Think about It," Jack Seigle followed with sixty-second spots showing Burns in action, playing on the 1970 legislative program.

A sample: "The Burns one-hundred-million-dollar housing program . . . is the strongest housing legislation this state has ever seen. In fact, it is the most comprehensive in the nation." State construction of a new Honolulu stadium, another 1970 legislative act, combined Burns the old sportsman with fast-paced baseball action. "John Burns didn't make a lot of speeches. He went to bat for us, and he got the job done. That is the kind of governor he is. Think about It." Just at that moment, a batter swung hard, connected solidly, and then—stop-action. It was one of those swings which one knew was good for a double, or triple, or perhaps a home run.

For the environment, the governor was pictured on the grass, clad in sports clothes, tumbling and tossing with his grandchildren.

"Every father and every grandfather has special reasons for wanting a beautiful world.

"That's one reason why Governor Burns, working with the state legislature, got us the most comprehensive program of environmental control our state has ever seen," an office of environmental quality control, a half-million dollars to start mass transit, an off-shore runway to cut jet noise from the airport, pesticide control —all 1970 legislation.

An oceanography ad spliced Governor Burns supporting the new industry to Grandfather Burns and the little children watching the porpoise show at Sea Life Park.

On they went—the TV ads showing Burns laboring at his desk in the dark of the night, Burns in a yellow hard-hat talking to construction workers, Burns talking to students, Burns talking at a neighborhood meeting, Burns philosophizing on the back steps of his house ("I represent every single solid citizen of the state. . . ."), Burns pushing the First Lady in her wheelchair.

Perhaps the best of them all was a collage of testimonials, which in sixty seconds ran through one-liners by sixteen people, mostly Burns' staff members and political allies: ". . . the man of change . . . brilliant . . . very knowledgeable . . . people somehow seem to forget the blood, sweat, and tears . . . great governors encourage all of us. . . ."

Dan Inouye closed it: "If you get to know him, you'd like him."

18
Catching a Wave

No doubt for John Burns these days were the darkest of the campaign, but had he bothered—as he said he had not—to tune in his television set on August 27, he might have been heartened. This was the date of the first showing of a half-hour film on John Burns, the result of many months of work by the San Francisco firm of Medion Inc.

Its title was: *To Catch a Wave.*

The film was released in the middle of the land use commission controversy, at a time when Burns' own poll found him and Gill running even—in deadlock.

Honolulu's political reporters, at least a few of them, at the time were groping for new ways to cover electronic campaigning, but typically the major headlines and stories of August 27 were devoted to yet another of the platform gatherings which Burns had missed. On this particular day Sam King, addressing the Chamber of Commerce, had been quoted as charging that Burns had "seriously damaged the most priceless of all executive resources, the public confidence.

"We don't have a credibility gap in Hawaii," King contended. "We have a credibility chasm." King proceeded to make one of his more cogent speeches, this one on ethics. His Republican primary opponent, D. Hebden Porteus, hacked away at student unrest, promising that if he were governor he would deal more vigorously than had John Burns with disruptive student protestors at the university.

Tom Gill got the laugh of the day. Gill said he was sorry that Burns—Jack, as Gill invariably referred to him—had not attended, but that this businessmen's audience might see Burns on television that night. Gill added, "I understand some of you helped pay for it." This no doubt being true, the audience laughed, and Gill seemed to have pleased himself with his quick wit.

Gill was only vaguely aware that in May of 1970, Medion Inc., under Lennen and Newell Pacific contract, had dispatched a film crew from San Francisco. For two weeks, the local agency had guided a Medion crew through some two hundred interviews, covering Burns' family friends, administrators, and political allies.

In the process the Medion crew shot twelve miles of film at sixteen millimeter, which, according to television technicians, was enough for more than thirty-six hours of viewing time. The editing process, therefore, had discarded seventy-two of every seventy-three feet of film, retaining only the most incisive footage. The result was more than biography—it was impressionistic artistry. Because it moved so fast, much is lost in point by point description; it was the net impression which made *To Catch a Wave.* In its variation of pace, color, and emotional appeal, it drove home a mystique. It drove home the otherwise inexplicable charisma of a man who would not state his own case, of a lofty father figure who also was part of the humblest of the crowd: steadfast, enduring, self-effacing, if stern then also warm of heart.

While highbrows would dismiss *To Catch a Wave* as syrup and nonsense, more to the point was the fact that the highbrow vote in a Democratic primary amounted to very little. *To Catch a Wave* was good because it was not highbrow, because it was sprinkled generously with halting English and fluent pidgin, because in a convincing way it conveyed how the Great Father belonged to the people.

The opening scene flashed on the governor driving over the Pali, then on the governor dedicating a space laboratory, then on Burns in his office talking into a telephone: "Arthur, I've established that some people was going over to Maui. We have troubles on Maui?" Fadeout Burns, cut to Fujio Matsuda, Burns' transportation director: "I don't think he's just dreaming up a utopia that we can never achieve. He's thinking about an achieveable future for us." Fadeout Fujio Matsuda, cut to the ever-present Dan Aoki: "When you're riding on top of a wave, you just sit on the wave. You just go. . . ." You just go.

The waves rolled in, a brilliant blue, the epitome of beloved and idyllic Hawaii, as the Beach Boys came across in loud rock . . . catch a wave.

David McClung, sitting in the majesty of the senate chamber over which he presided, marveled aloud at the governor's capacity for "staying on top of almost everything that's going on in this government."

Then there followed more of Burns at work: ". . . so you folks are going to have to have a closer relationship and a basic understanding of what might be. . . ."

On the Capitol steps, Burns was confronted by critical students who transmitted very harsh vibrations. Why had he not signed the abortion bill? "Because I personally differ very much with it. If it was left to me entirely, I would have vetoed it."

But then why had he not vetoed it?

"Because it wouldn't do any good. . . . The Bishop deals in blacks and whites. It's wrong or right. I don't deal in there. I've got to deal in shades of grey."

Oceanographer Tap Pryor led the viewer through the mysteries of the Pacific, telling how Burns had supported the exploration: "He's absolutely dedicated. He's, he's, got personal integrity. He can take any kind of criticism to do what he thinks is right. He never pushes himself. He's always given the credit out around, work, all kinds of things. People don't realize how much of a human he is. He really loves people."

Daniel Inouye expanded on love: "I'm convinced that this guy has had a love affair . . . with Hawaii. It's actually a love affair. He's in love with the people. He's in love with Hawaii."

Inouye, over breakfast with his political father, unfolded a citizen's letter concerning a park which, Inouye was certain, the governor would consider carefully. The U.S. senator then proceeded to tell Burns about his four-year-old son, cut off in Washington from Hawaii, so that the boy had to take swimming lessons: "Of course it's inconceivable for someone from Hawaii not knowing how to swim. So I asked him what happened. He said, 'Well, I went to the big boys' pool,' and he jumped in and he sank."

Burns chuckled. Gubernatorial aide Ed Rohrbough explained that Burns has a sense of humor, but "he's no Bob Hope." Burns followed with a joke about a gambling bust in the old cop days.

Then Burns' son, James Seishiro Burns: "Back in the old days I don't recall my father laughing when I was a little boy. I really don't. I recall him as one serious human being. . . . Obviously now that I reflect back on it he must have had a million problems."

Then Burns' brother, Edward: "He finished up high school here at St. Louis, started at the University and was working part-time for the *Star-Bulletin* and, uh, he met his wife Bea."

The fragile First Lady recalled the courting days of forty years ago. "I was very much impressed because Jack put his coat down on the sand for me to sit on."

Burns himself talked about raising the boys: "As they grew up they were assigned jobs around the areas. The smallest boy, he had the front yard, circling around the house. The oldest boy had the back yard, to keep it trimmed."

Ed Burns again: "During his first years of his political efforts, until he got elected delegate, I would say this was nip-and-tuck as far as income and getting along was concerned."

The First Lady: "There he was, just a young man with a completely paralyzed wife. We lost one child. . . ."

Son James Seishiro again: "In my mother's case, she finally decided, for whatever reasons, and I'm sure it was because my father stood behind her—she decided that she was going to make the best of it. And she always has."

Governor Burns: "She did her full job in raising the children. . . . In fact I did less than most fathers. . . ."

Nadao Yoshinaga, in the senate chambers, his voice as always coming through gut-level, trembling on the edge of rage: "In spite of the hurts he suffered, in spite of the guys who tried to destroy him, in spite of the fact that he believes some guys are still bad— basically he believes that most people, possibly all people, most people are honest, kind, loving people."

Part-Hawaiian Myron Thompson, driving in his car, talked about a strong feeling on Burns' part for history: "He has a book on his desk that he keeps pretty close to. It's the writing of some of King Kalakaua's memoirs. And he refers to that book. . . ."

Nadao Yoshinaga again: "I think he is a difficult man to get to know. I don't know whether it's because it's the kind of upbringing he had—the military style here, police officer. I don't know if it's because of the nature . . . he actually is a shy man. I don't know whether it's because he feels surrounded a good deal by people with college education—that he seems to have this insecurity.

"I don't know. Maybe that's the reason he looks so tough, so hard, so stone-faced."

Then statehood. So many had been skeptical. So many had thought statehood would never come. Even Aoki, the truest of the true believers, had been uncertain: "Even at that time, working alongside him, I had great doubts whether he was going to get statehood, until one day he came in and he said, 'Dan,' he says, 'All the ducks are laid. There is nothing more we can do. It's all in the hands of God.' "

More doubting students followed, students who could not understand what if anything Burns had done as governor. Aide Bill Cook and Shunichi Kimura, mayor of Hawaii, explained this away.

First Bill Cook: "Very frequently I've known of things that have occurred in the administration that I thought would be extremely newsworthy. Trying to get him to agree to me putting out a release on them was like pulling teeth.

"He would say, 'It's the game, not the name,' and so the result was it went unnoticed."

Mayor Kimura, sitting by the lava rock shore of his island, recalled Burns saying, " 'I'm a workhorse, not a showhorse.' And this is typical of the governor."

John Burns on Burns pursued this theme: "If anything I can be it's an organizer. And I do it better in small groups where you can do it, rather than in the mass media.

"I'm not a mass media type of individual.

"I don't like it.

"I don't like the stage.

"I don't like the posing."

One of Burns' long-time campaign workers, "Major" Okada of Waipahu, told how he had coached Jack on handling the stage: "Don't be like me, you know. Don't wear only aloha shirt. You're running for high office. Learn how to wear necktie and coat and be a little bit dignified.

"So he said he never forget that, you know. He always wear necktie and coat when he ran for office."

Finally James Burns, again: "My view of my father when I was small was he was God, he was king, he could do no wrong. I'm sure he swore, but I never heard him swear. I'm sure he's as human as the next man, but he always, at least within my view, controlled himself to the point where I never saw him do anything wrong— except, perhaps, lose that Irish temper once in a while."

John Burns nonetheless appeared to be human, seated on his back steps, dressed in an aloha shirt, his face muscles taut, his voice quavering in temper: "Taking a stand is anything anybody can do. The governor or chief executive of the nation is not a guy going around taking stands. That's the way to absolve yourself of any responsibility is taking a stand. . . . Any damn fool can take stands.

"And I say damn fool," his voice rising. "Any fool can take a stand.

"Does that make sense? Take stands?"

To Catch a Wave faded in soft music, leaving the governor pruning a tree in his lawn, remarking gently to his Beatrice on the fruits and blossoms.

With one foot of every seventy-three feet of film saved from the wastebasket, this was John Anthony Burns: above it all, a part of it all; a kinglike figure who swore and garbled his syntax; a lover of Hawaii, in spite of those who had tried to destroy him; a giant of integrity who disavowed taking stands.

To Catch a Wave played nine times before October the third, five on prime time, and with each time slot being carefully selected so as not to bump any of the favorite TV shows.

Adding six time slots in the general, Lennen and Newell would claim that *To Catch a Wave* reached six of every ten voters.

To combat Burns' eighteen one-minute TV spots and *To Catch a Wave*, Tom Gill had eight one-minute spot ads. Whereas Burns' were carefully phased for a crescendo effect, Gill's dribbled out of the darkroom in no apparent pattern. Burns' *Think about It* series had started in May; Gill's ads weren't on the air until after his July kickoff.

Still, given Gill's skimpy budget, he secured a reasonably smooth ad run, although not so tightly edited as Burns', nor so fast-paced, but warming Gill up and also portraying him as a man of action. The essential aim of Gill's ads was the same as Burns'; that is, to tug at the voter's emotions. Gill, instead of rolling on the lawn, strolled through the woods with his family. But the relative shortage of film and lack of precision editing showed through. In one ad, in which Gill paused to toss a football with a son, one of Gill's passes careened off to the boy's left. It was the kind of pass which demands a mumbled apology—the vigorous lieutenant governor looked like a dud with a football.

Production costs told part of the story. For this, Burns had laid out $152,000, compared to Gill's $14,500—Burns' TV production budget amounted to three-fourths of Gill's entire campaign budget. While the difference in spending on air time was substantial, it was not nearly so great as for production. Burns spent $68,586 for TV time, plus $32,214 for radio time, for a total of just over $100,000.

By comparison Gill spent $34,800 for TV time and $20,500 for radio time, for a total of $55,300.

Put another way, Burns spent just shy of twice what Gill spent on putting his message across, and Burns outspent Gill ten times over in producing the message.

While the Burns campaign blitzed the air waves, some of Gill's people clung hopefully to the idea of a backlash against the lavishness of Burns' TV, particularly in light of Burns avoiding Gill on the campaign platform. During the closing months of September, when Burns sidestepped meeting Gill personally on six separate occasions, Gill took the opportunity to play on the idea, charging that problems are not solved by "hiding behind TV tubes."

"I regret my loneliness up here. I understand I break up every meeting Jack plans to attend, just by accepting."

Gill's running mate, Vincent Yano, also came in with a biting attack: "I'm becoming increasingly bothered, because today you can buy an election. I hate to think this is going to happen in Hawaii. Are we going to buy candidates on the basis of a slick image? If this is the way we're going to have people elected, it's a pretty sad state of affairs."

Yano said that after watching *To Catch a Wave,* he had found himself wondering, "How can I help this nice old man?"

Sam King for his part described Burns as the canned candidate, "hiding behind the silver screen.

"I feel that it is not only a public official's responsibility to stand up and speak out on the issues—it is his duty," King said. "There are a number of issues we should be discussing, but so far the opposition has retreated behind the silver screen, backed up by a battery of advertising men and movie makers. I am told that this is known as the canned candidate approach to campaigning, but I don't buy the idea of packaged politicians."

The Burns forces simply ignored the barrage, forging ahead with new variations of electronic packaging. One innovation extended electronics to the neighborhood coffee hour circuit through a multipurpose system dubbed the "Aikane" program—the word *aikane* meaning friend in Hawaiian. Burns' neighborhood workers took out Aikane booklets from headquarters, in turn enlisting acquaintances as new aikanes, and listing in the booklets the new names, addresses, and telephone numbers.

The filled Aikane booklets were sorted at headquarters, and when a sufficient number of names had been collected, a campaign worker would organize a coffee hour featuring—if Burns were absent—either an extra filmstrip of *To Catch a Wave* or Don Horio's tape-narrated slide show.

Beyond organizing and expanding the mailing list for campaign literature, perhaps the most effective dimension of the Aikane drive was to heighten a supporter's sense of identity and involvement—a part of the Burns family. Although a stock item in campaigning, Burns' brochures also were remarkable, simply because of their variety, bulk, and cost. Lennen and Newell produced three different booklets on Burns, one in high-cost color, and an array of one-sheet flyers, some simply reinforcing the generalizations of the TV ads, others bursting with statistical details. For example, during the Burns years, the amount of money spent on each school student had almost doubled; salaries for beginning teachers had gone up 70 per cent; the number of classrooms had climbed from 5,400 to 7,400. Passenger traffic at the airport had increased five times over, airport cargo had tripled, appropriations for airport construction had gone from less than $2 million to over $73 million, and so on. Going into October, Burns had spent $89,000 on brochures and another $24,000 on posters, well over four times Gill's total of $24,400.

19

The Strange Calm

With less than a month of campaign time left until voting day, in early September polls on the Democratic primary race showed John Burns and Tom Gill still in a dead heat, some polls with a slight edge for Burns, others with a slight edge for Tom Gill. In these several polls, the number of undecided voters remained remarkably high, 10 to 15 per cent. Perhaps because of this, a curious calm, a sense of quiet desperation, descended on this battle, in marked contrast to the hot months of July and August—the month of September turned out to be peculiarly dull, even though it was the homestretch.

Burns, after his emotional speech on September 3 following Wilbert Choi's death, generally reverted to the role of the quiet man of Washington Place.

Gill continued criticizing the lavishness of Burns' television campaign, and also Burns' absence from the platform. But for the most part Gill drifted back more and more to his old issue speeches —housing, mass transit, and so forth, by now so oft-repeated that they were no longer news, his campaign gems dulled by overexposure, and also by everyone more or less agreeing with him.

The campaign, because of its unprecedented early start, had been going on for several months, and a sense of numbness seemed to pervade the public, the press, and sometimes even the campaigners. It was a month for foot-slogging. The media campaigns ground on. Burns' troops mounted a massive door-to-door drive distributing brochures. Gill's did likewise, led by kids, who were up as early as four and five in the morning shoving Gill propaganda into the hands of bus riders.

By now the rightness of their cause was for them such an established fact that perhaps they did not wonder overly long at the symbolism of a Gill fund-raiser in early September. While ever the critic of the fat-cats, Tom Gill staged his own $100-a-plate dinner in his desperation for campaign money. The assumed moral superiority of campaigning on a shoe-string budget, the in-touch Democratic party politics of stew and rice for a dollar, now was dead for certain. Gill's explanation—that this wasn't his decision but rather the decision of his finance managers, that there was no suggestion of favoritism for financial supporters—sounded as lame as the other finance disclaimers of 1970.

Most of Gill's late money was channeled into doubling his advertising run in the Japanese press and the Japanese-language stations, Gill strategists by now being actively concerned that the AJA vote was drifting.

Finally on September 21 Gill, knowing that he had not gone over the top in the preceding several weeks as he had expected, pushed Burns for a televised debate—something which most entrenched politicians have avoided since 1960, when Richard Nixon accepted John Kennedy's challenge to debate with such negative consequences.

In a letter written for public consumption and addressed to his opponent, Gill started with a "Dear Jack."

Gill said: "This campaign has been subject to mounting criticism because of the excessive amounts of money spent on slick public relations. The voters have been deprived of the time-honored opportunity to see and hear major candidates in face-to-face appearances where they may respond to the same questions, and be judged on their answers.

"Unfortunately . . . you have studiously avoided any such appearances with me."

Gill ticked off the platform confrontations which Burns had missed, assured Burns that the encounters had been friendly and reiterated how lonely he had been on stage.

"More important is the fact that it casts a cloud on the Democrats, who in the past have always been willing to discuss both their differences and programs openly and with all who were interested.

"The purpose of this note is to give you a chance to correct this deficiency before the primary."

And, condescendingly, Gill added, "Please don't take this as an attempt to embarrass you in any way. I don't think it should. You are perfectly capable of handling yourself in public. . . ."

Burns' response, like Gill's, was written for the public and addressed to his opponent. In contrast to Gill's "Dear Jack," Burns started with a stately "Dear Mr. Lieutenant Governor."

Unfortunately, Burns said, his campaign schedule would not allow him to engage in a television debate.

But, further, "Let's be frank about this public question-answer period you propose. You know, and I know, that in a very real sense, we have been 'campaigning' for four years.

"I have used deeds.

"My campaigning has been to serve Hawaii's people with all my heart and soul and all the special abilities—such as they may be —which the Almighty has given me to use."

The people knew where he stood, having watched him as delegate, as governor for eight years, as one who had worked closely with the legislature for "the poor, the jobless, the educationally deprived, the middle-income families, as well as all other segments of our society, and for the environment of Hawaii."

Burns cited his coffee hours, media interviews, and Island-hopping, disagreeing "with you strongly for implying in your letter that the people of Hawaii have not had a chance to meet with me face to face, or to question me. ... I have answered countless questions, and there are very few new ones to be asked."

Burns, privately so distrustful of the press, went on to say that Hawaii's press had given more and better coverage to politics and government than "any state in the Union, in my opinion."

The governor closed his letter to Gill as he did letters he wrote everyone: "Aloha, and may the Almighty be with you and yours always."

The Saturday night that Gill proposed for the debate, September 26, Burns left Honolulu to campaign on the tiny Island of Molokai.

Gill went ahead with a solo act to what must have been a small TV audience, bereft as the show was of the drama of Burns and Gill squaring off face-to-face. Gill came off smoothly, injected several deft one-line jokes, and explained in understandable terms some of the intricacies of housing, land use, mass transit, and the like.

It was one of Gill's best performances, and some of his people were anxious to rerun the hour show, Ed Joesting in particular. But it was too late to buy time slots.

Time had run out, and in this campaign only one spark of drama was left, the last swing of the candidates through the Neighbor Islands.

While the much-acclaimed Burns-Gill fight dragged tediously through the closing weeks of September, Sam King in the Republican primary came under increasing fire from Hebden Porteus. Although not apparent at the time, this thrust by Porteus—while not surprising in light of King's lead, nor in light of King's having gone back on his word to Porteus—would create a sensation on primary election night, and also would heavily influence the general election.

King found Porteus still doggedly pursuing him, making of him the antithesis of law and order. At first King had ignored the challenge, rejecting Porteus' demand for a TV debate by calling on Porteus to join him in attacking the "Burns-Gill administration." This was a verbal illusion necessitated by King's not knowing whom he would face after October 3.

King's apparent intent was to continuously ride such mainstream issues as housing and pollution, being personally cast as more dynamic and in tune with the times than John Burns, more approachable and reasonable than Tom Gill. But, pressed by Porteus, King had wavered to protect his political right flank.

King's most vulnerable point was the marijuana issue, and here Porteus attacked hardest. King, before announcing his candidacy, had been quoted as saying, "I do not think possession of marijuana should be a crime," adding that he nonetheless opposed the use of marijuana and supported continued prosecution of distributors. Once a candidate, King rolled back from that position, contending that the reporter had misunderstood, but that he—King—hadn't bothered to set the record straight at the time, not knowing that he would become a political candidate.

Further, King said, what he had meant to convey was that mere possession of marijuana should not be a "serious crime."

King then fell back to the position of a judicial council which he had participated in as a judge.

The council had reviewed the entire penal code, recommending far-reaching changes for legislative consideration, and the section on marijuana had proposed that possession of a kilo (2.2 pounds) should be a felony, and that possession of anything less than a kilo should be a misdemeanor.

Understanding that a kilo is a great deal of marijuana, Jack Orr, Porteus' press secretary from Spencer-Roberts, had bought a kilo of tobacco and had rolled the entire kilo into marijuana-sized cigarettes. Then Porteus had called a press conference to attack King's new kilo-or-less position on the evil stuff.

As the cameras rolled, Porteus dumped Orr's boxful of marijuana onto a table, making a veritable little mountain, six or so inches in height.

Porteus wanted to know if this much marijuana was not enough to justify a felony rap. Or if someone was going to smoke all of this stuff by himself. Or would this possessor not in fact be a pusher, spreading a dirty business.

Of course, Porteus went on, a youngster should not be harshly punished "for possession of two marijuana cigarettes or trying marijuana out of curiosity.

"But possession of a kilo of marijuana is definitely a different story."

King, in a sort of rear-guard action, bought full-page advertisements in both the *Honolulu* and *Beacon* magazines, which circulate mainly in affluent and therefore largely Republican homes.

Headlined "Sam King Speaks Out on Marijuana," the copy had led off by quoting King as saying, "Marijuana is unquestionably bad for our young people."

People who followed the details of the esoteric issue far enough found King actually going Porteus one better on policing marijuana traffic; King proposed that the airports be fully patrolled by watchdogs to sniff it out.

Hebden Porteus was not to be outdone.

Although forced off the air in August for lack of money, which had been largely shut off by King's entry and the unfavorable polls, Porteus had TV advertisements back on the air through September, laced with "scare" images. There was, for example, a sixty-second spot revolving around what purported to be the frightening distortion of reality caused by psychedelics. And even though there had been no student riots in Hawaii, the Porteus ads nonetheless flashed on scenes of student rioters—the suggestion being that it could happen in Hawaii.

In his personal campaigning, Porteus completed the remarkable transformation from master conciliator to outspoken advocate with lines such as, "Let me make one thing clear to you, and that is this." Or, "I'm making myself extremely clear on a lot of issues."

Or, "I believe the people of this state are tired of wishy-washy positions, being on one side of an issue today, on another side tomorrow." Porteus also was given to portraying himself as "fed up" with any number of things, with crime, with permissiveness, with the encroachment on Island life of the hippies. Mainland hippies in 1970 were a strangely compelling issue, particularly in the rural areas where many had chosen to live.

On September 19, Porteus ran a ten-hour, all-night talkathon, hammering away on such favorite themes as stiffer penalties for prostitutes. ("If it's in jail, it's not for sale.")

And then on September 24, Porteus mass-mailed a brochure called "Compare" to every Republican household.

From one side of the brochure, Heb Porteus beamed over a caption which quoted D. G. Anderson as saying, "Heb Porteus is a moderate. You'll find him in the main stream." King was on the opposite side over a caption quoting former Governor Quinn: "King leans more to the liberal side."

Four of the six "Compare" points dwelt on the permissiveness issue.

On marijuana (again): Porteus opposed legalization, but King was stuck with his old statement: "I do not think possession of marijuana should be a crime. . . ."

On hippies: Porteus opposed a hippie aid station. King was advocating one.

On judicial sentencing: Porteus wanted "firmness in the judiciary," while King, completely out of context, was quoted as saying, "When I was on the bench I would never send anyone to jail if I could help it." In fact, King had said he disliked sending anyone to Oahu Prison because he considered it a snakepit.

On adultery: Porteus favored upholding "the integrity of the family unit," while King by contrast supported legal recognition of common-law marriage. In conveniently overlooking the fact that common-law marriage is not adultery, this portrayed King as the friend of adulterers—none of whom presumably were of Republican stock.

At the bottom of this brochure, Sam King's inflammatory charge of the 1954 campaign was quoted: "No one is accusing all Democrats of being Communists, but they are politically obligated to the Communists." So the split-level implication of the brochure was that King was at once too liberal to represent Republicanism and too reactionary to attract Democratic voters in the general election campaign.

Yet another Porteus advertisement in this closing drive appealed to the hard-core rightists behind David Watumull, the third candidate. If they did not vote for Porteus, they would be saddled with a liberal in the candidacy of Sam King, the advertisement contended.

Sam King, in return, issued a statement bemoaning Hebden Porteus' advisors inducing Porteus to such low tactics: "Mudslinging is the trademark of the other party, and can only lead to party disharmony," King said. "I can only interpret this action as a frantic eleventh-hour, desperation move."

To cap this eleventh-hour drive, Porteus released a private poll which showed him within striking distance of King, a poll which scarcely anyone took seriously.

20
Last Days

It was early Thursday, October 1, 1970, just two days before the casting of votes in Hawaii's primary election.

On the morning flight to Hilo from Honolulu, one wondered absently over how long the campaign had dragged on, over how impersonal this conflict had turned out to be, and at the sense of battle fatigue which had infected the Oahu headquarters of the candidates.

In reality, the Hilo stop meant the campaign was in its death throes. But Hilo was still a small town, had just 27,000 people, and it pulsed with an infectious excitement, as if the votes of this Neighbor Island town would decide the fate of the candidates. In this new era of technological campaigning, six-figure campaign budgets, constant polling, and professional strategists, Hilo provided a ritual ending—the Grand Rally.

In Hilo, Thursday night was Republican night, to be followed on election eve by Democratic night. The crowd began gathering toward sundown on Thursday, converging on the bandstand at Mooheau Park, a clearing on the edge of Hilo Bay, where the tidal wave had struck in 1961. Seated on the bandstand, Hebden Porteus and Sam King somehow looked more important, more impressive, than they had in Honolulu. The Hawaii county band was playing, and the American flag was on prominent display—it was blown over once by a gust, but was quickly uprighted. And if God was dead in Honolulu, He lived on the Neighbor Islands. The rally started with a prayer to the Almighty, rendered by the mother of Elroy Osorio, a Republican candidate for the state senate. There also was a drawing for prizes, and Elroy Osorio's sister won a free weekend at the plush Mauna Kea Beach hotel on the Big Island's west coast. When Sam King's wife Anne won a ham, someone from the back of the crowd yelled, "This thing's been juiced." Hebden

Porteus, following a long line of local candidates, began his speech by saying he had been thinking of "demanding equal ham." In the crowd Porteus had a following of ranchers, wearing their straw cowboy hats, and they chuckled obligingly.

The gist of the Porteus speech, although toned down, was a reiteration of the "Compare" brochure, first gouging Sam King for drifting about on law and order, then gouging King as a proponent of far-out liberalism. Porteus for his part opposed "setting aside a beach where people swim naked." He likewise opposed common-law marriage—"I say let them go through a ceremony." Finally Porteus claimed "a welling up of feeling that I'm talking about things that are worrying people."

Sam King marched the political high road, contending to have revitalized the Republican party while simultaneously observing the Eleventh Republican Commandment: "Never speak evil of a fellow Republican."

That same Thursday night John Burns was on Maui and Tom Gill was on Kauai. At the Maui rally Burns, usually so stoical, surveyed a huge crowd with tears in his eyes, saying, "I don't deserve it."

The governor went on to touch briefly on campaign spending, noting that Gill's newspaper ads had been running far more heavily than his own. But, above money, Burns said, he wanted to stress that it was the loyal foot troops who mattered most.

"This manpower, based on faith and generous trust, cannot be bought by any amount of money," Burns said. "I look upon this aspect of the campaign as being incomparably more valuable than whatever money is being spent for television and newspaper advertising. Nobody can place any dollar value on the human effort that has been put in this campaign."

While Burns was warming up on Maui, Gill on Kauai was at last talking in his lowest key, telling a Lihue rally that people have been "saying bad things this season, but this week we will show how big we are." Strangely, given all that Gill had said in the past, Tom Gill allowed that Burns had been doing a good job as governor, but that the world was moving into a tangle of new problems, "moving in directions few of us can understand from day to day."

Then both Burns and Gill headed for Hilo, Gill arriving on the Big Island early Friday to be chauffeured around such hinterland towns as Kealakekua, Kailua-Kona, Naalehu, and Captain Cook. In Captain Cook, Gill was walking main-street shaking hands when a kid yelled from a school bus, "Hey, Meester Gill—you smile better than on TV."

John Burns in the morning toured Hilo's new county building, where he was greeted warmly. Then he ate lunch with several of his more prominent Big Island supporters, including the Island's young mayor, Shunichi Kimura. Like many people, Kimura had been torn both politically and personally by the Burns-Gill confrontation—he felt, on the one hand, a deep loyalty to Burns, but was more in tune with Tom Gill on many policy questions, particularly on the important question of placing tighter controls on development. On this last day of the campaign, Kimura was still stewing over his role, planning to boycott the night's rally in favor of a public dedication in the distant Kohala district. "Is this going to look like I'm copping out," Kimura kept asking his friends, and finally, convinced that indeed it appeared ridiculous, he decided on a quick return to the night's event.

During the hastily arranged lunch with Kimura and others, the governor was subdued, seemingly fatigued by the Island-hopping swing and by the emotional strain of the campaign. He replenished himself with a sizeable slice of pineapple, sandwiched between two pieces of bread. Then, following lunch, Burns and Mayor Kimura motored to a second restaurant, where U.S. Senator Inouye was holding forth on the merits of his candidate for the U.S. Senate, broadcaster Cecil Heftel. During this part of Inouye's talk, Burns ducked quietly into the restaurant's kitchen, shaking hands with the cooks, waitresses, and dishwashers.

When Burns had settled at a table in the back of the dining room, Inouye turned his talk to him, recalling the first gubernatorial campaign of 1959, when Burns had been so long delayed in returning from Washington to enter the race. This inside story, Inouye said, had never been told. Inouye went on to relate how in 1959, as soon as the statehood bill passed, he had called the then Delegate Burns in Washington, urging him to return immediately for a victory parade, "the return of the conquering hero," as Inouye put it. "Lo and behold, this man said no." Burns instead had taken his wife to the college graduation of their son James Burns, born to this paralyzed woman at the risk of her own life.

It had been her fondest dream, Inouye said, to live to see James graduate from college, and so it was that John Burns had chosen a private moment over the victory parade. "This is what took Burns away from Hawaii," what had chafed Gill and other Democrats in that year of defeat. John Burns, who had listened impassively, noiselessly tapping his fingers on the table top, slightly lowered his head at the end of Inouye's vignette. The luncheon gathering dispersed, and Burns continued his rounds at Hilo's new shopping center, while Inouye took Heftel downtown for display.

This allowed a few spare moments before the night's rally to peruse the frantic run of advertising in the two Honolulu dailies, particularly to note that the Burns agency of Lennen and Newell, with its exclusive control of media advertising, now had put a finishing touch on the campaign. In one advertisement, Burns was pictured behind his desk, looking as he did very much the part of a chief executive, intent, pencil in hand, captioned: "The Quiet Man of Washington Place." Also, "He is quiet, almost shy in manner. His philosophy is one of achievement, not self promotion. Where others seek the limelight, he avoids it." This advertisement cited spending on education as having increased fivefold in five years, and it also cited the 1970 housing law. A second advertisement showed a smiling John Burns standing erectly behind his wife Bea in her wheelchair—(only later would Lennen and Newell's Jack Seigle describe the newspaper campaign as "designed to hit the voter right where he lives—emotion.") Further back in the newspaper was a simple notice in bold type which urged, "Give Hawaii 30 Minutes Tonight."

"Watch Channel 13—At 7:30 P.M."

"It's important!"

On the eve of voting day, Seigle had decided to show *To Catch a Wave* one last time.

Gill's newspaper advertising, like Burns', was designed for its emotional appeal, but in contrast the Gill ads were fragmented.

A full-page Tom Gill smiled out at the reader, Gill wearing an aloha shirt, presumably as part of the effort to soften the lieutenant governor's image. Two other maverick Gill ads slashed and cut.

"Can money buy the office of governor?" asked Gill's splinter group of AFL-CIO unions.

"Yes it can. Governorships have been bought on the Mainland and now the same thing is being tried in Hawaii." The ad mentioned slick TV, then added: "We do not believe the voters should allow a candidate to be seen only on carefully selected television commercials and movies and be unwilling to stand on an open platform with his opponent."

The Honolulu Young Democrats exclaimed, "Hawaii CAN still be a paradise!" But, "Apathy is ruining our Islands."

"Our State faces problems which only Tom Gill as Governor and Vince Yano as Lt. Governor can solve."

For diversion, there also was an advertisement placed by Art Rutledge, Gill's labor ally, ripping into David McClung, the pro-Burns party chairman, who at the moment was sweating out reelection to the state senate.

Honolulu Mayor Frank F. Fasi, fighting his own little battles in city council races, was publishing full-page spreads condemning council candidates endorsed by the Burns-allied ILWU and AFL-CIO.

Such, then, was the newspaper reading on the day before the election.

After dinner it was rally time, and this night over a thousand people flocked to the bandstand at Mooheau Park, the crowd being obviously split into the two camps, pro-Burns and pro-Gill. Burns arrived before Gill and took his place behind the podium, dressed in a dark suit and tie. Then Gill came in, dressed in slacks and a short-sleeved white shirt with tie. Both were draped with maile leis.

They shook hands. "Hi, Tom." The words formed on Burns' lips. The two men had not seen one another for weeks, and this was their first and last meeting on a campaign platform—this was it. There was in the vast crowd an extraordinary sense of tension, heightening the illusion that the election's outcome after so many months would turn on events of the last moment. To the best knowledge of almost everyone there, based on an array of polls, Gill was assumed to still be holding his lead on his home base of Oahu, while Burns was considered to be substantially ahead on the Neighbor Islands. Even someone as close to the Burns campaign as Dan Inouye, for example, had said that day that Burns could only win by bringing in the Neighbor Islands on a big margin.

There was a breeze from Hilo Bay this Friday night, as there had been the night before, and the crowd was alive with banners and balloons. Burns and Gill, after shaking hands, sat down in adjoining chairs on the platform. Neither looked at ease, listening first to the lesser political figures, then to their respective candidates for lieutenant governor, Vincent Yano and George Ariyoshi. There was a strange twist to the night in that what was said by Ariyoshi and Yano told at least as much about the campaign as what Burns and Gill were to say later.

George Ariyoshi, the candidate of the incumbent, again turned to the past, to 1954, to the old days when many people in the Islands were in the grip of the plantation system. "I recall the days when our people were divided," Ariyoshi said.

"I recall the days when jobs were not available to all of us on an equal basis. I recall the days when no matter how able and how competent and how qualified people were, they could get up only to a certain level.

". . . And we were really divided into the first string and second string. And most of us could only qualify for the second string. And all this disturbed me very much."

As Ariyoshi had said so many times, John Burns had urged him into politics in 1954, and "I am very proud of the fact that in 1954 I did get involved."

Again, as at his kickoff dinner, Ariyoshi turned to his aspirations as a child who grew up in the tenement district of Honolulu. "I happened to make a decision when I was in the eighth grade to want to become a lawyer.

"And I remember going to my Dad and telling him, 'Pop, I want to become a lawyer.' And I remember my father, who was then a stevedore, who told me that I could have the shirt off his back in order to make my dreams come possible."

Now, Ariyoshi said, Hawaii was prospering, was united, its education system open so that diligent young people "can become anything and everything they want to."

The postplantation record spoke for itself. A governor's administration, Ariyoshi concluded, which could help bring about such change "is the best demonstrative record of the ability of government and people to meet the problems of the future, just as we have for the problems of the past."

Then Vincent Yano followed in the Gill vein, much as Ariyoshi had given a Burns speech.

Inevitably, Yano ranged over several of Gill's major issues, housing, traffic, and ethics in government: On housing, "We are falling behind daily. The family earning ten to twenty thousand dollars a year is unable to purchase a home today . . . yet we have had the necessary law in the book for years." And while traffic was not yet a Big Island problem, "the horrible traffic conditions in

Honolulu is grim evidence of our lack of planning and foresight. It is certainly tragic that of the billions of dollars we spent for super freeways that we didn't spend some of it for mass transit." Finally, on ethics, Yano recalled that Burns had vetoed an ethics bill which had received a prior clearance from Burns' own attorney general, and Yano asked, "Are we going to accept occasional irregularities and unethical conduct as normal . . . or do you have the right to demand and expect something more?"

Yano's speech moved from issues to core values, making it clear that he was talking of a very basic change in direction.

In Yano's words there could be heard the echo of generational conflict, and of agonizing questions about the relevance of the past to the future. Yano said, "We have emphasized consumer production, more spending, increasing technology, and an ever-increasing gross national product. Here in Hawaii we have major progress in the same terms—more highways, buildings, schools, land development." But, "Is this really progress? Are we going to stop this mad rush for material accomplishments, more gadgets, new inventions, and take a much needed break. . . . Are we going to measure success in terms of how much money we have, how big a house we have, or how many cars we own? With our vastly increased store of knowledge, are we going to continue our insane overuse of our precious, limited natural resources?"

Yano's closing remark would be from the Gill viewpoint wildly ironic: "When you scare people, they turn the other way and vote for the candidate who smiles and assures them that somehow everything will turn out all right."

To which Yano added, "We can't afford that luxury any more."

It was getting late, and babies slept in the arms of their mothers, but the crowd stayed, waiting for the main event.

For Burns, the applause was thunderous.

After acknowledging the rally's chairman, the sixty-one-year-old Burns turned to the forty-eight-year-old Gill and addressed him as "Mister Lieutenant Governor."

And then Burns gave the most traditional of Hawaiian greetings for an Island crowd: "Aloha. Aloha nui kakou. Alo-o-o-o-o-ha."

He talked of walking through Hilo that day, particularly of walking through its new shopping centers.

"And was I impressed. I was really impressed." When first elected in 1962, Burns said, "I can remember the empty stores. I can remember that the people didn't quite have the optimistic look that they have today. I can remember when I asked the storekeeper how was business? Wasn't very good. I can remember these things.

"As I went today there was a different look. We had an optimistic look. We had a look of hope, a feeling that we could answer our problems, and that we were meeting our problems."

Burns then slipped into the coded appeal for the vote of Neighbor Islanders, who so often see themselves as stranded from the center of power, populous Oahu.

"Hawaii is not one island," Burns said. "Hawaii is eight islands. The people of Hawaii are not the people of the City and County of Honolulu, but they're the people of the County of Hawaii, the County of Maui, the County of Kauai and the people of the City and County of Honolulu. We are one people."

Burns pressed the point. "Back in 1962, every Neighbor Island county was going downhill—sliding down from . . . 1946. As of today, every Neighbor Island county has gone up. People are working, people are employed, and people are able to support themselves."

Burns then humbly thanked the crowd for the high privilege of the governorship, and said, "I have tried to repay that trust and confidence you imposed on me"—again the theme of trust, loyalty, and of mutual obligation. "Hawaii is really an impossible dream, a dream of all people—race, color, and creed—working together, living together and causing for themselves a life in the future and a destiny among people of the Pacific.

"This is Hawaii. This is the place I believe in. And these are the people I believe in."

And here Burns' voice lowered, and the face muscles seemed to tighten.

"You have seen—and you know throughout the campaign—the things that have been done in the last eight years."

"Is this, then, the time to change, to stop that growth and progress, and to move to another hand . . . ?"

And then, "Mahalo. God bless everyone."

For the primary, Burns had finished campaigning.

Following Gill's introduction, the applause was hearty, but not quite so intense as it had been for Burns. As he had done on Kauai the night before, Gill again came on low-keyed, but the contrast to Burns' style still came through.

Addressed by his senior as "Mister Lieutenant Governor," Gill turned slightly over his shoulder to where the governor was sitting and said, "Glad to welcome Jack to the platform. It's real nice to see him."

Gill, being fond of quoting Shakespeare, then attempted an intricate twist on the story of Julius Caesar—Gill, in a paraphrase, bastardizing the eulogy delivered by Mark Antony, who at the great Caesar's funeral had rallied the people of Rome against Brutus.

Tom Gill, perhaps not content to be merely an honorable man, as was Brutus, dropped the dagger and leaped to the funeral bier, telling this Island crowd of people: "We are here to praise our friends, not to bury our enemies."

"We are here to say that we are proud, and I'm proud, of the record of the Democratic party in the last fifteen or twenty years.

"I think we've done well. I want to tell you here and now that I think Governor Burns has done well during his term in office. And I congratulate him for it."

The die had been cast. Gill could only hope to win, and the idea was to soften the hard lines within the party. "I want to tell you further that the party that has the ability to spring anew, meet the problems of the future—the solutions of the future—is the Democratic party. And this is the way it's always been, and this is the way it's always going to be.

". . . Friends, the point that I think we should make is that we have come a long way, but we have a long, long way to go.

"We have come through the battles of the fifties for equality of opportunity. We have come through the battles of the sixties, for the time when we were going to see our state develop and become a modern American society." But, "We are now facing the uncertainties and tribulations of the seventies, where an entirely new set of rules is being imposed.

"That result which was good yesterday may not be good today. . . . Many of the things we have done and done with all our hearts and minds are now doubtful and uncertain.

"Today is the beginning of a new decade. The seventies are going to require all of us to put our minds and hearts to the most severe test that we have ever faced."

Gill made a last appeal for starting the decade with "new talents, and certainly with new hope in your hearts." He added, "Because they're going to be a very tough period of years."

Gill turned and shook hands with John Burns a last time. They had a moment to talk—still seeming to feel uneasy in one another's presence—before their supporters rescued them, engulfing them, grabbing their hands, piling around their shoulders more leis. It seemed only appropriate when they drifted off the platform in opposite directions.

In Honolulu that night, Rick Egged and a few others in the Burns organization could see the down-to-the-wire atmosphere of Hilo for what it was—an illusion. They awaited the next day reasonably confident of victory, because in his last poll before the primary, Rick Egged had found that the largest voter group in the Democratic primary, Burns' traditional AJA support, had gradually swung from an even Burns-Gill split to being solidly pro-Burns. Specifically, the statewide sampling of 2,800 voters found AJAs coming down on the side of John Burns by a margin of 58.2 per cent to 34.8 per cent, while the Caucasian group—less than half the size of the AJA voter list—remained heavily pro-Gill, 59.2 per cent to 34.8 per cent. The balance, largely of Filipino-American and part-Hawaiian background, leaned substantially toward Burns: Filipino-Americans by 54.8 per cent to 40 per cent; Part-Hawaiians by 49.9 per cent to 41 per cent. The number of people professing to be undecided in the election had shrunk dramatically and, as if unconvinced by Gill, had opted for the familiar.

21

The Primary

Before the 1968 elections, the outcome of a vote had been a matter of suspense until long past midnight. The precincts had counted their votes by hand, and then had called the results in to Iolani Palace, where the running tally was chalked on a big board, the politicians and the press waiting and watching anxiously. Now in the new era of technology it was different. Tom Gill, as lieutenant governor, had computerized the voting system. To vote on Oahu or in Hilo, one merely punched a perforated hole beside a candidate's name, then dropped the ballot in a box. The guarded ballot boxes were driven to computer centers, and the press of the button yielded an election printout—the result of a year's campaign. If in theory the system was less prone to error, it also was less fun.

On the election day of 1970, both John Burns and Tom Gill rose early in Hilo. Gill took the first flight to Honolulu, looking out the window en route for a glimpse of the sun, for the sort of day when marginal and irregular voters would go to the polls to vote down John Burns, the candidate of the Democratic regulars. Burns took the next plane, having stayed over in Hilo long enough to attend his daily mass at St. Joseph's Church. There had been a light rain throughout much of the Island chain on this Saturday morning, October 3, but by midmorning the sky cleared and the sun shone brightly, an invitation to the irregulars—who have notoriously poor voting habits—to come to the polling booths. For one, Royce Higa, Gill's manager, felt reasonably assured of victory when he saw the sun. In 1970, however, there was a variable factor in voter turnout which was almost as unpredictable as the weather. This was the so-called closed primary, first instituted in 1968. The intent of it was to restrict Republican voters to the Republican primary, and Democratic voters to the Democratic primary. In effect it forced a person to disclose a party affiliation, therefore was widely resented, and in 1968 the voter turnout had dropped to 63 per cent. This contrasted sharply to the turnouts of 1954 and the years that had followed, turnouts which ran in the phenomenally high ranges of the eighties and nineties. On October 3, 1970, the percentage of voter participation would improve over 1968, but not greatly— from the low of 63 per cent in 1968, participation rose to 70 per cent of those registered and eligible. Because computerization allowed such an early vote count, by six o'clock that evening the senate chamber in the new Capitol was jammed with reporters. Television rigs covered most of the senate chamber floor, while the written press scattered around the fringe at tables—this was TV's story. At the nearby University of Hawaii computer center a technician secured a first printout, which was confined to the island of Oahu, and it was rushed to the Capitol. By 7:30 P.M., Dr. Dan W. Tuttle, who in precomputer times had created a sensation by calling elections on the basis of skimpy results, appeared on the television screen with a clipboard in hand and announced: "That's the ball game, unless there has been a massive computer error."

This was the ball game, because John Burns was leading Tom Gill on Oahu, where Gill always had been strongest—the Neighbor Island results, when they trickled in, would only broaden the Burns margin. Tom Gill, in his Capitol office on the fifth floor, surrounded by his family, knew there had been no massive computer error—Gill had devised the system, and he considered it foolproof.

Gill had lost.

Gill shortly went down to the senate chamber to the awaiting press corps and conceded defeat, adding, in a comment on the coming general election, "I'm a Democrat and I'll vote the Democratic ticket," but refused to specify that he would vote for John Burns. From the Capitol, Gill went to his King Street headquarters and was mobbed, hugged, and decked with leis by his followers. Many wept. Gill spoke briefly, stoically, attempting to lighten the gloom, saying, "Cheer up. Nothing is that bad." Defiantly many of the young sang *We Shall Overcome,* the civil rights protest anthem of the 1960s. "Deep in my heart Lord, I do believe—that we shall overcome—someday." Bitterness seeped through the headquarters, in remarks such as, "Winning an election boils down to one thing—money. Money equals power." And, "Just watch television, and it'll show you how to vote." There was a hint of bitterness in Gill himself. When asked if he was satisfied that he had done all he could, Gill said, "I don't know if I'd do anything different, outside of having another half-million dollars." From his headquarters Tom Gill went home and made plans for the next day —to hike in the mountains with his son.

He had defined the issues of the campaign long before, had played a large role in remolding public thought, had galvanized a mass following, had led all the early polls by wide margins, and had lost the election.

Of the 154,000 people who voted in the 1970 Democratic primary, Burns was given 82,000 votes, Gill only 69,000 votes. George Fontes, the eccentric who had run as a protest candidate in 1966, received the balance of 3,000 votes, a seventh of his 1966 total.

On the Republican side, the narrow margin of Sam King's victory was as much of a surprise as John Burns' solid margin over Tom Gill. Sam King, so long considered certain to overwhelm Porteus, had staggered through the primary campaign on a slim plurality, some 800 votes shy of the combined totals of Hebden Porteus and the ultrarightist David Watumull. The breakdown was 20,600 for King, 17,900 for Porteus, 3,300 for Watumull.

For Sam King, the showing was bad enough to raise speculation that had David Watumull not been in the race, Hebden Porteus might have won the nomination. The Porteus camp was quick to point this out, and also to heatedly blame the trial-heat polls for slowing down Porteus—particularly the widely publicized polls published by the *Honolulu Star-Bulletin*.* The Republican gubernatorial nomination, once considered such a valuable commodity, had plunged immeasurably in value.

In the lieutenant governor's race, Ralph Kiyosaki took the Republican nomination with 22,000 votes over Richard Sutton's 14,300 votes.

On the Democratic side, Burns' candidate, George Ariyoshi, swamped Vincent Yano by a margin of 80,000 to 40,000, with the

*For independent public service polling, 1970 was a bad year; many polls, including the *Star-Bulletin*'s, missed the mark. This may cast a shadow on the validity of polling in Hawaii for years to come. The last published *Star-Bulletin* poll before the primary showed King running away with the Republican nomination, and Burns and Gill in a dead heat. A never-published poll conducted in the campaign's final week picked up a strong surge for Gill, suggesting a substantial Gill victory. Mayor Frank F. Fasi, with his own polling group, predicted on election day a Gill victory—Fasi apparently picking up the same surge. One can only speculate that Gill had a large constituency who never actually voted—among short-time residents, the young, and the poor, whose sketchy voting habits have been documented nationally. The upwardly mobile middle class and the union-influenced working class vote far more consistently, and among these groups Burns had a substantial majority. As predictive work, Rick Egged's polls taken for Burns were amazingly accurate.

balance of 25,000 votes going to Honolulu City Councilman Charles Campbell.

The spotlight of the election night fell on John Burns, because he was the nominee of the majority Democratic party, because he had survived a dramatic challenge, because he not only had survived but had triumphed by a surprisingly solid margin, and also because of Sam King's lackluster vote total. John Burns, at sixty-one, having spent three decades in politics, having organized the modern Democratic party, having served two terms as delegate and two terms as governor, again was the man of the moment.

That afternoon, while his political fate was being decided, John Burns had napped. Around 6:30 he had risen, dressed, and then was picked up by his most illustrious protege, Daniel Inouye. First they had gone to Kuakini Hospital to see Nadao Yoshinaga, who that day had gone swimming off Ewa Beach, encountered a shark, and been stricken by a severe heart attack. Burns also visited a second man who, like Yoshinaga, had contributed enormously to the success of the campaign, Robert Oshiro, who had been brought down and hospitalized by the strain of the campaign. While saddened by the ill health of his two friends, John Burns was delighted by the people's vote of confidence, and he was expansive in the celebration of victory. When Burns entered his campaign headquarters on King Street, it erupted, and a smiling John Burns shook every hand, warmly thanking his people for their help, introducing one to another, "Meet my alarming friends." After greeting many people, and after enduring the explosion of flash bulbs and the glare of television lights, Burns walked down the street to Gill headquarters, but he found that his adversary had left. He talked with several of Gill's supporters, then at 1:30 in the morning, he and Inouye and others in his entourage made a ritual visit to the nearby Alakea Grill, the plain all-night coffee shop a block from the Capitol. This place held a special meaning for Burns and his people, because they had gone there in defeat on election night in 1959, when Burns first had run for the new state's governorship.

Inouye asked, "Remember?" and Burns nodded, perhaps remembering particularly that after his 1959 defeat he had been widely regarded as a political has-been, and that in 1970 he also had been prematurely written off into oblivion by many people. On this night in 1970, surrounded by his son James, by the George Ariyoshis, and others, Burns had further words of praise for his campaign work force: "You did a hell of a job. Who has people like I've got? And you should see the troops I have in the field," estimating the number at 10,000. "They said Gill had the backing of the kids, but you should see the young people I have. They just walked in and volunteered. And they've worked hard."

The conversation turned briefly to money and to *To Catch a Wave.* Burns said he had not yet seen the film, but of his television campaign generally he said, "We had to have it. It was the only way to present our record to the people." For his late-night breakfast, Burns ate scrambled eggs, crisp bacon, hashed-brown potatoes, and burnt toast, and then at three o'clock in the morning Burns got away for what every political figure, campaign worker, and newsman in Hawaii needed most—a night's sleep. He not only had won—he had won in grand style.

John Burns not only had come through the primary with momentum, but had done so without the expected dogfight. While Tom Gill had drawn hard lines as the aggressor, Burns had done nothing to escalate the sense of conflict in the primary. And as Burns had endured the primary, so had the attraction of the Democratic party label for the voters of Hawaii. Throughout the year, poll after poll had probed voter attachments to the two political parties, and invariably two of four voters would say Democratic. Only one of four would say Republican. The fourth would have no opinion, leaning neither way, and was probably the least likely of the four to actually vote. So despite two decades of internecine combat, culminating in the clash between Burns and Gill, the label of the party had retained its appeal, and seemed in fact to be as popular as it had been in the initial triumph of 1954.

Very early in 1970, Sam King had said that unless he won the governorship, Hawaii not only would be a one-party state but would continue as a one-party state for twenty years. Now, surveying his situation, King might have thought that Hawaii *already* was a one-party state—King's prospects were that bleak, the Republican party that frail. On a personal level, King's image had suffered since that early spring day when he had doffed the black robe of the judiciary. Following his go-round with Porteus, Sam King seemed as weather-beaten as a long-time politician. In May, Rick Egged's trial-heat poll had showed an edge of 2 percentage points for King in a projected Burns-King runoff. But immediately following the primary, Burns looked like a runaway in the Egged poll: Burns at 50 per cent, King at 37 per cent, and 13 per cent undecided.

King had to rebuild momentum, had to organize a coalition of the disenchanted, and additionally had to attract people who already inclined toward voting for Burns. Further, King had only a month to do all this: Hawaii's primary and general elections fall in a shorter time span than do elections in any other state in the nation. King's only possible opening was an appeal to the 69,000 people who on October 3 had voted in the Democratic primary for Gill, coupled to a solid campaign for independents who had not voted in the partisan primaries. King could take this course, and also hope that lightning would strike.

On October 6, the Tuesday following the primary, King started his general election campaign by decrying stagnation in the Burns administration, a speech Tom Gill could have written. "Experience teaches us that entrenched, unopposed power tends to become apathetic, inefficient, and possessive," King said. "This has happened in Hawaii." Further, whatever good may have resulted from the 1954 Democratic movement, "over the past few years executive action has slowed down. People involved in the administration have slowed down, and needed programs have come to a standstill.

"A rather dead calm prevails over the government of our state. The Burns administration is tired." This in substance was pretty much King's approach, a critical but fairly subdued approach, until mid-October, when he would explode.

The Tuesday night of King's first speech, Burns and George Ariyoshi campaigned by going to the prize fights at the Honolulu International Center. But appearances aside, Burns had not been idle in reaching out for the Gill vote—as King was doing so openly. On election night Burns had described Gill as a man of large talents, and had said that Gill "has a great contribution to make." The next day, a Sunday, the governor had dialed the Gill residence, had asked for Mr. Gill, but Lois Gill had said her husband was out hiking with the children.

The governor said he was sorry that he had just missed the Gills twice the night before, first at their headquarters, then in the senate chambers. For her part Mrs. Gill said, "Now it's over. We wish you luck." The governor thanked her and said he had always thought of her as "a good trooper." As the conversation closed, Mrs. Gill said she was certain her husband would be in his office the next morning. The governor said he might take off work half a day, but that he would be sure to see the lieutenant governor later. Tom Gill, like Burns and King, was aware that by virtue of 69,000 votes, and despite the defeat, he retained some modest measure of political influence, and Gill still had a few moments left on the public stage. In essence his strategy was to calm down his own following in order to play for commitments on issues from the nominees.

While Burns did not make it to Gill's office that Monday following the primary, Cindy Yokono did. The twenty-three-year-old Youth For Gill chairman thought she would cheer up Gill. Instead she broke down in tears. Cindy Yokono told Gill they had done their best, yet the voters had not come their way, that because of this she felt alienated, thinking that the people had been so stupid. Cindy Yokono had told Gill, "Tom, you're so patient, but maybe we ought to take to the streets." Gill countered, "What would we have then? We'd just have chaos." Particularly, Cindy Yokono was embittered by the heavy nisei vote for Burns, thinking that the transitional AJA generation was so steeped in the concept of loyalty that it was blinded to the need for a change in direction.

Gill in his turn said that the times had not been right for a new liberal program, that much of the generation which had emerged from the plantations now thought, "We've made it, why can't you?" In this exchange between Gill and his young campaign worker, Gill then ranged over the history of social change in Hawaii and across the country, suggesting that it usually is a slow and evolutionary process. To this he added: "If not me, then your generation will put into effect what we wanted to do." Cindy Yokono would sit out the rest of the gubernatorial campaign, but would work in the Manoa area for Gill-aligned legislative candidates, as would many of those close to Tom Gill.

Following this encounter, Gill also granted a newspaper interview, in which he said his most immediate concern was how the young people took the defeat. He said, "If they survive it and learn from it, then that's great. If they don't, we've lost something very valuable. It's not a question of whether I lose active supporters. That's not important. I don't want to see them drop out of the political process. In ten or fifteen years they should be running this place, and they're very different from what we've got now." Gill also used the interview to pass the word to his people to relax for a few days: "The first week after an election is too early for people to make rational decisions. Emotions are high. It's better for people to have time to think about it."

Gill himself waited until 11:15 Friday morning, when John Burns made the short walk across the top floor of the Capitol to Gill's office. The two talked for about ten minutes, then Burns emerged to face waiting reporters, describing the meeting as friendly but saying nothing more. Gill ducked out the side door, apparently wanting to avoid comment on the conversation for the time being. In fact, negotiations were in progress. For his part Gill subsequently drafted a statement. Burns reviewed it and made several changes, questioning—for example—whether the housing problem was as severe as described by Gill in his draft. They then settled on the 1970 Legislature's description, that Hawaii was lagging by 40,000 housing units. And on Wednesday, eleven days following the primary election, John A. Burns and George Ariyoshi affixed their signatures to this statement. Its contents, which would sharply alter the tone and direction of the general election campaign, were to appear in the newspapers on Friday, October 16, midway in the brief general election campaign.

22
The General

From primary night on, a sense of frustration and desperation brewed in Republican Sam King's campaign. King himself, increasingly irritated by Burns' tactics, would erupt in bitter anger on October 16th. Events were going badly for King.

For openers, most of Gill's work force—far from bolting en masse to King—was following Gill's cue by sitting tight on the gubernatorial campaign. Badly dispirited, they held several meetings to nurse their wounds, then gradually scattered either to the beach or to the legislative campaigns of liberal Democrats. Gill himself was becoming increasingly involved in Cecil Heftel's battle against Hiram Fong for the U.S. Senate seat.

(The broadcaster Heftel, a millionaire and owner of Hawaii's largest TV station, KGMB, and also Dan Inouye's political protege, was proving himself an adept campaigner, making the U.S. Senate fight suddenly as much of a conversation piece as the Burns-King race.)*

The only visible support King had garnered from the Gill camp was a favorable introduction to some of Gill's workers at a postprimary luau, a last-minute endorsement from Art Rutledge, and the endorsement of a committee of university faculty (offset by a second committee, including Gill's Allen Trubitt, which endorsed Burns). The old Republican scenario of reaping victory from a

*Inouye pulled all the stops for Cecil Heftel, provoking a Fong allegation that Inouye was trying to cut him down with a two-pronged ethnic pincer—Inouye, the pride of the 1954 AJAs, pushing for the haole newcomer Heftel. When Fong finally returned to Washington to again take the oath of office, he created a national scene. He refused Inouye the standard role as fellow Hawaii senator of escorting him down the senate aisle. Unlike Inouye, Burns scarcely lifted a finger for Heftel, other than to make a *pro forma* eleventh-hour party endorsement. It is notable that Burns and Fong have a close working relationship, that both are tied to the ILWU (one of many reasons the union is the keystone of consensus), and that in turn the Fong forces did virtually nothing for Burns' opponent, Sam King. *Quid pro quo,* many thought. Simply put, the Establishment in Hawaii by 1970 was bipartisan, rhetoric notwithstanding.

Burns-Gill fight wasn't really panning out, and King also was plagued by disunity within his own party. Many of Hebden Porteus' workers joined Hiram Fong's campaign, and at least one group of Porteus backers not surprisingly met with Burns to volunteer support.

King met personally with Fong and went away expecting a resounding endorsement which was never forthcoming. One notch down the ladder, King's aides drafted a statement for Fong lieutenant Wadsworth Yee taking Burns to task on the Magic Island affair of 1969, but the statement languished on Yee's desk for a week and finally was issued by Republican State Rep. Andrew Poepoe. In yet another exercise in frustration, Phil Spalding reentered the picture as Republican national committeeman, searching for a dramatic event that would turn the tide in King's favor.

Spalding left for the Mainland hoping for two things: First, money for King from the Republican National Committee and, second, a demonstration of support by President Nixon.

Discussion centered on an airport rally, for which Richard Nixon would fly 5,500 miles from Washington in a show of interest in Hawaii and aloha for King.

This, Spalding believed, would dramatize the idea of an open line between Hawaii's Capitol and the White House, as had been the case when Burns' old friend, Lyndon Johnson, had been president. Spalding pressed the matter even though Nixon had lost the Islands by 50,000 votes in 1968, and despite the fact that King was privately sour on Nixon—an old score dating back to King's party chairmanship in 1953.

For his part, King remembered pleading with the then Vice-President Nixon, in the name of saving the party in Hawaii, to push hard in Congress for immediate passage of statehood and for confirmation of AJA Shiro Kashiwa to a federal judgeship. Neither materialized.

Nonetheless, Spalding discussed his 1970 gambit with Murray Chotiner, Nixon's old California political operative who had moved on to Nixon's White House staff.

Spalding outlined his appeal to Chotiner, who countered by saying, "The president doesn't move on generalities. Give me numbers." Spalding divulged a poll which showed King trailing. But Spalding insisted that support for King was picking up, and that enough voters remained undecided to give King a shot at victory.

Spalding felt that Murray Chotiner's attitude was encouraging, but he subsequently heard nothing from the Nixon aide.

Next Spalding tried a Jack Wrather of Los Angeles, who sat with Spalding on the party's national finance committee. Wrather relayed the answer, which was no.

The answer, Spalding reported Wrather as saying, "came from the very highest level," presumably meaning Nixon. So the president was not to grace Hawaii by involving himself in the gubernatorial race.

Next, Spalding asked Wrather, what of the possibility of the party turning loose money for King's campaign? Wrather replied that the party was interested in controlling the U.S. Senate. Gubernatorial races were low priority, and the party would pour money into Hawaii only if convinced of one thing—that Senator Fong was really in trouble.

Spalding said, "I've got to say Hiram is running a lousy campaign, but he still isn't going to lose."

Spalding returned to Hawaii with nothing from either Nixon or the national party, although he had raised a sizeable piece of change from Mainland business contacts, estimated in excess of $50,000.

King was pouring money into media advertising at a furious pace, outspending Burns, but the effort was amateurish by comparison. It was the result, one could speculate, of the chaotic shifting from one local agency to another, and from one national agency to another. King's TV advertising, for example, now hinged on something resembling a daily "news report," a camera crew following King on his day's hike, then hastily pasting together sixty seconds of "Sam the Man" in action.*

By contrast, Burns' advertising strategy never wavered from the course set six months earlier by Jack Seigle and Joe Napolitan.

A dash of Burns' running mate, George Ariyoshi, was simply injected into the one-minute spots and into *To Catch a Wave*, augmented by a five-minute show on Mrs. Burns, which was directed at the afternoon housewives' audience.

The platform encounters were a repeat of the primary campaign, with Burns only once appearing with King.

*Regarding Sam the Man, also regarding the hackneyed tone of the King campaign, baseball had its Stan "The Man" Musial and Sam "The Man" Jones, also known as "Toothpick" Jones. These things King's Bill Bachran recalled one day at King headquarters while searching his mind for the origin of the phrase. Bachran also partially credited Sam the Barbasol man, who had done the Barbasol commercials in the great days of radio. For a reporter's benefit, Bachran sang a line of Sam the Man: "Barbasol. Barbasol. Wets your whiskers, wets your chin."

Otherwise, Ariyoshi appeared on Burns' behalf, on occasion with a comical effect.

Ariyoshi said he had no apologies to make for Burns' absence, since Burns was dedicated to keeping the state government running smoothly despite the campaign. "During working hours," Ariyoshi said solemnly "you won't find him out campaigning." At that very moment, Burns was at the Royal Hawaiian Hotel in Waikiki addressing the Rotary Club, talking decidedly Gillish issues— housing, land use, and the environment.

King complained bitterly. At the next King-Ariyoshi encounter, King told a student group, "I think it shows disrespect for a major political party to send a substitute of lower rank," meaning Ariyoshi. "To me, this is insolence."

When King got around to reading the day's newspapers, October 16, he was much angrier. The reason was an "Open Letter to the People of Hawaii," signed by Burns and Ariyoshi, which Gill had drafted following his meeting with Burns.

The letter began, "Among the basic issues of this election are housing, proper land use, protection of the environment, transportation, and the highest possible standard of ethics in government.

"These issues must be met with continued imagination and determination in the next few years if our Hawaii is to survive as a pleasant and livable place. . . ."

Excerpts: On housing, ". . . future needs are far in excess of the average number of units being built each year. . . . In addition to encouraging the private housing market, the State must use its own land, and condemn land if necessary, to build attractive, durable and economically integrated communities. . . . In building our housing, we must respect and treasure our most limited natural resource, the land."

On land use, "Rezoning of good agricultural land must be prevented wherever possible. We must eliminate conflicts of interest wherever they may be found, particularly in sensitive agencies such as the Land Use Commission; those members with interests, direct or indirect, in land developments affected by land use zoning, should disclose those interests, and if in serious conflict, resign."

On air and water pollution, "The pressures of development and an increasing population in recent years have begun to seriously depreciate the quality of our air and water. . . . Strong and effective monitoring followed by vigorous enforcement is necessary."

On mass transit, "The State is fully prepared to actively cooperate with the City and County of Honolulu in establishing at the earliest possible date, a modern, non-pollutive mass transit system."

On government ethics, "We need a strong and effective ethics code. It should be enforceable and fair. There should be a continuing, careful review of all functions of State government where favoritism, undue advantage, or conflicts of interest are possible. . . ."

Burns and Ariyoshi closed the letter by saying, "We hold these goals and actions essential to the proper administration of the State. We will put the full force of our administration behind them."

Gill immediately commended the position statement, having written most of it, and said it should be reassuring to those people who had voted for him in the primary.

Gill, however, qualified his statement with an innuendo, that regardless of the position statement, voters must also decide for themselves on the relative sincerity of the two nominees, Burns and King.

King, until that day, had been attacking the Burns administration as tired. After reading the "Open Letter," King threw away his standard script, announcing that now, "There is only one issue —credibility." King continued, "It's obvious he," meaning Burns, "is willing to employ any tactic, any deception, or any ploy to confuse the people into electing him to another four years in office."

A subsequent King ad picked up Burns' line from *To Catch a Wave* about any damn fool taking a stand. "Of course, when Governor Burns finds it politically expedient, he pretends to take a stand. Like last week when he signed a piece of paper on things he's been ignoring for years. . . ." And, "The Governor never liked Tom Gill . . . he made that very clear for four long years. But now he pretends to like everything Tom Gill stands for." Fred Rohlfing charged that Burns was dancing to Gill's tune so inconsistently that, "If the people can buy this line, they will get what the Burns administration has stood for all along—an Oahu covered by cement, ticky-tack expensive homes, and freeways to nowhere."

Burns remained unruffled. In one of his rare on-the-record remarks to a reporter, he brushed off King's assault by saying "he's grasping at straws."

Perhaps this would have been either the high or low point of the general election campaign, depending on one's point of view, except that in eight days the people of Hawaii were to be brutally shocked, and the "Open Letter" was to be largely forgotten.

Anxiety over organized crime had built up gradually during the long months of the primary campaign, played on first by Hebden Porteus, then—following Porteus' lead—by Sam King.

In fact an accelerating rash of gangland murders had made it all too clear that by 1970 the stakes in Hawaii were high for control of gambling, prostitution, drugs, and the fencing of stolen goods. In midsummer, the press had spelled out the emergence of a centralized crime syndicate, plagued, albeit, by continuing struggles for power.

The most recent victim had been a Francis Burke, a syndicate lieutenant with Mainland mob contacts, who had dreamed of new heights of sophistication in Island racketeering. Dreaming oversized dreams, Burke on October 21, 1970, had been murdered in broad daylight on Chinatown's Maunakea Street, keeling over beneath a loan company sign which advised, "We can help." In the general view of things, only another hoodlum was dead, a man who had lived in a netherworld remote from Hawaii's social mainstream. To be sure, Burke's death created something of a sensation, but Sen. David McClung probably voiced the conventional wisdom when he told newsmen at their Columbia Inn watering place, "One thing you can say about Honolulu, they never hurt anybody who's innocent. They only shoot each other." Sam King nonetheless pressed the issue, running a full-page advertisement in the *Star-Bulletin* under a headline which said, "Governor Burns Tragic Failure: Crime." In fact crime control was not a state responsibility but a county responsibility, with King insisting on state involvement. Noting that in the Burke murder Honolulu had just witnessed its seventeenth gangland killing in recent years, King restated his proposal for a statewide crime-fighting unit.

From this point, October 23, eleven days prior to the general election, crime would totally dominate public thought, not because of the Burke murder but because of another. In cold political terms, the tragedy of October 23 perhaps was King's last opening, if indeed one was possible.

On this day the popular Larry N. Kuriyama was biding time until his reelection, mending political fences, and also promoting an issue he took most seriously, that being the crime issue. Larry Kuriyama was forty-nine years old, was unopposed for reelection to the state senate, and during the eleven years of his public life had never lost a legislative race. Kuriyama had been one of the leaders of the 1962 Democratic legislative attack on the Republican Governor Quinn, helping to pave the way for John Burns' first gubernatorial victory. But by 1970 Kuriyama had become disenchanted, and in the closing days of the primary campaign had cut a radio tape endorsing Tom Gill. At the time Kuriyama's statement went all but unnoticed, a small bit in the last-moment confusion of things, being played mainly on the Japanese-language stations in Gill's attempt to shore up the AJA vote. In the tape Kuriyama had said, "Time is running out," and had called for vigorous action on the problems facing Hawaii, placing organized crime at the top of the list. Having taken the losing side, Kuriyama nonetheless felt keenly about the Democratic party, and on the night of October 23 he participated in a Democratic rally in Pacific Palisades, where he had chatted amiably with the Democratic nominee, John Burns. Then, after declining an invitation to join friends for coffee, Kuriyama motored to his home in Aiea Heights, wheeled his automobile into the darkened garage, stopped, turned off the ignition, and began to climb out of the car.

From the darkness five bullets tore into him, and Larry Kuriyama was dead.

The resulting sense of shock and grief was both widespread and acute, not only because Larry Kuriyama had been a well-liked and respected man, having devoted most of his public service to improving the University of Hawaii, but also because he was a high state official.

If a state senator's life could be so abruptly snuffed out, then no one was immune.

The circumstances of the murder suggested the work of a professional contract gunman and, by extension, the involvement of an element of the crime mob.

Sam King heard the news in Hilo early the next morning and boarded a plane for Honolulu, thinking, as he later recalled it, that this was possibly the turning point, the calamity to open people's eyes and reverse the Burns tide. Had King not, just the day before, issued his latest warning against organized crime?

One of King's staff members, Ted Kurrus, a writer, rose about 7:30 the morning after the shooting, a Saturday, and read about it in the newspaper. Like many in the King camp, Kurrus believed, as he would put it, that "there's got to be something to turn this campaign around." Kurrus called headquarters, saying that Kuriyama's death might be it, and on this point there was general agreement. He immediately drove across the Pali to Honolulu, and was joined about nine in the morning by several top King people —among them Ed Brennan, the campaign manager; and Mike Novelli, from the Weiner agency in California. Kuriyama had been dead about ten hours. There was some sort of consensus that King should make a hard-hitting statement on this turn of events.

Ted Kurrus drafted a statement for King, redrafted it, and then joined a group who presented it to Sam King in King's office.

According to Kurrus, King was somewhat reluctant about the timing and wording, but King himself would recall no such hesitation on his part.

King held his news conference on Saturday afternoon, fifteen hours after the senator's death. And the Sunday newspaper headlined, on the front page, "It's Burns' fault—King," although King would complain about the headline's wording.

Also resuming the attack on Burns' credibility, King again picked up the punchline of the half-hour Burns documentary, *To Catch a Wave*. If Burns had taken a stand on organized crime, King said, Larry Kuriyama "could well be alive today, and our state at peace instead of at war with organized crime."

The implication was clear enough—King was attempting to lay the slaying at the governor's doorstep.

King went on: "While gangsters' cars are being bombed, while organized crime thumbs its nose in our faces, while public officials are being murdered, and when reports on unethical conduct are being hidden in a drawer [a reference to the land use commission investigation]," the people must recognize—it's time for a change.

The governor, King added, should come out from behind his television set and address himself to the question of the crime wave.

Burns for his part said nothing, but as chief executive and titular leader of Kuriyama's political party he stayed close to the funeral proceedings. Burns had talked to Kuriyama just minutes before the shooting. He also had gone to Kuriyama's home the next morning to offer his sympathy to the senator's family.

Privately, on Monday, outside the senate chamber where Kuriyama's body lay in state, Burns remarked that he would rather lose the election than indulge in campaign rhetoric over this tragedy.

Burns, with Gill and six other men, stood honor guard, forming a lane through which Kuriyama's body was carried from the Capitol. It was an overcast day, and a chill wind blew down from the mountains into the faces of the pallbearers. The funeral at nearby Hosoi Mortuary lasted more than two hours, as 2,000 people filed past to burn *oshoko,* a Buddhist offering of incense, the smoke drifting upward in a symbolic pathway to heaven.

The mood was horrible.

Burns sat by himself in a row reserved for dignitaries, several chairs removed from the only other two people in the row, Lois and Tom Gill.

When the time came, Burns walked slowly forward, stopping to bow toward the altar and toward the casket of Larry Kuriyama. Delivering the statement of the community's condolence to the family, Burns addressed himself to the grief-stricken widow and the five children who sat to her left, saying, "My grief I share with you is deeply personal." Referring to the late husband and father, Burns went on: "We labored together in the vineyard for many years."

The next day, at the graveside in Punchbowl Cemetery, Burns presented the folded flag from the coffin to Mrs. Kuriyama.

King, meanwhile, pursued his campaign at Punahou School, where Kuriyama's oldest children were students. To loud applause, one of the Punahou students condemned King for blaming Burns, contending that King's statement was "totally uncalled for and in poor taste."

On Wednesday, King called yet another press conference, arguing that condemnations of his statement were a "desperate attempt to shift blame . . . to divert attention from the crisis we are now facing.

"Burns and his political henchmen have tried to pretend that organized crime does not exist in Hawaii."

In a further exercise in desperation, the King campaign pulled together a fifteen-minute film and released it in the final week, a scatter-shot piece of work called *Eight Long Years.* It depicted Burns as a stick-figure magician "who can make things disappear before your very eyes."

Now you see it, now you don't: "The trick is to fool the people —that's magic." The film skipped over Magic Island, crowded schools, crowded highways, dust from a rock quarry, Francis Burke's body, and Jack Burns on the golf course. At one point, a long-legged prostitute—arrested in a Waikiki bust—was shown turning her backside to the camera, flipping her dress up.

And King again implied that Burns should be held accountable for Kuriyama's death, refusing to back down. While estimates of the impact of King's attack varied, everywhere one heard, "I was thinking about voting for him—but not now."

When D. G. Anderson heard of the Kuriyama statement, he was appalled.

Fred Rohlfing, who had played such a major role in bringing King in as a candidate, was at home when he heard of it, turned to his wife and said, "There goes the election."

Senior Republican Art Woolaway was riding in his car when he heard King on the radio and he thought to himself, "This is going to cost him the ball game."

Later Woolaway would say, "Jesus, knowing the temper of the voters here—it was just too personal. I knew it.

"I really believe Sam didn't intend it that way. But, right or wrong, I shuddered."

An unpublished poll taken at the time asked whether respondents agreed or disagreed with King's charge that had Burns "taken a stand," Kuriyama might be alive. Women rejected the notion three to one. Men rejected it almost four to one. The general view, it seemed, was that King—who in 1954 had charged that all Democrats were under the influence of Communists—had in 1970 made another such blunder.

King himself, after all was done, insisted that the Kuriyama statement hadn't hurt him, and pressed the point that after the primary he had made a net gain in the polls. When asked about the wording of the statement, King said: "If that sentence hadn't been in there, they would have picked some other sentence for criticism."

There was left in this campaign yet one more dismal episode, a last-moment release of the attorney general's investigation into the land use commission. King, in his attack on Burns' credibility, had alluded to investigative reports "being hidden in a drawer," meaning the drawer of the governor's desk. And subsequently King several times had demanded the report's release, so that the people could be fully informed before the day of voting.

Then John Burns, surprisingly in light of his having implicated a reporter in Commissioner Wilbert Choi's death, also in light of his attitude toward protection of reputations, on October 29 ordered the report to be released. In substance Attorney General Bertram Kanbara's findings confirmed the points made by the press on the three land use commission members and to them added a fourth, an Amfac corporation executive who on six occasions had voted favorably on Amfac rezoning applications. In sum, Kanbara found that on the nine-member commission no fewer than four members at one time or another—and by their own actions—had been in a conflict-of-interest situation.

Kanbara, despite the delicate situation, had thoroughly covered all questions, and in some instances had cited English common law where Hawaii's ethics law had not fully defined a conflict of interest. King nonetheless dismissed the Kanbara report as a whitewash job.

If the Kanbara report's release, and King's reaction, had further poisoned the atmosphere of the campaign season, few among King's people thought it would alter the outcome of the election. Nor did it.

This time there was no suspense, no sense of drama—a victory for John Burns was a foregone conclusion. In this long year, the general election was anticlimax.

On November 3, the only pending question was the margin of Burns' victory.

It turned out to be a landslide, 137,800 votes to 101,200 votes. And John Burns, who had been in such dire straits eighteen months earlier, was reelected to govern Hawaii through 1974.

Epilogue

As it turned out, John Burns had an alarming number of friends. When his prospects for reelection were darkest, his basic elements of support held fast. His campaign strategy was set early, and it moved forward toward election day like a slow-motion tidal wave. By the time Tom Gill had been defeated in the primary, the weird meandering of the Republicans had all but made the general election a closed question.

The outcome no doubt was in large measure a tribute to one who had served long and well. But there also were less savory yet vital elements to this campaign—the appeals to ethnicity, the staggering cost, and the electronic manipulation of both image and fact.

In the battle to retain John Burns in office, Robert Oshiro, Burns' manager, reported spending $980,000, or just $20,000 shy of a million dollars. This was slightly more than the combined total reported by Gill and the two Republicans, King and Hebden Porteus. In the crucial Democratic primary contest, Burns outspent Gill by a margin of almost 3½-to-1, $697,000 to $205,000.

On a per vote basis, Burns spent $8.50 apiece appealing to his 82,400 voters, compared to Gill's spending $3 apiece on his 69,000 voters.

Counting both the primary and general election campaigns, Burns outspent Sam King by $420,000, although Burns actually spent slightly less than King in the thirty-one-day general election campaign, $275,000 to $278,000.

On a per vote basis, Burns spent $7.10 compared to King's $5.60. In the all-important Democratic primary, more than half of the Democratic legislators openly supported Burns. Dan Inouye, his prize protege, whose mass popularity was unrivaled, stuck by him with a passion. George Ariyoshi pulled all the stops for Burns, playing on the emotion-charged first-class citizen line. And Ariyoshi was stumping in the field early, three months before Vincent Yano belatedly leaped in to campaign for Gill.

Burns' union base considerably outweighed Gill's in the primary, and Arthur Rutledge was the only union leader to oppose Burns in the general. The ILWU in particular again proved its effectiveness.

What mattered most is problematical—it could be debated endlessly. Burns himself attributed the outcome largely to the many people who worked for him in the field, and up to a point he was right: of the four major organizations, his was superior in both numbers and discipline. And while much of the framework was supplied by the patronage which is an incumbent's, many people were motivated solely by their sense of obligation and high regard for John Burns. Conversely, Burns was given to downplaying, if not dismissing, the media effort, contending that its principal effect was to bolster morale and to give his people a talking point.

Jack Seigle, Lennen and Newell Pacific, continued talking long after the campaign was over, revealing much of the inner strategy of the media plan while reaping recognition far beyond the shores of Hawaii. Following the general election, the Burns campaign was one of six American campaigns reviewed by the American Association of Political Consultants. Then it was one of two campaigns—and the only American campaign—reviewed by a meeting of the International Association of Political Consultants. Subsequently the sixty-second collage of testimonials was awarded top honors for political advertising at the fourth annual International Film Festival, one of four prize-winning productions by Medion Inc., of San Francisco.

Ultimately, the victory of the Burns campaign rested on the shoring up of his traditional strength among non-Caucasians, and most importantly among AJA voters.

As noted previously, Democratic AJAs were about evenly divided in midsummer between Burns and Gill, but had swung behind the incumbent governor on a two-to-one split by primary voting day.

For the go-round with King, on the nights of October 27 and 28, less than a week before the general election, Rick Egged of the Burns camp ran yet another poll which sampled 2,800 voters statewide. It pointed to a Burns victory on the strength of a heavy AJA vote and an equally wide margin for Burns in the much smaller Filipino-American community. The Egged poll also showed a slight edge for Burns among voters of Chinese descent. Burns trailed King among Hawaiians and Part-Hawaiians by a razor-thin margin, and he trailed King by a slightly wider margin among haoles.

Of those who disclosed their voting intentions, the breakdown was as follows:

AJA: For Burns, 59.2%. For King, 34.8%.

Haole: For Burns, 45.3%. For King, 49.7%

Hawaiian/Part-Hawaiian: For King, 46.9%. For Burns, 47.9%.

Filipino: For Burns, 61%. For King, 33.1%.

Chinese: For Burns, 48.2%. For King, 41.9%.

Others (Samoan, Korean, Black, etc.): For Burns, 55.1%. For King, 38.9%.

Among those who shaped modern Hawaii, Burns endured as number one, *ichiban,* as well-nigh larger than life: the triumphant party chairman, two-term delegate to Congress, and now three-term governor. Burns talks of retiring in 1974, but he will be under pressure to run for a fourth term. Partly this is because his organization is starting to divide between David McClung and Burns' heir apparent, Lt. Gov. George Ariyoshi. Part of the reason is as before: the regime is again unpopular and it faces another strong challenge in 1974. Tom Gill probably will run again, and Frank Fasi also aspires to the governorship. If Burns chooses to retire, there could be a four-way race for the Democratic nomination: Ariyoshi, McClung, Fasi, and Gill. So the drama of 1970 could be followed by carnival in 1974.

This again will give the Republicans a chance to revive the two-party system by winning the governorship.

But in broad terms 1970 confirmed that the large conflicts in Hawaii are acted out through the factional politics of the Democratic party.

Democrats of one sort or another control not only the State Capitol but also the four county governments and three of Hawaii's four congressional seats. The only Republican in top office is still Hiram L. Fong, who defeated the politically unknown Cecil Heftel by a scant 8,000 votes. The state legislature again is lop-sidedly Democratic, the majority party holding 17 of 25 senate seats and 34 of 51 seats in the House of Representatives. Since 1970 these Democrat legislators have divided not so neatly into two competing factions as into multiple cliques, agreeing neither on leadership nor on program—this is a time of drift and regrouping.

The murderer of Larry N. Kuriyama has not been brought to justice.

The economy has fallen off sharply since election day. Unemployment has doubled. The urban malaise and the destruction of the environment are less easily escaped, less easily ignored, each day. The housing problem has grown worse, although now it is seldom discussed. Internecine war continues within the Hawaii crime syndicate, while the Mainland syndicate probes for further openings, eager for the start of a vast casino operation in Hawaii.

During the 1970 campaign, a stronger ethnic current began to run. It seemed to flow from a sense of apprehension. So far as it was a reaction to the Mainland migration, it flowed from the memory of past wrongs. But if today some AJAs in particular feel threatened, if some Caucasians feel shut out politically, and if many Hawaiians and Filipino-Americans are evolving a stronger ethnic sense, the foremost fact is that these currents ripple in a sea of good will and multiracial *aloha.*

The multiracial way is the everyday reality for most people: in work, in play, in neighborhood association, and often in kinship and marriage. Yet it now is axiomatic that this way of life can only be properly nurtured in a congenial physical environment and by a responsive political system—grave questions facing all of America.

On quality of life, a brief vignette: in speech after speech, ecologist Tony Hodges asks people, "Do you think life in Hawaii is better now than it was five years ago?" Only a few say yes. Then, "Do you think life in Hawaii will be better," definition unspecified, "five years from now?" No one says yes, "even at the Optimist Club," as Hodges puts it.

If this is the contemporary mood, then *Hawaii still isn't such a bad place to live.* On the contrary, most of Hawaii is still a paradise; and its people a last best hope in the strife-torn global community.

And Hawaii is still young, still imbued with a spirit of experimentation, an appreciation of nature's gifts, and a pride in place and in self. If this be the prevailing spirit, then the promise of Hawaii will become reality, the life of the land will be preserved *i ka pono;* and Hawaii will give birth to a more truly egalitarian and pluralistic society, and to a new cosmopolitan race of mankind.

May 17, 1972   TOM COFFMAN

Epilogue II, 1973

Unlike most things in politics, the sources of John Burns' campaign fund long remained a truly well-kept secret. Answers emerged in the research for articles on campaign finance, which were published in the *Honolulu Star-Bulletin* in February 1973: Burns raised much of his million-dollar fund from the construction and development industries, and from such related interests as real estate and banking. He also raised large sums from architects and engineers who do a heavy business in nonbid state contracts. He raised it from people who operate businesses in public places on state concession. And he raised a six-figure sum from his political appointees. The fund was called *tanomoshi,* a Japanese word for an informal savings and loan.

Index